Catholic Cycle of Prayer

2020-2021

Let all the world in ev'ry corner sing,
My God and King!
--George Herbert, 1633

Walsingham Publishing

About the Cycle of Prayer

The Catholic Cycle of Prayer assigns a date within the cycle to each Catholic diocese, archdiocese, ordinariate, eparchy, archeparchy, exarchy, and other similar structure. The faithful are encouraged to pray together with other faithful throughout the world with special intention for the clergy and people of each diocese, covering every part of the Catholic Church throughout the world once during each year.

A cycle year begins on the Day of Pentecost, the birthday of the Church, and runs through the Eve of Pentecost in the following year. Because the date of Pentecost varies with the date of Easter, the length of a cycle year varies from year to year. For each new cycle year, a completely random "shuffle" of diocese-to-date assignments is calculated so that each diocese has an equal chance of appearing on any particular day of the year.

The 2020-2021 cycle assigns the 3,169 dioceses to the 357 days from March 31st, 2020 to May 22nd, 2021. As a result, 8 or 9 dioceses appear on each day. It is suggested to pray for the first 4 or 5 dioceses in the morning, and the second 4 in the evening. This can be done at mass, during the daily office, or at any other time of prayer.

The Cycle of Prayer is a project of Walsingham Publishing, and is dedicated to Our Blessed Lady, Mary, Mother of the Church. On the cover is the icon of the Feodorovskaya Mother of God by Fabergé, created in 1908 as a gift to the Grand Duchess Maria Pavlovna the Younger (1890-1958) on the occasion of her wedding to Prince Willem of Sweden, Duke of Sodermanland. The icon belongs to the *Russian Icon Museum* in Clinton, Massachusetts.

Walsingham Publishing thanks the administrator of the "Catholic-Hierarchy" website for maintaining the up-to-date list of dioceses used to create this Cycle of Prayer.

May

Sun, 31 May 2020
  Morning
    Melkite Greek Catholic Archeparchy of Caesarea Philippi, Lebanon
    Suburbicarian See of Frascati, Italy
    Diocese of Phát Diệm, Viet Nam
    Diocese of Sanyuan, China
  Evening
    Archdiocese of Anqing, China
    Diocese of Puerto Iguazú, Argentina
    Archdiocese of Rhodes, Greece
    Territorial Abbey of Saint-Maurice, Switzerland

June

Mon, 01 June 2020
  Morning
    Apostolic Vicariate of Alexandria of Egypt-Eliopoli di Egitto-Port-Said
    Diocese of Grenoble-Vienne, France
    Diocese of Paranavaí, Parana, Brazil
    Diocese of Pesqueira, Pernambuco, Brazil
    Diocese of San Marcos de Arica, Chile
  Evening
    Archdiocese of Johannesburg, South Africa
    Diocese of Owando, Republic of the Congo
    Diocese of Queenstown, South Africa
    Diocese of San Bernardo, Chile

Tue, 02 June 2020
  Morning
    Eritrean Catholic Eparchy of Barentu, Eritrea
    Diocese of Cheongju, South Korea
    Archdiocese of Chongqing, China
    Diocese of Manzini, Swaziland
    Archdiocese of Medellín, Colombia
  Evening
    Diocese of Hildesheim, Germany
    Diocese of Nha Trang, Viet Nam
    Archdiocese of Rabaul, Papua New Guinea
    Diocese of Tournai, Belgium

Wed, 03 June 2020
  Morning
    Diocese of Brescia, Italy
    Archdiocese of Florence, Italy
    Diocese of Ho, Ghana
    Archdiocese of Nanjing, China
    Diocese of Paranaguá, Parana, Brazil
  Evening
    Ruthenian Catholic Eparchy of Holy Protection of Mary of Phoenix, Arizona, USA
    Syrian Catholic Eparchy of Cairo, Egypt
    Diocese of Naha, Japan
    Diocese of Naval, Philippines

Thu, 04 June 2020
  Morning
    Archdiocese of Athens, Greece

    Diocese of Chişinău, Moldova
    Diocese of Moundou, Chad
    Archdiocese of Port of Spain, Trinidad and Tobago, Antilles
    Diocese of Rottenburg-Stuttgart, Germany
  Evening
    Archdiocese of Alba Iulia, Romania
    Diocese of Gbarnga, Liberia
    Diocese of Rondonópolis - Guiratinga, Mato Grosso, Brazil
    Diocese of Yongping, China

Fri, 05 June 2020
  Morning
    Diocese of Agboville, Côte d'Ivoire
    Diocese of Huejutla, Hidalgo, México
    Diocese of Miarinarivo, Madagascar
    Diocese of Presidente Prudente, Sao Paulo, Brazil
    Archdiocese of Siracusa, Italy
  Evening
    Diocese of Linhai, China
    Diocese of Opole, Poland
    Archdiocese of Sens, France
    Diocese of Valleyfield, Québec, Canada

Sat, 06 June 2020
  Morning
    Diocese of Beja, Portugal
    Diocese of Eisenstadt, Austria
    Diocese of Machala, Ecuador
    Diocese of Puerto Escondido, Oaxaca, México
    Diocese of Wallis et Futuna, Wallis and Futuna
  Evening
    Apostolic Vicariate of Aguarico, Ecuador
    Diocese of Avezzano, Italy
    Diocese of Haarlem-Amsterdam, Netherlands
    Archdiocese of Tijuana, Baja California Norte, México

Sun, 07 June 2020
  Morning
    Diocese of Barinas, Venezuela
    Syrian Catholic Archdiocese of Damas, Syria
    Diocese of Gubbio, Italy
    Diocese of Huancavélica, Peru
    Diocese of Kitui, Kenya
  Evening
    Diocese of Lae, Papua New Guinea
    Bulgarian Catholic Eparchy of Saint John XXIII of Sofia, Bulgaria
    Diocese of San Cristóbal de Venezuela
    Diocese of Sokoto, Nigeria

Mon, 08 June 2020
  Morning
    Diocese of Bonfim, Bahia, Brazil
    Diocese of Istmina-Tadó, Colombia
    Diocese of Keimoes-Upington, South Africa
    Diocese of Palm Beach, Florida, USA
  Evening
    Diocese of Azul, Argentina
    Diocese of Ciudad Obregón, Sonora, México
    Diocese of Lisala, Democratic Republic of the Congo

Diocese of Tzaneen, South Africa
Tue, 09 June 2020
  Morning
    Chaldean Catholic Diocese of Aqrā, Iraq
    Diocese of Keningau, Malaysia
    Diocese of Münster, Germany
    Diocese of Nsukka, Nigeria
    Diocese of Xianxian, China
  Evening
    Territorial Prelature of Alto Xingu-Tucumã, Para, Brazil
    Diocese of Gulbarga, India
    Diocese of Nice, France
    Archdiocese of Turin, Italy
Wed, 10 June 2020
  Morning
    Syro-Malabar Catholic Diocese of Adilabad, India
    Diocese of Chapecó, Santa Catarina, Brazil
    Diocese of Irapuato, Guanajuato, México
    Archdiocese of Naples, Italy
    Archdiocese of Tegucigalpa, Honduras
  Evening
    Diocese of Chilpancingo-Chilapa, Guerrero, México
    Diocese of León en Nicaragua
    Diocese of Mazara del Vallo, Italy
    Diocese of Simla and Chandigarh, India
Thu, 11 June 2020
  Morning
    Diocese of Aizawl, India
    Diocese of Jaipur, India
    Archdiocese of Kisumu, Kenya
    Diocese of Mongomo, Equatorial Guinea
    Diocese of Roraima, Roraima, Brazil
  Evening
    Diocese of Bà Rịa, Viet Nam
    Archdiocese of Buenos Aires, Argentina
    Diocese of Denpasar, Indonesia
    Diocese of Mohale's Hoek, Lesotho
Fri, 12 June 2020
  Morning
    Maronite Catholic Archeparchy of Antélias, Lebanon
    Diocese of Crema, Italy
    Apostolic Administration of Harbin, China
    Diocese of Kinkala, Republic of the Congo
    Diocese of Marbel, Philippines
  Evening
    Diocese of Bettiah, India
    Archdiocese of Porto Alegre, Rio Grande do Sul, Brazil
    Maronite Catholic Eparchy of Saïdā, Lebanon
    Diocese of Tui-Vigo, Spain
Sat, 13 June 2020
  Morning
    Archdiocese of Antananarivo, Madagascar
    Apostolic Vicariate of Phnom-Penh, Cambodia
    Diocese of São Raimundo Nonato, Piaui, Brazil
    Diocese of Tainan, Taiwan

Archdiocese of Vitória, Espirito Santo, Brazil
  Evening
    Diocese of Caxias do Maranhão, Brazil
    Diocese of Galle, Sri Lanka
    Apostolic Prefecture of Qiqihar, China
    Diocese of Tiruchirapalli, India

Sun, 14 June 2020
  Morning
    Archdiocese of Antequera, Oaxaca, México
    Military Ordinariate of El Salvador
    Diocese of Guarenas, Venezuela
    Archdiocese of Maringá, Parana, Brazil
    Diocese of Phan Thiết, Viet Nam
  Evening
    Diocese of Anápolis, Goias, Brazil
    Diocese of Inongo, Democratic Republic of the Congo
    Archdiocese of Rijeka, Croatia
    Diocese of São João del Rei, Minas Gerais, Brazil

Mon, 15 June 2020
  Morning
    Archdiocese of Ayacucho o Huamanga, Peru
    Archdiocese of Cambrai, France
    Diocese of Châlons, France
    Diocese of Colatina, Espirito Santo, Brazil
    Diocese of Tapachula, Chiapas, México
  Evening
    Diocese of Crateús, Ceara, Brazil
    Archdiocese of Saint-Boniface, Manitoba, Canada
    Diocese of San Jose in California, USA
    Archdiocese of Tucumán, Argentina

Tue, 16 June 2020
  Morning
    Diocese of Charlottetown, Prince Edward Island, Canada
    Archdiocese of Oklahoma City, Oklahoma, USA
    Diocese of Orlu, Nigeria
    Diocese of Tulle, France
  Evening
    Archdiocese of Fuzhou, China
    Diocese of Maroua-Mokolo, Cameroon
    Diocese of Soacha, Colombia
    Archdiocese of Toledo, Spain

Wed, 17 June 2020
  Morning
    Diocese of Calicut, India
    Diocese of Clonfert, Ireland
    Syro-Malabar Catholic Diocese of Irinjalakuda, India
    Archdiocese of Olinda e Recife, Pernambuco, Brazil
    Melkite Greek Catholic Archeparchy of Zahleh e Furzol, Lebanon
  Evening
    Diocese of Cabimas, Venezuela
    Chaldean Catholic Diocese of Shahpour, Iran
    Diocese of San Angelo, Texas, USA
    Diocese of Tianjin, China

Thu, 18 June 2020
  Morning
    Archdiocese of Feira de Santana, Bahia, Brazil
    Diocese of Ndalatando, Angola
    Diocese of Obuasi, Ghana
    Melkite Greek Catholic Archeparchy of Petra e Filadelfia, Jordan
    Diocese of San Cristóbal de Las Casas, Chiapas, México
  Evening
    Diocese of Balasore, India
    Diocese of Grand Island, Nebraska, USA
    Diocese of La Rioja, Argentina
    Diocese of Parañaque, Philippines

Fri, 19 June 2020
  Morning
    Ukrainian Catholic Eparchy of Buchach, Ukraine
    Diocese of Guanare, Venezuela
    Diocese of Kondoa, Tanzania
    Diocese of Lichinga, Mozambique
    Diocese of Urdaneta, Philippines
  Evening
    Diocese of Darjeeling, India
    Diocese of Gweru, Zimbabwe
    Archdiocese of Ibagué, Colombia
    Archdiocese of Managua, Nicaragua

Sat, 20 June 2020
  Morning
    Diocese of Aversa, Italy
    Diocese of Hradec Králové, Czech Republic
    Diocese of Parramatta, Australia
    Diocese of Shaoguan, China
    Diocese of Spiš, Slovakia
  Evening
    Archdiocese of Alger, Algeria
    Diocese of San Juan de la Maguana, Dominican Republic
    Archdiocese of Songea, Tanzania
    Diocese of Zamość-Lubaczów, Poland

Sun, 21 June 2020
  Morning
    Apostolic Vicariate of Camiri, Bolivia
    Archdiocese of Louisville, Kentucky, USA
    Diocese of Nuevo Casas Grandes, Chihuahua, México
    Diocese of Pasig, Philippines
    Diocese of Zhumadian, China
  Evening
    Diocese of Bouar, Central African Republic
    Archdiocese of Brindisi-Ostuni, Italy
    Archdiocese of Curitiba, Parana, Brazil
    Diocese of Jataí, Goias, Brazil

Mon, 22 June 2020
  Morning
    Diocese of Alleppey, India
    Diocese of Chengde, China
    Apostolic Administration of São João Maria Vianney, Rio de Janeiro, Brazil
    Diocese of Saskatoon, Saskatchewan, Canada
    Diocese of Wrexham, Wales

Evening
- Diocese of Huehuetenango, Guatemala
- Diocese of Karaganda, Kazakhstan
- Diocese of Le Puy-en-Velay, France
- Diocese of Tarahumara, Chihuahua, México

Tue, 23 June 2020
Morning
- Diocese of Bondoukou, Côte d'Ivoire
- Diocese of Butare, Rwanda
- Diocese of Mangochi, Malawi
- Archdiocese of Thành-Phô Hồ Chí Minh, Viet Nam
- Diocese of Villarrica del Espíritu Santo, Paraguay

Evening
- Melkite Greek Catholic Archdiocese of Alep, Syria
- Archdiocese of Baghdad, Iraq
- Archdiocese of Mercedes-Luján, Argentina
- Diocese of Ouesso, Republic of the Congo

Wed, 24 June 2020
Morning
- Diocese of Benjamín Aceval, Paraguay
- Diocese of Estância, Sergipe, Brazil
- Diocese of Mexicali, Baja California Norte, México
- Diocese of Tarma, Peru

Evening
- Diocese of Argyll and The Isles, Scotland
- Military Ordinariate of Lithuania
- Archdiocese of Parakou, Benin
- Diocese of São José dos Pinhais, Parana, Brazil

Thu, 25 June 2020
Morning
- Archdiocese of Baltimore, Maryland, USA
- Diocese of Brooklyn, New York, USA
- Archdiocese of Chihuahua, México
- Diocese of Nyundo, Rwanda
- Diocese of Pemba, Mozambique

Evening
- Diocese of Alotau-Sideia, Papua New Guinea
- Diocese of Biloxi, Mississippi, USA
- Diocese of Metuchen, New Jersey, USA
- Diocese of Padua, Italy

Fri, 26 June 2020
Morning
- Diocese of Bungoma, Kenya
- Diocese of Derry, Ireland
- Diocese of Elbląg, Poland
- Apostolic Administration of Kazakhstan and Central Asia for the Faithful of the Byzantine Rite
- Diocese of Mendi, Papua New Guinea

Evening
- Territorial Prelature of Borba, Amazonas, Brazil
- Territorial Prelature of El Salto, Durango, México
- Diocese of Holguín, Cuba
- Diocese of Nicolet, Québec, Canada

Sat, 27 June 2020
Morning
- Archdiocese of Colombo, Sri Lanka

    Archdiocese of Gatineau, Québec, Canada
    Archdiocese of Lomé, Togo
    Ukrainian Catholic Eparchy of Saint Vladimir-Le-Grand de Paris
    Diocese of Springfield in Massachusetts, USA
  Evening
    Diocese of Ambositra, Madagascar
    Archdiocese of Grouard-McLennan, Alberta, Canada
    Diocese of Purnea, India
    Diocese of Wichita, Kansas, USA

Sun, 28 June 2020
  Morning
    Territorial Prelature of Chuquibamba, Peru
    Military Ordinariate of Ecuador
    Diocese of Ouahigouya, Burkina Faso
    Diocese of Penedo, Alagoas, Brazil
    Diocese of Santander, Spain
  Evening
    Diocese of Dolisie, Republic of the Congo
    Diocese of Laredo, Texas, USA
    Archdiocese of Liverpool, England
    Archdiocese of Lyon, France

Mon, 29 June 2020
  Morning
    Diocese of Comayagua, Honduras
    Diocese of Córdoba, Spain
    Diocese of Málaga, Spain
    Personal Prelature of Opus Dei, N/A
    Diocese of Santiago del Estero, Argentina
  Evening
    Diocese of Islamabad-Rawalpindi, Pakistan
    Diocese of Malindi, Kenya
    Archdiocese of Palermo, Italy
    Diocese of Zaria, Nigeria

Tue, 30 June 2020
  Morning
    Syrian Catholic Archeparchy of Alep, Syria
    Diocese of Bunbury, Australia
    Diocese of Cloyne, Ireland
    Diocese of Lezhë, Albania
    Diocese of Nakuru, Kenya
  Evening
    Diocese of Barreiras, Bahia, Brazil
    Archdiocese of Garoua, Cameroon
    Diocese of Leshan, China
    Diocese of São Luís de Montes Belos, Goias, Brazil

July

Wed, 01 July 2020
- Morning
  - Archdiocese of Foggia-Bovino, Italy
  - Diocese of Jayapura, Indonesia
  - Archdiocese of Naxos, Andros, Tinos e Mykonos, Greece
  - Diocese of Popokabaka, Democratic Republic of the Congo
  - Diocese of Yongjia/Wenzhou, China
- Evening
  - Diocese of Bragança-Miranda, Portugal
  - Apostolic Vicariate of Ñuflo de Chávez, Bolivia
  - Personal Ordinariate of Our Lady of Walsingham, England
  - Diocese of São Gabriel da Cachoeira, Amazonas, Brazil

Thu, 02 July 2020
- Morning
  - Archdiocese of Aracajú, Sergipe, Brazil
  - Apostolic Vicariate of Benghazi, Libya
  - Diocese of Cabanatuan, Philippines
  - Diocese of Helsinki, Finland
  - Diocese of Quelimane, Mozambique
- Evening
  - Diocese of Cartagena en España
  - Archdiocese of Lille, France
  - Archdiocese of Lilongwe, Malawi
  - Diocese of Oradea Mare, Romania

Fri, 03 July 2020
- Morning
  - Diocese of Duque de Caxias, Rio de Janeiro, Brazil
  - Diocese of Osório, Rio Grande do Sul, Brazil
  - Archdiocese of Passo Fundo, Rio Grande do Sul, Brazil
  - Apostolic Prefecture of Yueyang, China
- Evening
  - Archdiocese of Antofagasta, Chile
  - Diocese of Coari, Amazonas, Brazil
  - Diocese of Tanjore, India
  - Diocese of Tuxpan, Veracruz, México

Sat, 04 July 2020
- Morning
  - Diocese of Biella, Italy
  - Diocese of Jales, Sao Paulo, Brazil
  - Diocese of Krk, Croatia
  - Russian Catholic Apostolic Exarchate of Russia
  - Diocese of Yoro, Honduras
- Evening
  - Syrian Catholic Patriarchal Exarchate of Jerusalem, Palestine
  - Diocese of Mtwara, Tanzania
  - Ukrainian Catholic Eparchy of Saint Josaphat in Parma, USA
  - Diocese of Suzhou, China

Sun, 05 July 2020
- Morning
  - Diocese of Bafang, Cameroon
  - Diocese of Bom Jesus do Gurguéia, Piaui, Brazil
  - Diocese of Chilaw, Sri Lanka

   Archdiocese of Cincinnati, Ohio, USA
   Archdiocese of Natal, Rio Grande do Norte, Brazil
  Evening
   Diocese of Crete, Greece
   Diocese of Lucera-Troia, Italy
   Diocese of Pinar del Rio, Cuba
   Diocese of Taubaté, Sao Paulo, Brazil

Mon, 06 July 2020
  Morning
   Diocese of Barra do Garças, Mato Grosso, Brazil
   Syrian Catholic Eparchy of Beirut, Lebanon
   Diocese of Evry-Corbeil-Essonnes, France
   Diocese of Kansas City-Saint Joseph, Missouri, USA
   Diocese of Tacuarembó, Uruguay
  Evening
   Diocese of Kerry, Ireland
   Diocese of Nanterre, France
   Diocese of Tilarán-Liberia, Costa Rica
   Diocese of Vicenza, Italy

Tue, 07 July 2020
  Morning
   Apostolic Vicariate of Bontoc-Lagawe, Philippines
   Diocese of Copiapó, Chile
   Diocese of Locri-Gerace, Italy
   Diocese of Tuticorin, India
   Ukrainian Catholic Archeparchy of Winnipeg, Manitoba, Canada
  Evening
   Diocese of Barbastro-Monzón, Spain
   Archdiocese of Libreville, Gabon
   Archdiocese of Maputo, Mozambique
   Diocese of Tanga, Tanzania

Wed, 08 July 2020
  Morning
   Ordinariate of the Faithful of the Eastern Rites in Austria
   Diocese of Bayombong, Philippines
   Diocese of Loikaw, Myanmar
   Diocese of Rourkela, India
   Syrian Catholic Patriarchal Dependent Territory of Sudan and South Sudan
  Evening
   Archdiocese of Bucaramanga, Colombia
   Archdiocese of Manfredonia-Vieste-San Giovanni Rotondo, Italy
   Diocese of Speyer, Germany
   Diocese of Spokane, Washington, USA

Thu, 09 July 2020
  Morning
   Diocese of Edéa, Cameroon
   Diocese of Nuestra Señora de la Altagracia en Higüey, Dominican Republic
   Diocese of São Miguel Paulista, Sao Paulo, Brazil
   Ordinariate of the Faithful of the Eastern Rites in Spain
   Diocese of Tubarão, Santa Catarina, Brazil
  Evening
   Diocese of Basse-Terre, Guadeloupe, Antilles
   Diocese of Maumere, Indonesia
   Diocese of Rulenge-Ngara, Tanzania
   Diocese of Trieste, Italy

Fri, 10 July 2020
  Morning
    Diocese of Ascoli Piceno, Italy
    Diocese of Djougou, Benin
    Diocese of Eséka, Cameroon
    Diocese of Osogbo, Nigeria
    Diocese of Zhengding, China
  Evening
    Diocese of Antwerp, Belgium
    Ukrainian Catholic Archeparchy of Lviv, Ukraine
    Diocese of Setúbal, Portugal
    Diocese of Xingtai, China

Sat, 11 July 2020
  Morning
    Archdiocese of Cuiabá, Mato Grosso, Brazil
    Diocese of Libmanan, Philippines
    Diocese of Raphoe, Ireland
    Archdiocese of Vancouver, British Columbia, Canada
  Evening
    Archdiocese of Bogotá, Colombia
    Diocese of Campos, Rio de Janeiro, Brazil
    Archdiocese of Nampula, Mozambique
    Archdiocese of Tuxtla Gutiérrez, Chiapas, México

Sun, 12 July 2020
  Morning
    Diocese of Broken Bay, Australia
    Maronite Catholic Apostolic Exarchate of Colombia
    Diocese of Maturín, Venezuela
    Diocese of Mazatlán, Sinaloa, México
    Diocese of Xiamen, China
  Evening
    Diocese of Barrancabermeja, Colombia
    Diocese of El Banco, Colombia
    Syro-Malabar Catholic Eparchy of Mananthavady, India
    Diocese of Miri, Malaysia

Mon, 13 July 2020
  Morning
    Archdiocese of Bloemfontein, South Africa
    Diocese of Bruges, Belgium
    Archdiocese of Guiyang, China
    Diocese of Pyay, Myanmar
    Diocese of Rajshahi, Bangladesh
  Evening
    Diocese of Granada en Colombia
    Coptic Catholic Eparchy of Sohag, Egypt
    Diocese of Tandag, Philippines
    Diocese of Willemstad, Netherlands Antilles, Antilles

Tue, 14 July 2020
  Morning
    Diocese of Apatzingán, Michoacán, México
    Archdiocese of Cap-Haïtien, Haïti
    Diocese of Jingxian, China
    Diocese of Pitigliano-Sovana-Orbetello, Italy
    Archdiocese of Veszprém, Hungary

Evening
- Syrian Catholic Archeparchy of Baghdad, Iraq
- Diocese of Dindigul, India
- Diocese of Hwalien, Taiwan
- Diocese of Kielce, Poland

Wed, 15 July 2020
Morning
- Diocese of Cairns, Australia
- Diocese of Caozhou/Heze, China
- Diocese of Concepción, Argentina
- Diocese of Kaohsiung, Taiwan
- Diocese of Sorsogon, Philippines

Evening
- Archdiocese of Albi, France
- Diocese of Brno, Czech Republic
- Diocese of Rimini, Italy
- Diocese of Tôlagnaro, Madagascar

Thu, 16 July 2020
Morning
- Archdiocese of Arequipa, Peru
- Diocese of Caicó, Rio Grande do Norte, Brazil
- Diocese of Chios, Greece
- Diocese of Shantou, China
- Diocese of Yokadouma, Cameroon

Evening
- Archdiocese of Douala, Cameroon
- Territorial Abbey of Montecassino, Italy
- Diocese of Nelson, British Columbia, Canada
- Diocese of Talca, Chile

Fri, 17 July 2020
Morning
- Diocese of Ciudad Lázaro Cárdenas, Michoacán, México
- Diocese of Muranga, Kenya
- Diocese of Ondjiva, Angola
- Slovakian Catholic Archdiocese of Prešov, Slovakia
- Archdiocese of Wrocław, Poland

Evening
- Archdiocese of Jakarta, Indonesia
- Diocese of Kilwa-Kasenga, Democratic Republic of the Congo
- Personal Ordinariate of Our Lady of the Southern Cross, Australia
- Diocese of Uije, Angola

Sat, 18 July 2020
Morning
- Diocese of Dedza, Malawi
- Diocese of Gallup, New Mexico, USA
- Diocese of Geita, Tanzania
- Territorial Prelature of Illapel, Chile
- Diocese of Primavera do Leste - Paranatinga, Mato Grosso, Brazil

Evening
- Diocese of Bereina, Papua New Guinea
- Archdiocese of Freiburg im Breisgau, Germany
- Diocese of Nîmes, France
- Archdiocese of Tunis, Tunisia

Sun, 19 July 2020
  Morning
    Archdiocese of Accra, Ghana
    Diocese of Maracay, Venezuela
    Diocese of Salgueiro, Pernambuco, Brazil
    Ukrainian Catholic Eparchy of Sokal-Zhovkva, Ukraine
  Evening
    Diocese of Dori, Burkina Faso
    Military Ordinariate of Paraguay
    Diocese of Plasencia, Spain
    Diocese of Vittorio Veneto, Italy

Mon, 20 July 2020
  Morning
    Diocese of Celje, Slovenia
    Diocese of Itapeva, Sao Paulo, Brazil
    Diocese of Kericho, Kenya
    Diocese of Meru, Kenya
    Diocese of Pécs, Hungary
  Evening
    Maronite Catholic Archeparchy of Damas, Syria
    Diocese of Melfi-Rapolla-Venosa, Italy
    Apostolic Vicariate of Northern Arabia, Kuwait
    Diocese of Santisimo Salvador de Bayamo y Manzanillo, Cuba

Tue, 21 July 2020
  Morning
    Coptic Catholic Eparchy of Lycopolis, Egypt
    Diocese of Ipil, Philippines
    Archdiocese of Kigali, Rwanda
    Diocese of Lleida, Spain
    Coptic Catholic Eparchy of Luqsor, Egypt
  Evening
    Diocese of Cahors, France
    Diocese of Lwena, Angola
    Diocese of Neuquén, Argentina
    Diocese of San Marcos, Guatemala

Wed, 22 July 2020
  Morning
    Diocese of Nashik, India
    Diocese of Riobamba, Ecuador
    Diocese of Saint-Etienne, France
    Territorial Prelature of São Félix, Mato Grosso, Brazil
    Ukrainian Catholic Archeparchy of São João Batista em Curitiba, Brazil
  Evening
    Diocese of Guarabira, Paraiba, Brazil
    Diocese of Namibe, Angola
    Diocese of Pamiers, France
    Diocese of Sonsón-Rionegro, Colombia

Thu, 23 July 2020
  Morning
    Diocese of Diébougou, Burkina Faso
    Diocese of Divinópolis, Minas Gerais, Brazil
    Territorial Prelature of Mission de France o Pontigny, France
    Territorial Abbey of Pannonhalma, Hungary
    Romanian Catholic Eparchy of Saint George's in Canton, USA

Evening
  Diocese of Chalan Kanoa, Northern Mariana Islands
  Diocese of Erexim, Rio Grande do Sul, Brazil
  Archdiocese of La Plata, Argentina
  Diocese of Santiago de Veraguas, Panama

Fri, 24 July 2020
  Morning
    Patriarchate of Lisbon, Portugal
    Archdiocese of Medan, Indonesia
    Diocese of Mweka, Democratic Republic of the Congo
    Diocese of Pekhon, Myanmar
    Diocese of Soissons, France
  Evening
    Diocese of Berhampur, India
    Armenian Catholic Patriarchate of Cilicia, Lebanon
    Apostolic Vicariate of Thessaloniki, Greece
    Apostolic Prefecture of Ulaanbaatar, Mongolia

Sat, 25 July 2020
  Morning
    Diocese of Dodge City, Kansas, USA
    Diocese of Lokossa, Benin
    Archdiocese of Teresina, Piaui, Brazil
    Diocese of Thái Bình, Viet Nam
    Diocese of Wiawso, Ghana
  Evening
    Archdiocese of Bangui, Central African Republic
    Archdiocese of Brazzaville, Republic of the Congo
    Diocese of Cornélio Procópio, Parana, Brazil
    Diocese of Guarapuava, Parana, Brazil

Sun, 26 July 2020
  Morning
    Diocese of Arlington, Virginia, USA
    Diocese of Montería, Colombia
    Diocese of Oliveira, Minas Gerais, Brazil
    Diocese of San Miguel, El Salvador
    Archdiocese of San Salvador, El Salvador
  Evening
    Diocese of Joliet in Illinois, USA
    Diocese of Las Cruces, New Mexico, USA
    Diocese of Macerata-Tolentino-Recanati-Cingoli-Treia, Italy
    Diocese of Xai-Xai, Mozambique

Mon, 27 July 2020
  Morning
    Coptic Catholic Eparchy of Abu Qurqas, Egypt
    Archdiocese of Bhopal, India
    Diocese of Bissau, Guinea-Bissau
    Archdiocese of Coro, Venezuela
    Archdiocese of Vienna, Austria
  Evening
    Archdiocese of Gwangju, South Korea
    Diocese of Orense, Spain
    Diocese of Ruhengeri, Rwanda
    Diocese of Yan'an, China

Tue, 28 July 2020
- Morning
  - Diocese of Mananjary, Madagascar
  - Diocese of Pensacola-Tallahassee, Florida, USA
  - Syro-Malankara Catholic Eparchy of Saint Mary, Queen of Peace, USA
  - Military Ordinariate of Spain
- Evening
  - Diocese of Florida, Uruguay
  - Diocese of Isangi, Democratic Republic of the Congo
  - Diocese of Paisley, Scotland
  - Military Ordinariate of South Africa

Wed, 29 July 2020
- Morning
  - Diocese of Byumba, Rwanda
  - Diocese of Fada N'Gourma, Burkina Faso
  - Archdiocese of Lviv, Ukraine
  - Diocese of Ngozi, Burundi
  - Syro-Malabar Catholic Diocese of Thuckalay, India
- Evening
  - Diocese of Añatuya, Argentina
  - Diocese of Cruz Alta, Rio Grande do Sul, Brazil
  - Diocese of Fenyang, China
  - Syro-Malankara Catholic Eparchy of Muvattupuzha, India

Thu, 30 July 2020
- Morning
  - Diocese of Autlán, Jalisco, México
  - Syro-Malankara Catholic Eparchy of Marthandom, India
  - Diocese of Plymouth, England
  - Melkite Greek Catholic Eparchy of Saint-Sauveur de Montréal, Canada
  - Apostolic Prefecture of Zhaotong, China
- Evening
  - Diocese of Auchi, Nigeria
  - Diocese of Bafia, Cameroon
  - Diocese of Ndola, Zambia
  - Diocese of Palmeira dos Índios, Alagoas, Brazil

Fri, 31 July 2020
- Morning
  - Diocese of Baoding, China
  - Ordinariate of the Faithful of the Eastern Rites in France
  - Diocese of Leeds, England
  - Diocese of Wabag, Papua New Guinea
  - Archdiocese of Xi'an, China
- Evening
  - Diocese of Castanhal, Para, Brazil
  - Diocese of Georgetown, Guyana, Antilles
  - Diocese of Getafe, Spain
  - Archdiocese of the Military of the United States of America

August

Sat, 01 August 2020
  Morning
    Diocese of Buta, Democratic Republic of the Congo
    Diocese of Knoxville, Tennessee, USA
    Diocese of Nanchong, China
    Diocese of Saint-Jean-Longueuil, Québec, Canada
    Diocese of Santo André, Sao Paulo, Brazil
  Evening
    Archdiocese of Fort-de-France, Martinique, Antilles
    Diocese of Líbano-Honda, Colombia
    Territorial Abbey of Montevergine, Italy
    Diocese of Santa Cruz do Sul, Rio Grande do Sul, Brazil

Sun, 02 August 2020
  Morning
    Diocese of Jesi, Italy
    Diocese of Mzuzu, Malawi
    Archdiocese of Pontianak, Indonesia
    Diocese of Radom, Poland
    Diocese of Tshumbe, Democratic Republic of the Congo
  Evening
    Diocese of Atlacomulco, México, México
    Diocese of Belize City-Belmopan, Belize, Antilles
    Archdiocese of Kampala, Uganda
    Slovakian Catholic Eparchy of Košice, Slovakia

Mon, 03 August 2020
  Morning
    Ethiopian Catholic Eparchy of Adigrat, Ethiopia
    Diocese of Bacabal, Maranhão, Brazil
    Diocese of Syros, Greece
    Diocese of Talibon, Philippines
    Diocese of Vanimo, Papua New Guinea
  Evening
    Ethiopian Catholic Eparchy of Emdeber, Ethiopia
    Diocese of Nancy, France
    Archdiocese of Patna, India
    Diocese of San Carlos de Ancud, Chile

Tue, 04 August 2020
  Morning
    Diocese of Bangassou, Central African Republic
    Archdiocese of Denver, Colorado, USA
    Diocese of La Dorada-Guaduas, Colombia
    Archdiocese of Saint Paul and Minneapolis, Minnesota, USA
    Archdiocese of Yucatán, México
  Evening
    Diocese of Gap, France
    Diocese of Malang, Indonesia
    Diocese of Rodez, France
    Diocese of Texcoco, México, México

Wed, 05 August 2020
  Morning
    Diocese of Baucau, Timor-Leste
    Diocese of Kakamega, Kenya

   Diocese of Santa Rosa, Argentina
   Diocese of Yanzhou, China
  Evening
   Diocese of Lokoja, Nigeria
   Diocese of San Marco Argentano-Scalea, Italy
   Diocese of São Carlos, Sao Paulo, Brazil
   Diocese of Syracuse, New York, USA

Thu, 06 August 2020
  Morning
   Diocese of Choluteca, Honduras
   Diocese of Kasese, Uganda
   Diocese of Laohekou, China
   Diocese of Muyinga, Burundi
   Diocese of San Pedro de Macorís, Dominican Republic
  Evening
   Diocese of Amboina, Indonesia
   Diocese of Bubanza, Burundi
   Diocese of Coimbra, Portugal
   Diocese of Girardota, Colombia

Fri, 07 August 2020
  Morning
   Diocese of Cheju, South Korea
   Diocese of Fargo, North Dakota, USA
   Diocese of Kankan, Guinea
   Diocese of Mantova, Italy
   Archdiocese of Monrovia, Liberia
  Evening
   Diocese of Bergamo, Italy
   Archdiocese of Dar-es-Salaam, Tanzania
   Diocese of Hengyang, China
   Archdiocese of Southwark, England

Sat, 08 August 2020
  Morning
   Diocese of Dharmapuri, India
   Archdiocese of Évora, Portugal
   Diocese of San, Mali
   Archdiocese of Siena-Colle di Val d'Elsa-Montalcino, Italy
   Diocese of Sofia e Plovdiv, Bulgaria
  Evening
   Military Ordinariate of Belgium
   Diocese of Hải Phòng, Viet Nam
   Diocese of Iringa, Tanzania
   Diocese of Salem, India

Sun, 09 August 2020
  Morning
   Archdiocese of Częstochowa, Poland
   Syro-Malabar Catholic Archdiocese of Ernakulam-Angamaly, India
   Diocese of Groningen-Leeuwarden, Netherlands
   Archdiocese of Monreale, Italy
   Diocese of Viana, Maranhão, Brazil
  Evening
   Diocese of Farafangana, Madagascar
   Diocese of Fort Portal, Uganda
   Diocese of Lamego, Portugal
   Diocese of San Vicente del Caguán, Colombia

Mon, 10 August 2020
  Morning
    Diocese of Kangding, China
    Diocese of La Spezia-Sarzana-Brugnato, Italy
    Diocese of Mogadiscio, Somalia
    Archdiocese of Nanning, China
    Diocese of Nuevo Laredo, Tamaulipas, México
  Evening
    Archdiocese of Goiânia, Goias, Brazil
    Diocese of Larantuka, Indonesia
    Diocese of Ratnapura, Sri Lanka
    Maronite Catholic Archeparchy of Tyr, Lebanon
Tue, 11 August 2020
  Morning
    Diocese of Buga, Colombia
    Diocese of Hoima, Uganda
    Diocese of Lismore, Australia
    Diocese of Matadi, Democratic Republic of the Congo
    Diocese of Tagum, Philippines
  Evening
    Diocese of Buéa, Cameroon
    Diocese of Essen, Germany
    Diocese of San Bartolomé de Chillán, Chile
    Diocese of Sintang, Indonesia
Wed, 12 August 2020
  Morning
    Archdiocese of Capiz, Philippines
    Armenian Catholic Patriarchal Exarchate of Jerusalem and Amman, Palestine
    Diocese of Nogales, Sonora, México
    Diocese of Porto, Portugal
    Diocese of San Pedro Sula, Honduras
  Evening
    Diocese of Aire et Dax, France
    Diocese of Masaka, Uganda
    Territorial Abbey of Monte Oliveto Maggiore, Italy
    Diocese of Toledo, Ohio, USA
Thu, 13 August 2020
  Morning
    Macedonian Catholic Eparchy of Beata Maria Vergine Assunta in Strumica-Skopje
    Diocese of Chiavari, Italy
    Maronite Catholic Eparchy of Our Lady of the Annunciation at Ibadan, Nigeria
    Diocese of San Miguel, Argentina
  Evening
    Archdiocese of Kisangani, Democratic Republic of the Congo
    Romanian Catholic Diocese of Lugoj, Romania
    Diocese of Moramanga, Madagascar
    Greek Catholic Eparchy of San Nicola di Ruski Krstur
Fri, 14 August 2020
  Morning
    Territorial Prelature of Chota, Peru
    Diocese of Kaolack, Senegal
    Diocese of Macau, China
    Diocese of Maiduguri, Nigeria
    Diocese of Montego Bay, Jamaica, Antilles

Evening
  Diocese of Belfort-Montbéliard, France
  Diocese of Jullundur, India
  Diocese of Mariannhill, South Africa
  Melkite Greek Catholic Eparchy of Nossa Senhora do Paraíso em São Paulo, Sao Paulo, Brazil
Sat, 15 August 2020
  Morning
    Armenian Catholic Eparchy of Ispahan, Iran
    Diocese of Mackenzie-Fort Smith, Northwest Territories, Canada
    Diocese of Mont-Laurier, Québec, Canada
    Diocese of Tunduru-Masasi, Tanzania
    Diocese of Uvira, Democratic Republic of the Congo
  Evening
    Diocese of Río Gallegos, Argentina
    Armenian Catholic Eparchy of San Gregorio de Narek en Buenos Aires, Argentina
    Diocese of Vilkaviškis, Lithuania
    Diocese of Yanji, China
Sun, 16 August 2020
  Morning
    Diocese of Enugu, Nigeria
    Apostolic Vicariate of Esmeraldas, Ecuador
    Melkite Greek Catholic Archeparchy of Latakia, Syria
    Diocese of Marquette, Michigan, USA
    Diocese of Pinheiro, Maranhão, Brazil
  Evening
    Apostolic Vicariate of Jaén en Peru o San Francisco Javier
    Diocese of Oeiras, Piaui, Brazil
    Archdiocese of Oristano, Italy
    Diocese of Sincelejo, Colombia
Mon, 17 August 2020
  Morning
    Diocese of Adria-Rovigo, Italy
    Diocese of Allahabad, India
    Diocese of Celaya, Guanajuato, México
    Archdiocese of Jinan, China
    Apostolic Prefecture of Tongzhou, China
  Evening
    Archdiocese of Imphal, India
    Diocese of Jackson, Mississippi, USA
    Diocese of Pankshin, Nigeria
    Diocese of Rockford, Illinois, USA
Tue, 18 August 2020
  Morning
    Diocese of Cefalù, Italy
    Diocese of Izcalli, México, México
    Archdiocese of Portland in Oregon, USA
    Archdiocese of Regina, Saskatchewan, Canada
    Territorial Prelature of Sicuani, Peru
  Evening
    Diocese of Guadix, Spain
    Maronite Catholic Eparchy of Joubbé, Sarba e Jounieh, Lebanon
    Archdiocese of Messina-Lipari-Santa Lucia del Mela, Italy
    Diocese of Riohacha, Colombia

Wed, 19 August 2020
- Morning
  - Armenian Catholic Archeparchy of Baghdad, Iraq
  - Archdiocese of Durango, México
  - Diocese of Limeira, Sao Paulo, Brazil
  - Diocese of 's Hertogenbosch, Netherlands
  - Diocese of Witbank, South Africa
- Evening
  - Diocese of Jericó, Colombia
  - Archdiocese of Korhogo, Côte d'Ivoire
  - Diocese of Massa Marittima-Piombino, Italy
  - Diocese of Rotterdam, Netherlands

Thu, 20 August 2020
- Morning
  - Diocese of Altoona-Johnstown, Pennsylvania, USA
  - Archdiocese of Bangalore, India
  - Archdiocese of Kingston in Jamaica, Antilles
  - Diocese of Šibenik, Croatia
  - Diocese of Terni-Narni-Amelia, Italy
- Evening
  - Archdiocese of Dakar, Senegal
  - Diocese of Mandeville, Jamaica, Antilles
  - Diocese of Santa Rosa, USA
  - Diocese of Shinyanga, Tanzania

Fri, 21 August 2020
- Morning
  - Diocese of Gizo, Solomon Islands
  - Diocese of Óbidos, Para, Brazil
  - Archdiocese of Sorrento-Castellammare di Stabia, Italy
  - Diocese of Wilcannia-Forbes, Australia
  - Diocese of Zacatecoluca, El Salvador
- Evening
  - Archdiocese of Brasília, Distrito Federal, Brazil
  - Apostolic Vicariate of Donkorkrom, Ghana
  - Diocese of Sosnowiec, Poland
  - Territorial Prelature of Tefé, Amazonas, Brazil

Sat, 22 August 2020
- Morning
  - Armenian Catholic Archeparchy of Alep, Syria
  - Diocese of San Martín, Argentina
  - Archdiocese of Santa Fe de la Vera Cruz, Argentina
  - Diocese of Teramo-Atri, Italy
- Evening
  - Archdiocese of Cape Coast, Ghana
  - Romanian Catholic Archdiocese of Făgăraş şi Alba Iulia, Romania
  - Diocese of Waterford and Lismore, Ireland
  - Archdiocese of Zaragoza, Spain

Sun, 23 August 2020
- Morning
  - Diocese of Baroda, India
  - Archdiocese of Ibadan, Nigeria
  - Diocese of Kyōto, Japan
  - Archdiocese of Nagpur, India
  - Diocese of Quy Nhơn, Viet Nam

Evening
- Diocese of Montelibano, Colombia
- Syro-Malabar Catholic Diocese of Rajkot, India
- Diocese of Rēzekne-Aglona, Latvia
- Diocese of San Bernardino, California, USA

Mon, 24 August 2020
Morning
- Diocese of Cerreto Sannita-Telese-Sant'Agata de' Goti, Italy
- Diocese of Jardim, Mato Grosso do Sul, Brazil
- Chaldean Catholic Eparchy of Mar Addai of Toronto, Canada
- Diocese of Skopje, North Macedonia
- Apostolic Prefecture of Yixian, China

Evening
- Diocese of Danlí, Honduras
- Archdiocese of Florencia, Colombia
- Apostolic Vicariate of San Andrés y Providencia, Colombia
- Apostolic Vicariate of Taytay, Philippines

Tue, 25 August 2020
Morning
- Archdiocese of Cali, Colombia
- Archdiocese of Cuttack-Bhubaneswar, India
- Diocese of Jalapa, Guatemala
- Diocese of Morombe, Madagascar
- Archdiocese of Villavicencio, Colombia

Evening
- Diocese of Beihai, China
- Diocese of Joinville, Santa Catarina, Brazil
- Diocese of Montauban, France
- Diocese of Uruaçu, Goias, Brazil

Wed, 26 August 2020
Morning
- Diocese of Bjelovar-Križevci, Croatia
- Diocese of Broome, Australia
- Diocese of Cassano all'Jonio, Italy
- Archdiocese of Ottawa-Cornwall, Ontario, Canada
- Mission Sui Iuris of Turkmenistan

Evening
- Archdiocese of Bar, Montenegro
- Diocese of Chascomús, Argentina
- Diocese of Dali, China
- Diocese of Tombura-Yambio, South Sudan

Thu, 27 August 2020
Morning
- Diocese of Butembo-Beni, Democratic Republic of the Congo
- Archdiocese of Cagliari, Italy
- Diocese of Floriano, Piaui, Brazil
- Apostolic Vicariate of Harar, Ethiopia
- Archdiocese of Trento, Italy

Evening
- Diocese of Ebolowa, Cameroon
- Diocese of Melaka-Johor, Malaysia
- Diocese of Palangkaraya, Indonesia
- Diocese of Surigao, Philippines

Fri, 28 August 2020
- Morning
  - Diocese of Gary, Indiana, USA
  - Archdiocese of Keewatin-Le Pas, Manitoba, Canada
  - Diocese of Latina-Terracina-Sezze-Priverno, Italy
  - Diocese of Ogdensburg, New York, USA
  - Diocese of Techiman, Ghana
- Evening
  - Diocese of Bluefields, Nicaragua
  - Diocese of Reggio Emilia-Guastalla, Italy
  - Apostolic Vicariate of Trinidad, Colombia
  - Melkite Greek Catholic Archeparchy of Tripoli, Lebanon

Sat, 29 August 2020
- Morning
  - Syro-Malabar Catholic Eparchy of Chanda, India
  - Diocese of Chinhoyi, Zimbabwe
  - Archdiocese of Edmonton, Alberta, Canada
  - Diocese of Sankt Gallen, Switzerland
  - Apostolic Prefecture of Shaowu, China
- Evening
  - Diocese of Chalatenango, El Salvador
  - Diocese of Orán, Argentina
  - Diocese of Padang, Indonesia
  - Diocese of Thunder Bay, Ontario, Canada

Sun, 30 August 2020
- Morning
  - Diocese of Bagdogra, India
  - Archdiocese of Katowice, Poland
  - Diocese of Shuoxian, China
  - Diocese of Xochimilco, México, México
- Evening
  - Diocese of Barra do Piraí-Volta Redonda, Rio de Janeiro, Brazil
  - Archdiocese of Nueva Segovia, Philippines
  - Diocese of Pereira, Colombia
  - Diocese of Verona, Italy

Mon, 31 August 2020
- Morning
  - Diocese of Mainz, Germany
  - Diocese of Mansa, Zambia
  - Diocese of Noto, Italy
  - Diocese of Piedras Negras, Coahuila, México
  - Diocese of Rockville Centre, New York, USA
- Evening
  - Diocese of Concordia, Argentina
  - Diocese of Meath, Ireland
  - Diocese of Yibin, China
  - Maronite Catholic Eparchy of Zahleh, Lebanon

September

Tue, 01 September 2020
  Morning
    Diocese of Doba, Chad
    Diocese of Huelva, Spain
    Diocese of Margarita, Venezuela
    Diocese of Nakhon Ratchasima, Thailand
    Diocese of Troyes, France
  Evening
    Diocese of Leribe, Lesotho
    Archdiocese of Maseru, Lesotho
    Diocese of Saint-Claude, France
    Diocese of Sibolga, Indonesia

Wed, 02 September 2020
  Morning
    Diocese of Irecê, Bahia, Brazil
    Diocese of Mallorca, Spain
    Diocese of Same, Tanzania
    Diocese of Sikasso, Mali
    Diocese of Yantai, China
  Evening
    Diocese of Buffalo, New York, USA
    Military Ordinariate of Colombia
    Archdiocese of Indianapolis, Indiana, USA
    Diocese of Tsiroanomandidy, Madagascar

Thu, 03 September 2020
  Morning
    Diocese of Bunda, Tanzania
    Diocese of Gómez Palacio, Durango, México
    Diocese of Gumla, India
    Diocese of Molegbe, Democratic Republic of the Congo
    Diocese of Nicosia, Italy
  Evening
    Diocese of Koudougou, Burkina Faso
    Archdiocese of Pisa, Italy
    Apostolic Vicariate of Rundu, Namibia
    Diocese of Versailles, France

Fri, 04 September 2020
  Morning
    Diocese of Daejeon, South Korea
    Chaldean Catholic Archeparchy of Diarbekir, Turkey
    Diocese of Uromi, Nigeria
    Diocese of Wonju, South Korea
    Diocese of Zielona Góra-Gorzów, Poland
  Evening
    Diocese of Berbérati, Central African Republic
    Archdiocese of Lagos, Nigeria
    Archdiocese of N'Djaména, Chad
    Diocese of Santorini, Greece

Sat, 05 September 2020
  Morning
    Archdiocese of Poznań, Poland
    Diocese of Rutana, Burundi
    Diocese of San Benedetto del Tronto-Ripatransone-Montalto, Italy

    Diocese of Umuarama, Parana, Brazil
    Diocese of Wilmington, Delaware, USA
  Evening
    Diocese of Gaoua, Burkina Faso
    Diocese of Itumbiara, Goias, Brazil
    Diocese of Musoma, Tanzania
    Diocese of Teófilo Otoni, Minas Gerais, Brazil

Sun, 06 September 2020
  Morning
    Maronite Catholic Archeparchy of Beirut, Lebanon
    Diocese of Isernia-Venafro, Italy
    Diocese of Prato, Italy
    Ukrainian Catholic Eparchy of Stryj, Ukraine
    Diocese of Wollongong, Australia
  Evening
    Patriarchate of East Indies, India
    Diocese of Mahajanga, Madagascar
    Diocese of Pavia, Italy
    Chaldean Catholic Eparchy of Saint Peter the Apostle of San Diego, USA

Mon, 07 September 2020
  Morning
    Diocese of Ciudad Real, Spain
    Archdiocese of Fianarantsoa, Madagascar
    Diocese of Patti, Italy
    Diocese of Teruel y Albarracín, Spain
  Evening
    Diocese of Ariano Irpino-Lacedonia, Italy
    Archdiocese of Karachi, Pakistan
    Diocese of Rzeszów, Poland
    Diocese of San Rafael, Argentina

Tue, 08 September 2020
  Morning
    Diocese of Bom Jesus da Lapa, Bahia, Brazil
    Diocese of Gospić-Senj, Croatia
    Diocese of Jefferson City, Missouri, USA
    Apostolic Vicariate of Reyes, Bolivia
    Diocese of San Vicente, El Salvador
  Evening
    Archdiocese of Chieti-Vasto, Italy
    Diocese of Ciego de Ávila, Cuba
    Archdiocese of Madras and Mylapore, India
    Diocese of Maralal, Kenya

Wed, 09 September 2020
  Morning
    Diocese of Eluru, India
    Diocese of Mao-Monte Cristi, Dominican Republic
    Suburbicarian See of Porto-Santa Rufina, Italy
    Archdiocese of Salerno-Campagna-Acerno, Italy
    Diocese of Santíssima Conceição do Araguaia, Brazil
  Evening
    Archdiocese of Barranquilla, Colombia
    Archdiocese of Khartoum, Sudan
    Archdiocese of Samarinda, Indonesia
    Apostolic Vicariate of Tabuk, Philippines

Thu, 10 September 2020
  Morning
    Diocese of Bismarck, North Dakota, USA
    Territorial Prelature of Huautla, Oaxaca, México
    Diocese of Karonga, Malawi
    Diocese of San Carlos de Bariloche, Argentina
    Apostolic Vicariate of Tucupita, Venezuela
  Evening
    Diocese of Asti, Italy
    Diocese of Kilmore, Ireland
    Diocese of Osma-Soria, Spain
    Diocese of Singida, Tanzania
Fri, 11 September 2020
  Morning
    Diocese of Colón-Kuna Yala, Panama
    Syrian Catholic Archeparchy of Hadiab-Erbil, Iraq
    Diocese of Joaçaba, Santa Catarina, Brazil
    Diocese of Nanyang, China
    Diocese of Raiganj, India
  Evening
    Diocese of Ambikapur, India
    Diocese of Springfield-Cape Girardeau, Missouri, USA
    Diocese of Tlapa, Guerrero, México
    Archdiocese of Tororo, Uganda
Sat, 12 September 2020
  Morning
    Diocese of Calbayog, Philippines
    Diocese of Carabayllo, Peru
    Diocese of Encarnación, Paraguay
    Diocese of Gurué, Mozambique
    Diocese of Puerto Plata, Dominican Republic
  Evening
    Archdiocese of Kuala Lumpur, Malaysia
    Apostolic Vicariate of Paksé, Laos
    Apostolic Vicariate of Southern Arabia, Yemen
    Diocese of Yuci, China
Sun, 13 September 2020
  Morning
    Territorial Prelature of Corocoro, Bolivia
    Diocese of Doumé-Abong' Mbang, Cameroon
    Greek Catholic Apostolic Exarchate of Istanbul, Turkey
    Diocese of Keetmanshoop, Namibia
    Archdiocese of Sant'Angelo dei Lombardi-Conza-Nusco-Bisaccia, Italy
  Evening
    Diocese of Bragança Paulista, Sao Paulo, Brazil
    Territorial Prelature of Marajó, Para, Brazil
    Archdiocese of New Orleans, Louisiana, USA
    Diocese of Vacaria, Rio Grande do Sul, Brazil
Mon, 14 September 2020
  Morning
    Chaldean Catholic Patriarchate of Babylon, Iraq
    Diocese of Facatativá, Colombia
    Diocese of Kiyinda-Mityana, Uganda
    Diocese of Neiva, Colombia
    Diocese of San José de Mayo, Uruguay

Evening
    Archdiocese of Dubuque, Iowa, USA
    Diocese of Guanhães, Minas Gerais, Brazil
    Diocese of Sapporo, Japan
    Diocese of Udupi, India
Tue, 15 September 2020
  Morning
    Diocese of Ciudad del Este, Paraguay
    Archdiocese of Milan, Italy
    Diocese of Mukachevo, Ukraine
    Archdiocese of Porto Velho, Rondonia, Brazil
  Evening
    Diocese of Cleveland, Ohio, USA
    Diocese of Manokwari-Sorong, Indonesia
    Diocese of Quiché, Guatemala
    Diocese of San Luis, Argentina
Wed, 16 September 2020
  Morning
    Coptic Catholic Patriarchate of Alexandria, Egypt
    Apostolic Vicariate of Napo, Ecuador
    Apostolic Prefecture of Robe, Ethiopia
    Diocese of Sault Sainte Marie, Ontario, Canada
    Diocese of Temuco, Chile
  Evening
    Diocese of Hamilton in Bermuda, Antilles
    Diocese of Jilin, China
    Diocese of Siuna, Nicaragua
    Diocese of Tenkodogo, Burkina Faso
Thu, 17 September 2020
  Morning
    Diocese of Bareilly, India
    Diocese of Chifeng, China
    Archdiocese of Kingston, Ontario, Canada
    Diocese of Tacámbaro, Michoacán, México
    Diocese of Ugento-Santa Maria di Leuca, Italy
  Evening
    Diocese of Hearst-Moosonee, Ontario, Canada
    Diocese of Hwange, Zimbabwe
    Territorial Prelature of Isabela, Philippines
    Diocese of Nashville, Tennessee, USA
Fri, 18 September 2020
  Morning
    Diocese of Hong Kong, China
    Diocese of Lomas de Zamora, Argentina
    Diocese of Lorena, Sao Paulo, Brazil
    Archdiocese of Pretoria, South Africa
    Diocese of Žilina, Slovakia
  Evening
    Diocese of Andria, Italy
    Diocese of Gikongoro, Rwanda
    Syro-Malabar Catholic Eparchy of Saint Thomas the Apostle of Chicago, Illinois, USA
    Diocese of Trier, Germany
Sat, 19 September 2020
  Morning
    Diocese of Calahorra y La Calzada-Logroño, Spain

Diocese of Campanha, Minas Gerais, Brazil
　　Diocese of Guarulhos, Sao Paulo, Brazil
　　Diocese of La Rochelle, France
　　Archdiocese of Warmia, Poland
　Evening
　　Diocese of Chikwawa, Malawi
　　Archdiocese of Ferrara-Comacchio, Italy
　　Apostolic Vicariate of Galápagos, Ecuador
　　Archdiocese of Toamasina, Madagascar

Sun, 20 September 2020
　Morning
　　Apostolic Administration of Estonia
　　Diocese of Imola, Italy
　　Diocese of Les Cayes, Haïti
　　Diocese of Mongu, Zambia
　　Diocese of Vasai, India
　Evening
　　Diocese of Abaetetuba, Para, Brazil
　　Diocese of Fulda, Germany
　　Diocese of Saint-Jérôme, Québec, Canada
　　Apostolic Prefecture of Weihai, China

Mon, 21 September 2020
　Morning
　　Diocese of Anse-à-Veau et Miragoâne, Haïti
　　Diocese of Arras, France
　　Diocese of Guasdualito, Venezuela
　　Diocese of Santiago de María, El Salvador
　　Diocese of Viana, Angola
　Evening
　　Diocese of Jowai, India
　　Apostolic Vicariate of Nekemte, Ethiopia
　　Diocese of Saint-Louis du Sénégal
　　Diocese of San Sebastián, Spain

Tue, 22 September 2020
　Morning
　　Greek Catholic Diocese of Križevci, Croatia
　　Diocese of Matamoros, Tamaulipas, México
　　Diocese of Paulo Afonso, Bahia, Brazil
　　Diocese of Port-Gentil, Gabon
　　Diocese of Vannes, France
　Evening
　　Diocese of Kalamazoo, Michigan, USA
　　Diocese of Kurunegala, Sri Lanka
　　Diocese of Rockhampton, Australia
　　Armenian Catholic Ordinariate of Romania

Wed, 23 September 2020
　Morning
　　Diocese of Catanduva, Sao Paulo, Brazil
　　Diocese of Incheon, South Korea
　　Diocese of Petrolina, Pernambuco, Brazil
　　Diocese of Segorbe-Castellón de la Plana, Spain
　　Diocese of Tortosa, Spain
　Evening
　　Diocese of Frederico Westphalen, Rio Grande do Sul, Brazil
　　Archdiocese of Hamburg, Germany

Apostolic Vicariate of Ingwavuma, South Africa
Diocese of Laghouat, Algeria

Thu, 24 September 2020
  Morning
    Diocese of Ciudad Victoria, Tamaulipas, México
    Diocese of Dumaguete, Philippines
    Diocese of Pasto, Colombia
    Diocese of Pointe-Noire, Republic of the Congo
  Evening
    Diocese of Debrecen-Nyíregyháza, Hungary
    Diocese of San Francisco, Argentina
    Archdiocese of Westminster, England
    Diocese of Zárate-Campana, Argentina

Fri, 25 September 2020
  Morning
    Diocese of Ávila, Spain
    Diocese of Bongaigaon, India
    Diocese of Kenge, Democratic Republic of the Congo
    Diocese of Kindu, Democratic Republic of the Congo
    Archdiocese of Shillong, India
  Evening
    Diocese of Daet, Philippines
    Diocese of Jaffna, Sri Lanka
    Diocese of San Jacinto, Ecuador
    Diocese of Santissima Trinità in Almaty, Kazakhstan

Sat, 26 September 2020
  Morning
    Archdiocese of Barquisimeto, Venezuela
    Diocese of Charlotte, North Carolina, USA
    Diocese of Civitavecchia-Tarquinia, Italy
    Syro-Malabar Catholic Eparchy of Faridabad, India
    Archdiocese of Szczecin-Kamień, Poland
  Evening
    Diocese of Augsburg, Germany
    Diocese of Lutsk, Ukraine
    Diocese of Shendam, Nigeria
    Diocese of Wanxian, China

Sun, 27 September 2020
  Morning
    Diocese of Babahoyo, Ecuador
    Archdiocese of Boston, Massachusetts, USA
    Diocese of Gboko, Nigeria
    Diocese of Orvieto-Todi, Italy
    Diocese of Pelplin, Poland
  Evening
    Diocese of Agen, France
    Diocese of Beaumont, Texas, USA
    Diocese of Lafayette, Louisiana, USA
    Diocese of Zhouzhi, China

Mon, 28 September 2020
  Morning
    Diocese of Bauru, Sao Paulo, Brazil
    Diocese of Madison, Wisconsin, USA
    Archdiocese of Semarang, Indonesia
    Diocese of Shangqiu, China

Diocese of Shrewsbury, England
 Evening
  Apostolic Prefecture of Baojing, China
  Diocese of Itapipoca, Ceara, Brazil
  Diocese of Požega, Croatia
  Diocese of Senigallia, Italy

Tue, 29 September 2020
 Morning
  Diocese of Caguas, Puerto Rico
  Diocese of Conversano-Monopoli, Italy
  Syro-Malabar Catholic Eparchy of Idukki, India
  Diocese of Moroto, Uganda
  Diocese of Xiwanzi-Chongli, China
 Evening
  Diocese of Mbinga, Tanzania
  Diocese of Rouyn-Noranda, Québec, Canada
  Diocese of Rrëshen, Albania
  Melkite Greek Catholic Eparchy of Saint Michael's of Sydney, Australia

Wed, 30 September 2020
 Morning
  Diocese of Cristalândia, Goias, Brazil
  Diocese of San Justo, Argentina
  Diocese of Santa Clara, Cuba
  Diocese of Sobral, Ceara, Brazil
  Diocese of Telšiai, Lithuania
 Evening
  Diocese of Ch'unch'ŏn, South Korea
  Diocese of Maitland-Newcastle, Australia
  Diocese of Quixadá, Ceara, Brazil
  Apostolic Vicariate of San José del Amazonas, Peru

October

Thu, 01 October 2020
  Morning
    Territorial Prelature of Deán Funes, Argentina
    Diocese of Hamilton, Ontario, Canada
    Diocese of Leiria-Fátima, Portugal
    Diocese of Oberá, Argentina
    Diocese of Valledupar, Colombia
  Evening
    Melkite Greek Catholic Archdiocese of Beirut and Jbeil, Lebanon
    Archdiocese of Clermont, France
    Diocese of Gaborone, Botswana
    Diocese of Kontagora, Nigeria

Fri, 02 October 2020
  Morning
    Diocese of Belgaum, India
    Melkite Greek Catholic Patriarchal Dependent Territory of Egypt, Sudan, and South Sudan
    Diocese of Gumaca, Philippines
    Archdiocese of Mérida-Badajoz, Spain
  Evening
    Diocese of Atakpamé, Togo
    Archdiocese of Kumasi, Ghana
    Diocese of Raigarh, India
    Diocese of Sunyani, Ghana

Sat, 03 October 2020
  Morning
    Coptic Catholic Eparchy of Guizeh, Egypt
    Diocese of Jaca, Spain
    Diocese of Jequié, Bahia, Brazil
    Diocese of Murska Sobota, Slovenia
    Diocese of Reno, Nevada, USA
  Evening
    Archdiocese of Esztergom-Budapest, Hungary
    Diocese of Treviso, Italy
    Archdiocese of Urbino-Urbania-Sant'Angelo in Vado, Italy
    Diocese of Valença, Rio de Janeiro, Brazil

Sun, 04 October 2020
  Morning
    Diocese of Caltagirone, Italy
    Ukrainian Catholic Eparchy of Kamyanets-Podilskyi, Ukraine
    Archdiocese of Przemyśl, Poland
    Diocese of Sakania-Kipushi, Democratic Republic of the Congo
    Diocese of Tampico, Tamaulipas, México
  Evening
    Diocese of Khandwa, India
    Archdiocese of Lanzhou, China
    Diocese of Phoenix, Arizona, USA
    Diocese of Votuporanga, Sao Paulo, Brazil

Mon, 05 October 2020
  Morning
    Suburbicarian See of Albano, Italy
    Diocese of Crato, Ceara, Brazil
    Diocese of Manado, Indonesia

Diocese of Prince-Albert, Saskatchewan, Canada
Evening
Diocese of Altamura-Gravina-Acquaviva delle Fonti, Italy
Diocese of Bagé, Rio Grande do Sul, Brazil
Archdiocese of Cotabato, Philippines
Diocese of Registro, Sao Paulo, Brazil

Tue, 06 October 2020
Morning
Diocese of Almería, Spain
Diocese of Guaranda, Ecuador
Diocese of Ilagan, Philippines
Diocese of Odessa-Simferopol, Ukraine
Archdiocese of Saint John's, Newfoundland, Canada
Evening
Diocese of Barishal, Bangladesh
Diocese of Córdoba, Veracruz, México
Diocese of Formosa, Goias, Brazil
Armenian Catholic Archeparchy of Lviv, Ukraine

Wed, 07 October 2020
Morning
Diocese of Birmingham, Alabama, USA
Diocese of El Alto, Bolivia
Diocese of Jinotega, Nicaragua
Diocese of San Marino-Montefeltro, Italy
Diocese of Sumbawanga, Tanzania
Evening
Diocese of Burlington, Vermont, USA
Diocese of Ganzhou, China
Diocese of Manchester, New Hampshire, USA
Apostolic Vicariate of Soddo, Ethiopia

Thu, 08 October 2020
Morning
Diocese of Gamboma, Republic of the Congo
Diocese of Killala, Ireland
Ukrainian Catholic Archiepiscopal Exarchate of Krym, Ukraine
Archdiocese of Samoa-Apia, Samoa
Diocese of Veracruz, México
Evening
Diocese of Carolina, Maranhão, Brazil
Diocese of Cuernavaca, Morelos, México
Diocese of Meixian, China
Archdiocese of Shenyang, China

Fri, 09 October 2020
Morning
Diocese of Ambatondrazaka, Madagascar
Diocese of Andong, South Korea
Diocese of Coria-Cáceres, Spain
Archdiocese of Hobart, Australia
Diocese of Issele-Uku, Nigeria
Evening
Diocese of Angoulême, France
Diocese of Kabinda, Democratic Republic of the Congo
Syro-Malankara Catholic Eparchy of Saint John Chrysostom of Gurgaon, India
Diocese of San Lorenzo, Paraguay

Sat, 10 October 2020
- Morning
  - Archdiocese of Bujumbura, Burundi
  - Diocese of Feldkirch, Austria
  - Territorial Prelature of Santiago Apóstol de Huancané, Peru
  - Diocese of Stockholm, Sweden
- Evening
  - Diocese of Duitama-Sogamoso, Colombia
  - Diocese of Lai, Chad
  - Diocese of Saint John's-Basseterre, British Virgin Islands
  - Diocese of Uberlândia, Minas Gerais, Brazil

Sun, 11 October 2020
- Morning
  - Diocese of Belluno-Feltre, Italy
  - Archdiocese of Camagüey, Cuba
  - Diocese of Kerema, Papua New Guinea
  - Diocese of Makeni, Sierra Leone
  - Archdiocese of Modena-Nonantola, Italy
- Evening
  - Diocese of Great Falls-Billings, Montana, USA
  - Diocese of Ocaña, Colombia
  - Diocese of Savannah, Georgia, USA
  - Archdiocese of Yangon, Myanmar

Mon, 12 October 2020
- Morning
  - Diocese of Coxim, Mato Grosso do Sul, Brazil
  - Diocese of Cuautitlán, México, México
  - Apostolic Vicariate of Meki, Ethiopia
  - Apostolic Vicariate of Quetta, Pakistan
  - Diocese of Roermond, Netherlands
- Evening
  - Diocese of Eldoret, Kenya
  - Diocese of Fort Wayne-South Bend, Indiana, USA
  - Diocese of Mondovi, Italy
  - Archdiocese of Toulouse, France

Tue, 13 October 2020
- Morning
  - Archdiocese of Gaeta, Italy
  - Archdiocese of Granada, Spain
  - Maronite Catholic Archeparchy of Haifa and the Holy Land, Israel
  - Diocese of Jundiaí, Sao Paulo, Brazil
  - Archdiocese of Resistencia, Argentina
- Evening
  - Syro-Malankara Catholic Eparchy of Battery, India
  - Diocese of Buxar, India
  - Diocese of Chikmagalur, India
  - Military Ordinariate of Italy

Wed, 14 October 2020
- Morning
  - Archdiocese of Bamberg, Germany
  - Diocese of Chimoio, Mozambique
  - Archdiocese of Lusaka, Zambia
  - Archdiocese of Owerri, Nigeria
  - Archdiocese of Sydney, Australia

Evening
  Maronite Catholic Eparchy of Batrun, Lebanon
  Armenian Catholic Eparchy of Sainte-Croix-de-Paris, France
  Diocese of Saint Paul in Alberta, Canada
  Archdiocese of Tabora, Tanzania

Thu, 15 October 2020
  Morning
    Diocese of Fukuoka, Japan
    Archdiocese of México, Federal District
    Archdiocese of Port-au-Prince, Haïti
    Archdiocese of Trivandrum, India
    Diocese of Yingkou, China
  Evening
    Diocese of Amparo, Sao Paulo, Brazil
    Diocese of Kimberley, South Africa
    Apostolic Prefecture of Lixian, China
    Ruthenian Catholic Eparchy of Passaic, New Jersey, USA

Fri, 16 October 2020
  Morning
    Archdiocese of Beijing, China
    Apostolic Vicariate of Leticia, Colombia
    Ukrainian Catholic Archiepiscopal Exarchate of Lutsk, Ukraine
    Archdiocese of Mobile, Alabama, USA
    Archdiocese of Zadar, Croatia
  Evening
    Diocese of Erie, Pennsylvania, USA
    Archdiocese of Gniezno, Poland
    Military Ordinariate of Kenya
    Diocese of Sandomierz, Poland

Sat, 17 October 2020
  Morning
    Ruthenian Catholic Apostolic Exarchate of Czech Republic
    Diocese of Girardot, Colombia
    Archdiocese of Santiago de los Caballeros, Dominican Republic
    Diocese of Tibú, Colombia
    Archdiocese of Trani-Barletta-Bisceglie, Italy
  Evening
    Ukrainian Catholic Archeparchy of Philadelphia, Pennsylvania, USA
    Apostolic Vicariate of Puerto Gaitán, Colombia
    Diocese of Rustenburg, South Africa
    Diocese of Yinchuan, China

Sun, 18 October 2020
  Morning
    Diocese of Bafatá, Guinea-Bissau
    Diocese of Ketapang, Indonesia
    Diocese of Khunti, India
    Archdiocese of La Paz, Bolivia
    Diocese of Miao, India
  Evening
    Archdiocese of Bertoua, Cameroon
    Diocese of Dunedin, New Zealand
    Diocese of Oudtshoorn, South Africa
    Archdiocese of Tōkyō, Japan

Mon, 19 October 2020
  Morning
    Diocese of Apucarana, Parana, Brazil
    Russian Catholic Apostolic Exarchate of Harbin, China
    Diocese of Moulins, France
    Diocese of Oakland, California, USA
  Evening
    Diocese of Carúpano, Venezuela
    Diocese of Karwar, India
    Archdiocese of Riga, Latvia
    Diocese of Torit, South Sudan
Tue, 20 October 2020
  Morning
    Diocese of Nova Iguaçu, Rio de Janeiro, Brazil
    Diocese of Port-Vila, Vanuatu
    Archdiocese of Rabat, Morocco
    Diocese of Sainte-Anne-de-la-Pocatière, Québec, Canada
    Diocese of Suwon, South Korea
  Evening
    Archdiocese of Aparecida, Sao Paulo, Brazil
    Mission Sui Iuris of Funafuti, Tuvalu
    Diocese of San Isidro de El General, Costa Rica
    Diocese of Taichung, Taiwan
Wed, 21 October 2020
  Morning
    Archdiocese of Bologna, Italy
    Diocese of Chitré, Panama
    Melkite Greek Catholic Archdiocese of Damas, Syria
    Archdiocese of Huế, Viet Nam
    Diocese of Pathein, Myanmar
  Evening
    Archdiocese of Camerino-San Severino Marche, Italy
    Diocese of Matanzas, Cuba
    Archdiocese of Montevideo, Uruguay
    Diocese of Tarawa and Nauru, Kiribati
Thu, 22 October 2020
  Morning
    Diocese of Acireale, Italy
    Diocese of Banmaw, Myanmar
    Archdiocese of Besançon, France
    Suburbicarian See of Sabina-Poggio Mirteto, Italy
    Archdiocese of San Luis Potosí, México
  Evening
    Diocese of Kiayi, Taiwan
    Suburbicarian See of Palestrina, Italy
    Diocese of Prince George, British Columbia, Canada
    Archdiocese of Seattle, Washington, USA
Fri, 23 October 2020
  Morning
    Diocese of Đà Lạt, Viet Nam
    Apostolic Vicariate of Mitú, Colombia
    Military Ordinariate of New Zealand
    Diocese of Nueve de Julio, Argentina
    Diocese of Orihuela-Alicante, Spain

Evening
  Diocese of Granada, Nicaragua
  Archdiocese of Sorocaba, Sao Paulo, Brazil
  Syro-Malankara Catholic Archeparchy of Tiruvalla, India
  Diocese of Wuzhou, China
Sat, 24 October 2020
  Morning
    Diocese of Livingstone, Zambia
    Diocese of Ondo, Nigeria
    Diocese of Srijem, Serbia
    Diocese of Villarrica, Chile
    Diocese of Zamora, Michoacán, México
  Evening
    Diocese of Foligno, Italy
    Diocese of Idiofa, Democratic Republic of the Congo
    Archdiocese of Mendoza, Argentina
    Archdiocese of Toliara, Madagascar
Sun, 25 October 2020
  Morning
    Diocese of Annecy, France
    Diocese of Antipolo, Philippines
    Diocese of Bolzano-Bressanone, Italy
    Diocese of Málaga-Soatá, Colombia
    Diocese of Tucson, Arizona, USA
  Evening
    Diocese of Litoměřice, Czech Republic
    Diocese of Mostar-Duvno, Bosnia and Herzegovina
    Diocese of Paterson, New Jersey, USA
    Diocese of União da Vitória, Parana, Brazil
Mon, 26 October 2020
  Morning
    Diocese of Ambato, Ecuador
    Italo-Albanese Catholic Eparchy of Lungro degli Italo-Albanesi, Italy
    Apostolic Prefecture of Misurata, Libya
    Diocese of Papantla, Puebla, México
    Diocese of Zacapa y Santo Cristo de Esquipulas, Guatemala
  Evening
    Diocese of Caetité, Bahia, Brazil
    Diocese of Christchurch, New Zealand
    Diocese of Grosseto, Italy
    Diocese of Tianshui, China
Tue, 27 October 2020
  Morning
    Diocese of Bangued, Philippines
    Territorial Prelature of Bocas del Toro, Panama
    Archdiocese of Fermo, Italy
    Diocese of Vic, Spain
  Evening
    Diocese of Bo, Sierra Leone
    Diocese of Ikot Ekpene, Nigeria
    Archdiocese of Minsk-Mohilev, Belarus
    Ruthenian Catholic Eparchy of Mukachevo, Ukraine
Wed, 28 October 2020
  Morning
    Diocese of Como, Italy

    Diocese of Kontum, Viet Nam
    Syro-Malankara Catholic Eparchy of Saint Ephrem of Khadki, India
    Archdiocese of Saint Louis, Missouri, USA
    Diocese of Sylhet, Bangladesh
  Evening
    Diocese of Geraldton, Australia
    Diocese of Jalpaiguri, India
    Archdiocese of Popayán, Colombia
    Apostolic Vicariate of Puerto Ayacucho, Venezuela

Thu, 29 October 2020
  Morning
    Diocese of Ballarat, Australia
    Military Ordinariate of Korea
    Ukrainian Catholic Archeparchy of Kiev-Galicia, Ukraine
    Apostolic Administration of Kyrgyzstan
    Syro-Malabar Catholic Diocese of Thamarasserry, India
  Evening
    Diocese of Mouila, Gabon
    Archdiocese of Puebla de los Ángeles, Puebla, México
    Archdiocese of San Fernando, Philippines
    Diocese of Springfield in Illinois, USA

Fri, 30 October 2020
  Morning
    Diocese of Anlong, China
    Diocese of Itabuna, Bahia, Brazil
    Diocese of Mende, France
    Diocese of Sacramento, California, USA
    Apostolic Prefecture of Xinxiang, China
  Evening
    Archdiocese of Aix, France
    Diocese of Corner Brook and Labrador, Newfoundland, Canada
    Diocese of Joliette, Québec, Canada
    Military Ordinariate of Venezuela

Sat, 31 October 2020
  Morning
    Diocese of Assis, Sao Paulo, Brazil
    Armenian Catholic Archdiocese of Beirut, Lebanon
    Diocese of Orizaba, Veracruz, México
    Archdiocese of Puerto Montt, Chile
    Diocese of Zé-Doca, Maranhão, Brazil
  Evening
    Archdiocese of Campinas, Sao Paulo, Brazil
    Diocese of Ica, Peru
    Diocese of Sioux City, Iowa, USA
    Syro-Malabar Catholic Diocese of Ujjain, India

November

Sun, 01 November 2020
  Morning
    Archdiocese of Mbeya, Tanzania
    Diocese of Ossory, Ireland
    Apostolic Vicariate of Pucallpa, Peru
    Diocese of Saint Augustine, Florida, USA
    Diocese of Villa María, Argentina
  Evening
    Diocese of Jammu-Srinagar, India
    Syro-Malabar Catholic Archeparchy of Kottayam, India
    Diocese of San Juan Bautista de las Misiones, Paraguay
    Diocese of Sessa Aurunca, Italy

Mon, 02 November 2020
  Morning
    Ukrainian Catholic Eparchy of Imaculada Conceição in Prudentópolis, Brazil
    Diocese of Kumbakonam, India
    Diocese of London, Ontario, Canada
    Diocese of San Carlos, Philippines
    Diocese of Três Lagoas, Mato Grosso do Sul, Brazil
  Evening
    Diocese of Kayanga, Tanzania
    Diocese of Poona, India
    Diocese of San Andrés Tuxtla, Veracruz, México
    Diocese of Valparaíso, Chile

Tue, 03 November 2020
  Morning
    Apostolic Vicariate of Calapan, Philippines
    Diocese of Constantine, Algeria
    Diocese of Linyi, China
    Diocese of Piazza Armerina, Italy
    Diocese of Tyler, Texas, USA
  Evening
    Territorial Prelature of Aiquile, Bolivia
    Archdiocese of Anchorage-Juneau, Alaska, USA
    Diocese of Bridgeport, Connecticut, USA
    Apostolic Prefecture of Yuzhno Sakhalinsk, Russian Federation

Wed, 04 November 2020
  Morning
    Diocese of Batouri, Cameroon
    Military Ordinariate of Bolivia
    Diocese of Budweis, Czech Republic
    Archdiocese of Manila, Philippines
  Evening
    Diocese of Cruz das Almas, Bahia, Brazil
    Archdiocese of Los Angeles, California, USA
    Diocese of Sioux Falls, South Dakota, USA
    Diocese of Zhaoxian, China

Thu, 05 November 2020
  Morning
    Diocese of Malaybalay, Philippines
    Archdiocese of Nagasaki, Japan
    Diocese of Nola, Italy
    Diocese of Oruro, Bolivia

    Archdiocese of Tours, France
  Evening
    Syro-Malabar Catholic Eparchy of Bhadravathi, India
    Diocese of Carpi, Italy
    Diocese of Fossano, Italy
    Diocese of Yei, South Sudan

Fri, 06 November 2020
  Morning
    Diocese of Evreux, France
    Archdiocese of Galveston-Houston, Texas, USA
    Diocese of Kottar, India
    Diocese of Punta Arenas, Chile
    Apostolic Prefecture of Xinjiang-Urumqi, China
  Evening
    Archdiocese of Koupéla, Burkina Faso
    Archdiocese of León, Guanajuato, México
    Diocese of Myitkyina, Myanmar
    Apostolic Vicariate of San Miguel de Sucumbíos, Ecuador

Sat, 07 November 2020
  Morning
    Diocese of Comodoro Rivadavia, Argentina
    Diocese of Jhabua, India
    Diocese of La Paz en la Baja California Sur, México
    Diocese of Šiauliai, Lithuania
    Diocese of Viviers, France
  Evening
    Diocese of Bathurst in Canada, New Brunswick
    Diocese of Kitale, Kenya
    Diocese of Saint-Denis, France
    Diocese of Tanjungkarang, Indonesia

Sun, 08 November 2020
  Morning
    Diocese of Damongo, Ghana
    Maronite Catholic Patriarchal Exarchate of Jordan
    Diocese of Nongstoin, India
    Diocese of Poreč i Pula, Croatia
    Archdiocese of Rimouski, Québec, Canada
  Evening
    Diocese of Dallas, Texas, USA
    Diocese of Kavieng, Papua New Guinea
    Syro-Malankara Catholic Eparchy of Mavelikara, India
    Diocese of Quibdó, Colombia

Mon, 09 November 2020
  Morning
    Diocese of Fort-Liberté, Haïti
    Diocese of Hexham and Newcastle, England
    Diocese of Loja, Ecuador
    Diocese of Ragusa, Italy
    Diocese of Sées, France
  Evening
    Diocese of Avellino, Italy
    Diocese of Haimen, China
    Apostolic Vicariate of Izabal, Guatemala
    Archdiocese of Juiz de Fora, Minas Gerais, Brazil

Tue, 10 November 2020
- Morning
  - Diocese of Barahona, Dominican Republic
  - Diocese of Embu, Kenya
  - Diocese of Kingstown, Saint Vincent and Grenadines, Antilles
  - Diocese of Northampton, England
  - Diocese of Ponce, Puerto Rico
- Evening
  - Diocese of Autun, France
  - Archdiocese of Maribor, Slovenia
  - Diocese of Navrongo-Bolgatanga, Ghana
  - Diocese of Viseu, Portugal

Wed, 11 November 2020
- Morning
  - Diocese of Boac, Philippines
  - Archdiocese of Cuenca, Ecuador
  - Armenian Catholic Patriarchal Exarchate of Damas, Syria
  - Apostolic Vicariate of El Beni o Beni, Bolivia
  - Diocese of Hakha, Myanmar
- Evening
  - Diocese of Daming, China
  - Diocese of Dipolog, Philippines
  - Archdiocese of Mbandaka-Bikoro, Democratic Republic of the Congo
  - Diocese of Sapë, Albania

Thu, 12 November 2020
- Morning
  - Diocese of Impfondo, Republic of the Congo
  - Diocese of Isiro-Niangara, Democratic Republic of the Congo
  - Diocese of Nalgonda, India
  - Apostolic Vicariate of Pilcomayo, Paraguay
  - Diocese of San Carlos de Venezuela
- Evening
  - Diocese of Alba, Italy
  - Diocese of Bielsko-Żywiec, Poland
  - Archdiocese of Guadalajara, Jalisco, México
  - Diocese of Plzeň, Czech Republic

Fri, 13 November 2020
- Morning
  - Apostolic Vicariate of Alep, Syria
  - Diocese of Espinal, Colombia
  - Diocese of Nova Friburgo, Rio de Janeiro, Brazil
  - Diocese of Teano-Calvi, Italy
- Evening
  - Diocese of Coroico, Bolivia
  - Diocese of Janaúba, Minas Gerais, Brazil
  - Diocese of Ruteng, Indonesia
  - Diocese of San Pedro-en-Côte d'Ivoire

Sat, 14 November 2020
- Morning
  - Diocese of Caacupé, Paraguay
  - Diocese of Jelgava, Latvia
  - Diocese of Naviraí, Mato Grosso do Sul, Brazil
  - Diocese of Pala, Chad
  - Diocese of Warangal, India

Evening
   Diocese of Ahiara, Nigeria
   Diocese of Faenza-Modigliana, Italy
   Apostolic Prefecture of Haizhou, China
   Archdiocese of Hermosillo, Sonora, México

Sun, 15 November 2020
  Morning
   Diocese of Aosta, Italy
   Archdiocese of Benevento, Italy
   Diocese of Cuauhtémoc-Madera, Chihuahua, México
   Diocese of Dédougou, Burkina Faso
   Archdiocese of Split-Makarska, Croatia
  Evening
   Diocese of Grajaú, Maranhão, Brazil
   Apostolic Prefecture of Guilin, China
   Archdiocese of Hohhot, China
   Diocese of Ourinhos, Sao Paulo, Brazil

Mon, 16 November 2020
  Morning
   Diocese of Ales-Terralba, Italy
   Diocese of Baguio, Philippines
   Apostolic Vicariate of Derna, Libya
   Diocese of Salamanca, Spain
   Apostolic Vicariate of Vientiane, Laos
  Evening
   Archdiocese of Amalfi-Cava de' Tirreni, Italy
   Diocese of Arecibo, Puerto Rico
   Diocese of Mangalore, India
   Diocese of Tacna y Moquegua, Peru

Tue, 17 November 2020
  Morning
   Personal Ordinariate of The Chair of Saint Peter, USA
   Diocese of El Paso, Texas, USA
   Territorial Prelature of Itacoatiara, Amazonas, Brazil
   Diocese of Petrópolis, Rio de Janeiro, Brazil
   Diocese of Wewak, Papua New Guinea
  Evening
   Archdiocese of Gitega, Burundi
   Diocese of Mossoró, Rio Grande do Norte, Brazil
   Diocese of Wuhu, China
   Diocese of Yopougon, Côte d'Ivoire

Wed, 18 November 2020
  Morning
   Diocese of Bathurst, Australia
   Diocese of Le Mans, France
   Diocese of Masvingo, Zimbabwe
   Archdiocese of Palo, Philippines
   Apostolic Prefecture of Yangzhou, China
  Evening
   Archdiocese of Acapulco, Guerrero, México
   Diocese of Aliwal, South Africa
   Syro-Malabar Catholic Diocese of Palai, India
   Diocese of Ruyigi, Burundi

Thu, 19 November 2020
- Morning
  - Diocese of Aného, Togo
  - Diocese of Dumka, India
  - Archdiocese of Lanciano-Ortona, Italy
  - Diocese of Querétaro, México
  - Diocese of Yagoua, Cameroon
- Evening
  - Diocese of Borongan, Philippines
  - Archdiocese of Matera-Irsina, Italy
  - Apostolic Vicariate of San Jose in Mindoro, Philippines
  - Apostolic Prefecture of Shashi, China

Fri, 20 November 2020
- Morning
  - Armenian Catholic Archeparchy of Istanbul, Turkey
  - Archdiocese of Mombasa, Kenya
  - Diocese of Mopti, Mali
  - Maronite Catholic Eparchy of Saint Maron of Brooklyn, New York, USA
  - Diocese of Siping, China
- Evening
  - Diocese of Chiquinquirá, Colombia
  - Territorial Prelature of Humahuaca, Argentina
  - Diocese of Minna, Nigeria
  - Maronite Catholic Eparchy of Saint-Maron de Montréal, Canada

Sat, 21 November 2020
- Morning
  - Diocese of Ban Mê Thuột, Viet Nam
  - Archdiocese of Niamey, Niger
  - Diocese of Tulsa, Oklahoma, USA
  - Diocese of Virac, Philippines
- Evening
  - Diocese of Caruaru, Pernambuco, Brazil
  - Diocese of Cork and Ross, Ireland
  - Diocese of Kribi, Cameroon
  - Archdiocese of Melbourne, Australia

Sun, 22 November 2020
- Morning
  - Diocese of Agartala, India
  - Diocese of Ciudad Juárez, Chihuahua, México
  - Ukrainian Catholic Archiepiscopal Exarchate of Kharkiv, Ukraine
  - Diocese of Saint Catharines, Ontario, Canada
  - Diocese of Toowoomba, Australia
- Evening
  - Diocese of Magdeburg, Germany
  - Diocese of Périgueux, France
  - Archdiocese of Tulancingo, Hidalgo, México
  - Apostolic Vicariate of Yurimaguas, Peru

Mon, 23 November 2020
- Morning
  - Diocese of Covington, Kentucky, USA
  - Melkite Greek Catholic Patriarchal Exarchate of Iraq
  - Diocese of New Ulm, Minnesota, USA
  - Archdiocese of Santa Maria, Rio Grande do Sul, Brazil
  - Diocese of Teotihuacán, México, México

Evening
- Archdiocese of Gulu, Uganda
- Diocese of Lạng Sơn et Cao Bằng, Viet Nam
- Diocese of San Jose de Antique, Philippines
- Diocese of Teggiano-Policastro, Italy

Tue, 24 November 2020

Morning
- Diocese of Acqui, Italy
- Diocese of Iztapalapa, México, México
- Diocese of Lodi, Italy
- Archdiocese of Madre di Dio a Mosca, Russian Federation
- Diocese of San Pedro, Paraguay

Evening
- Melkite Greek Catholic Archeparchy of Baalbek, Lebanon
- Apostolic Vicariate of Rodrigues, Mauritius
- Diocese of Xinyang, China
- Diocese of Yuanling, China

Wed, 25 November 2020

Morning
- Diocese of Bridgetown, Barbados, Antilles
- Diocese of Little Rock, Arkansas, USA
- Diocese of Penang, Malaysia
- Diocese of Portsmouth, England
- Diocese of Santo Tomé, Argentina

Evening
- Archdiocese of Bamenda, Cameroon
- Diocese of Greensburg, Pennsylvania, USA
- Diocese of Muzaffarpur, India
- Diocese of Santa Rosa de Osos, Colombia

Thu, 26 November 2020

Morning
- Diocese of Amravati, India
- Military Ordinariate of Canada
- Diocese of Nouna, Burkina Faso
- Archdiocese of Oviedo, Spain
- Apostolic Vicariate of Puerto Maldonado, Peru

Evening
- Archdiocese of Chicago, Illinois, USA
- Diocese of Concordia-Pordenone, Italy
- Diocese of Gibraltar
- Diocese of Yongnian, China

Fri, 27 November 2020

Morning
- Apostolic Vicariate of Beirut, Lebanon
- Diocese of Gwalior, India
- Apostolic Vicariate of Hosanna, Ethiopia
- Diocese of Mayagüez, Puerto Rico
- Diocese of Port Victoria o Seychelles

Evening
- Diocese of Baie-Comeau, Québec, Canada
- Coptic Catholic Eparchy of Ismayliah, Egypt
- Diocese of Jixian, China
- Archdiocese of Maracaibo, Venezuela

Sat, 28 November 2020
- Morning
  - Archdiocese of Abuja, Nigeria
  - Archdiocese of Bulawayo, Zimbabwe
  - Diocese of Diamantino, Mato Grosso, Brazil
  - Diocese of Ostrava-Opava, Czech Republic
  - Diocese of San Francisco de Asís de Jutiapa, Guatemala
- Evening
  - Diocese of Banfora, Burkina Faso
  - Diocese of Carapeguá, Paraguay
  - Diocese of Dinajpur, Bangladesh
  - Diocese of Zanzibar, Tanzania

Sun, 29 November 2020
- Morning
  - Military Ordinariate of Bosnia and Herzegovina
  - Diocese of Engativá, Colombia
  - Diocese of Namur, Belgium
  - Diocese of Port-Bergé, Madagascar
- Evening
  - Diocese of Dundee, South Africa
  - Diocese of Long Xuyên, Viet Nam
  - Diocese of Rumbek, South Sudan
  - Archdiocese of Zagreb, Croatia

Mon, 30 November 2020
- Morning
  - Diocese of Hamilton in New Zealand
  - Diocese of Maintirano, Madagascar
  - Diocese of Nitra, Slovakia
  - Archdiocese of Santa Fe, New Mexico, USA
  - Diocese of Sisak, Croatia
- Evening
  - Diocese of Banjul, Gambia
  - Diocese of Budjala, Democratic Republic of the Congo
  - Archdiocese of Manaus, Amazonas, Brazil
  - Archdiocese of Tiranë-Durrës, Albania

December

Tue, 01 December 2020
  Morning
    Diocese of Batticaloa, Sri Lanka
    Diocese of Ifakara, Tanzania
    Diocese of Tepic, Nayarit, México
    Diocese of Vallo della Lucania, Italy
    Diocese of Xichang, China
  Evening
    Melkite Greek Catholic Archdiocese of Bosra e Haūrān, Syria
    Diocese of Bururi, Burundi
    Syro-Malankara Catholic Eparchy of Puthur, India
    Archdiocese of Taipei, Taiwan

Wed, 02 December 2020
  Morning
    Diocese of Cuenca, Spain
    Diocese of Harrisburg, Pennsylvania, USA
    Diocese of Iligan, Philippines
    Diocese of Ituiutaba, Minas Gerais, Brazil
    Diocese of Manga, Burkina Faso
  Evening
    Diocese of Alexandria, Louisiana, USA
    Diocese of Forli-Bertinoro, Italy
    Diocese of Francistown, Botswana
    Diocese of Motherwell, Scotland

Thu, 03 December 2020
  Morning
    Diocese of Győr, Hungary
    Syro-Malabar Catholic Diocese of Kalyan, India
    Diocese of Łomża, Poland
    Diocese of Luziânia, Goias, Brazil
    Diocese of Mutare, Zimbabwe
  Evening
    Archdiocese of Lubango, Angola
    Maronite Catholic Eparchy of Notre-Dame du Liban de Paris, France
    Ukrainian Catholic Archiepiscopal Exarchate of Odessa, Ukraine
    Diocese of Saint-Dié, France

Fri, 04 December 2020
  Morning
    Syrian Catholic Apostolic Exarchate of Canada
    Territorial Prelature of Caravelí, Peru
    Archdiocese of Concepción, Chile
    Diocese of Kano, Nigeria
    Archdiocese of Winnipeg, Manitoba, Canada
  Evening
    Diocese of Cabinda, Angola
    Melkite Greek Catholic Archdiocese of Homs, Syria
    Diocese of Mbalmayo, Cameroon
    Diocese of Sivagangai, India

Sat, 05 December 2020
  Morning
    Diocese of Austin, Texas, USA
    Archdiocese of Castries, Saint Lucia, Antilles
    Greek Catholic Apostolic Exarchate of Greece

    Diocese of Piacenza-Bobbio, Italy
    Diocese of Vác, Hungary
  Evening
    Diocese of Camaçari, Bahia, Brazil
    Diocese of Hongdong, China
    Diocese of Koszalin-Kołobrzeg, Poland
    Archdiocese of São Salvador da Bahia, Brazil

Sun, 06 December 2020
  Morning
    Diocese of Aguascalientes, México
    Chaldean Catholic Archeparchy of Ahwaz, Iran
    Diocese of Keta-Akatsi, Ghana
    Diocese of Tarazona, Spain
    Diocese of Warszawa-Praga, Poland
  Evening
    Archdiocese of Cascavel, Parana, Brazil
    Archdiocese of Huancayo, Peru
    Diocese of Ipameri, Goias, Brazil
    Diocese of Lugano, Switzerland

Mon, 07 December 2020
  Morning
    Archdiocese of Catania, Italy
    Diocese of Down and Connor, Ireland
    Archdiocese of Los Altos, Quetzaltenango-Totonicapán, Guatemala
    Territorial Prelature of Trondheim, Norway
  Evening
    Diocese of Corpus Christi, Texas, USA
    Diocese of Kandi, Benin
    Diocese of Osnabrück, Germany
    Diocese of Tura, India

Tue, 08 December 2020
  Morning
    Diocese of Jérémie, Haïti
    Diocese of Osorno, Chile
    Ordinariate of the Faithful of the Eastern Rites in Poland
    Diocese of Sant Feliu de Llobregat, Spain
    Diocese of São José dos Campos, Sao Paulo, Brazil
  Evening
    Diocese of Caraguatatuba, Sao Paulo, Brazil
    Diocese of Matagalpa, Nicaragua
    Archdiocese of Pelotas, Rio Grande do Sul, Brazil
    Diocese of Quimper and Léon, France

Wed, 09 December 2020
  Morning
    Diocese of Koper, Slovenia
    Diocese of Lancaster, England
    Diocese of Menevia, Wales
    Diocese of Odienné, Côte d'Ivoire
    Diocese of Sambalpur, India
  Evening
    Diocese of Duluth, Minnesota, USA
    Diocese of Ihosy, Madagascar
    Diocese of Segovia, Spain
    Diocese of Tulcán, Ecuador

Thu, 10 December 2020
- Morning
  - Archdiocese of Bouaké, Côte d'Ivoire
  - Diocese of Bragança do Pará, Brazil
  - Diocese of Luoyang, China
  - Diocese of Machakos, Kenya
  - Diocese of Rio Branco, Acre, Brazil
- Evening
  - Armenian Catholic Eparchy of Alexandria, Egypt
  - Diocese of Posadas, Argentina
  - Diocese of Regensburg, Germany
  - Archdiocese of Santiago de Compostela, Spain

Fri, 11 December 2020
- Morning
  - Apostolic Vicariate of Archipelago of the Comores
  - Diocese of Bambari, Central African Republic
  - Military Ordinariate of the Philippines
  - Diocese of Superior, Wisconsin, USA
  - Archdiocese of Vilnius, Lithuania
- Evening
  - Diocese of Aba, Nigeria
  - Diocese of Hưng Hóa, Viet Nam
  - Archdiocese of Raipur, India
  - Diocese of Wheeling-Charleston, West Virginia, USA

Sat, 12 December 2020
- Morning
  - Diocese of Baton Rouge, Louisiana, USA
  - Apostolic Prefecture of Hainan, China
  - Diocese of Manono, Democratic Republic of the Congo
  - Diocese of Mogi das Cruzes, Sao Paulo, Brazil
  - Diocese of Socorro y San Gil, Colombia
- Evening
  - Diocese of Darwin, Australia
  - Apostolic Vicariate of Jolo, Philippines
  - Archdiocese of San Francisco, California, USA
  - Archdiocese of Suva, Fiji

Sun, 13 December 2020
- Morning
  - Diocese of Jalingo, Nigeria
  - Maronite Catholic Eparchy of Jbeil, Lebanon
  - Diocese of Port-de-Paix, Haïti
  - Archdiocese of Ribeirão Preto, Sao Paulo, Brazil
  - Diocese of Rio do Sul, Santa Catarina, Brazil
- Evening
  - Diocese of Azcapotzalco, México, México
  - Diocese of Dunkeld, Scotland
  - Diocese of Novo Mesto, Slovenia
  - Diocese of San Fernando de La Union, Philippines

Mon, 14 December 2020
- Morning
  - Archdiocese of Belo Horizonte, Minas Gerais, Brazil
  - Archdiocese of Đakovo-Osijek, Croatia
  - Diocese of Świdnica, Poland
  - Syro-Malabar Catholic Archeparchy of Tellicherry, India
  - Diocese of Ziguinchor, Senegal

Evening
- Diocese of Kasongo, Democratic Republic of the Congo
- Apostolic Prefecture of Linqing, China
- Diocese of Perpignan-Elne, France
- Diocese of Tocantinópolis, Tocatins, Brazil

Tue, 15 December 2020
Morning
- Diocese of Barcelona, Venezuela
- Diocese of Fort Worth, Texas, USA
- Chaldean Catholic Archeparchy of Mossul, Iraq
- Diocese of Neyyattinkara, India
- Diocese of Valence, France

Evening
- Diocese of Ciudad Guzmán, Jalisco, México
- Archdiocese of Corrientes, Argentina
- Diocese of Victoria in Texas, USA
- Territorial Abbey of Wettingen-Mehrerau, Austria

Wed, 16 December 2020
Morning
- Diocese of Cochin, India
- Archdiocese of Genoa, Italy
- Diocese of Kabankalan, Philippines
- Diocese of Nellore, India

Evening
- Diocese of Diphu, India
- Diocese of Jerez de la Frontera, Spain
- Diocese of Mbanza Congo, Angola
- Diocese of Płock, Poland

Thu, 17 December 2020
Morning
- Archdiocese of Kaduna, Nigeria
- Diocese of Le Havre, France
- Diocese of Liepāja, Latvia
- Archdiocese of Łódź, Poland
- Archdiocese of Valladolid, Spain

Evening
- Syro-Malabar Catholic Archeparchy of Changanacherry, India
- Diocese of Eshowe, South Africa
- Diocese of Palmares, Pernambuco, Brazil
- Diocese of Trincomalee, Sri Lanka

Fri, 18 December 2020
Morning
- Diocese of Amarillo, Texas, USA
- Diocese of Cape Palmas, Liberia
- Archdiocese of Tanger, Morocco
- Archdiocese of Toluca, México, México
- Diocese of Umzimkulu, South Africa

Evening
- Diocese of Dourados, Mato Grosso do Sul, Brazil
- Diocese of San Felipe, Chile
- Diocese of San Fernando de Apure, Venezuela
- Apostolic Prefecture of Shiqian, China

Sat, 19 December 2020
Morning
- Archdiocese of Harare, Zimbabwe

    Archdiocese of Mbarara, Uganda
    Hungarian Catholic Eparchy of Miskolc, Hungary
    Archdiocese of Omaha, Nebraska, USA
    Diocese of Wagga Wagga, Australia
  Evening
    Diocese of Jasikan, Ghana
    Diocese of Mocoa-Sibundoy, Colombia
    Archdiocese of Newark, New Jersey, USA
    Diocese of Tehuacán, Puebla, México

Sun, 20 December 2020
  Morning
    Archdiocese of Beograd, Serbia
    Archdiocese of Calabar, Nigeria
    Chaldean Catholic Archdiocese of Kerkūk, Iraq
    Diocese of Oppido Mamertina-Palmi, Italy
    Diocese of Tarija, Bolivia
  Evening
    Diocese of Dassa-Zoumé, Benin
    Diocese of Luiza, Democratic Republic of the Congo
    Archdiocese of Pescara-Penne, Italy
    Diocese of Zipaquirá, Colombia

Mon, 21 December 2020
  Morning
    Diocese of Caxito, Angola
    Archdiocese of Honiara, Solomon Islands
    Chaldean Catholic Patriarchal Dependent Territory of Jordan
    Diocese of São Tomé e Príncipe
    Diocese of Satu Mare, Romania
  Evening
    Apostolic Vicariate of Istanbul, Turkey
    Archdiocese of Perth, Australia
    Archdiocese of Spoleto-Norcia, Italy
    Diocese of Sulmona-Valva, Italy

Tue, 22 December 2020
  Morning
    Diocese of Angra, Portugal
    Diocese of Floresta, Pernambuco, Brazil
    Diocese of Goma, Democratic Republic of the Congo
    Diocese of Green Bay, Wisconsin, USA
    Archdiocese of Pamplona y Tudela, Spain
  Evening
    Apostolic Vicariate of Jimma-Bonga, Ethiopia
    Diocese of Kabgayi, Rwanda
    Diocese of Kaposvár, Hungary
    Syro-Malabar Catholic Archdiocese of Trichur, India

Wed, 23 December 2020
  Morning
    Diocese of Apartadó, Colombia
    Diocese of Arundel and Brighton, England
    Syrian Catholic Archdiocese of Homs, Syria
    Diocese of Kuzhithurai, India
    Territorial Prelature of Tromsø, Norway
  Evening
    Diocese of Bhagalpur, India
    Diocese of Chartres, France

Diocese of Goya, Argentina
　Syro-Malankara Catholic Eparchy of Pathanamthitta, India
Thu, 24 December 2020
　Morning
　　Melkite Greek Catholic Archeparchy of Akka, Israel
　　Diocese of Armidale, Australia
　　Diocese of Ensenada, Baja California Norte, México
　　Diocese of Kurnool, India
　Evening
　　Diocese of Aveiro, Portugal
　　Diocese of Azogues, Ecuador
　　Diocese of Itaguaí, Rio de Janeiro, Brazil
　　Diocese of Kayes, Mali
Fri, 25 December 2020
　Morning
　　Diocese of Cachoeiro do Itapemirim, Espirito Santo, Brazil
　　Diocese of Cesena-Sarsina, Italy
　　Diocese of Chachapoyas, Peru
　　Diocese of Hanzhong, China
　　Diocese of Tabasco, México
　Evening
　　Archdiocese of Beira, Mozambique
　　Diocese of Campo Maior, Piaui, Brazil
　　Archdiocese of Gdańsk, Poland
　　Diocese of Savona-Noli, Italy
Sat, 26 December 2020
　Morning
　　Archdiocese of Cagayan de Oro, Philippines
　　Archdiocese of Chambéry, France
　　Diocese of Ebebiyin, Equatorial Guinea
　　Diocese of Taungngu, Myanmar
　　Diocese of Tortona, Italy
　Evening
　　Diocese of Katsina-Ala, Nigeria
　　Diocese of Nkongsamba, Cameroon
　　Diocese of Saint Cloud, Minnesota, USA
　　Mission Sui Iuris of Tadjikistan
Sun, 27 December 2020
　Morning
　　Diocese of Daltonganj, India
　　Diocese of Huacho, Peru
　　Diocese of Katiola, Côte d'Ivoire
　　Diocese of Palmira, Colombia
　　Diocese of Tambacounda, Senegal
　Evening
　　Diocese of Bellary, India
　　Archdiocese of Campobasso-Boiano, Italy
　　Archdiocese of Ciudad Bolívar, Venezuela
　　Diocese of Ibarra, Ecuador
Mon, 28 December 2020
　Morning
　　Syrian Catholic Patriarchal Exarchate of Bassorah e Golfo, Iraq
　　Diocese of Coatzacoalcos, Veracruz, México
　　Military Ordinariate of France
　　Diocese of Kumbo, Cameroon

       Diocese of Yujiang, China
    Evening
       Archdiocese of Antsiranana, Madagascar
       Archdiocese of Cotonou, Benin
       Diocese of Fidenza, Italy
       Diocese of Nantes, France
Tue, 29 December 2020
    Morning
       Diocese of Caçador, Santa Catarina, Brazil
       Diocese of Kalookan, Philippines
       Eritrean Catholic Eparchy of Keren, Eritrea
       Diocese of Lafia, Nigeria
       Diocese of Prizren-Prishtina, Serbia
    Evening
       Archdiocese of Delhi, India
       Diocese of Kenema, Sierra Leone
       Syro-Malabar Catholic Diocese of Kothamangalam, India
       Melkite Greek Catholic Archdiocese of Tyr, Lebanon
Wed, 30 December 2020
    Morning
       Diocese of Indore, India
       Diocese of Lages, Santa Catarina, Brazil
       Diocese of Nuoro, Italy
       Diocese of São José do Rio Preto, Sao Paulo, Brazil
       Diocese of Venice, Florida, USA
    Evening
       Diocese of El Obeid, Sudan
       Apostolic Prefecture of Falkland Islands o Malvinas
       Archdiocese of Kasama, Zambia
       Diocese of Wamba, Democratic Republic of the Congo
Thu, 31 December 2020
    Morning
       Diocese of Alessandria, Italy
       Archdiocese of Caceres, Philippines
       Diocese of Lansing, Michigan, USA
       Archdiocese of Onitsha, Nigeria
       Ukrainian Catholic Eparchy of Saints Peter and Paul of Melbourne, Australia
    Evening
       Diocese of Basel, Switzerland
       Archdiocese of Huambo, Angola
       Archdiocese of Izmir, Turkey
       Archdiocese of Ravenna-Cervia, Italy

January

Fri, 01 January 2021
  Morning
    Diocese of Clifton, England
    Diocese of Kyiv-Zhytomyr, Ukraine
    Diocese of Morón, Argentina
    Diocese of Peterborough, Ontario, Canada
  Evening
    Archdiocese of Canberra-Goulburn, Australia
    Diocese of Sonsonate, El Salvador
    Diocese of Susa, Italy
    Archdiocese of Taranto, Italy

Sat, 02 January 2021
  Morning
    Diocese of Castellaneta, Italy
    Diocese of Changde, China
    Diocese of Kabale, Uganda
    Diocese of Lake Charles, Louisiana, USA
    Diocese of Peoria, Illinois, USA
  Evening
    Diocese of Erfurt, Germany
    Military Ordinariate of Germany
    Diocese of Juazeiro, Bahia, Brazil
    Diocese of Warri, Nigeria

Sun, 03 January 2021
  Morning
    Chaldean Catholic Eparchy of Alep, Syria
    Diocese of Awka, Nigeria
    Diocese of Garissa, Kenya
    Diocese of Hallam, England
    Diocese of Ibiza, Spain
  Evening
    Diocese of Banjarmasin, Indonesia
    Diocese of Davenport, Iowa, USA
    Melkite Greek Catholic Eparchy of Nuestra Señora del Paraíso en México
    Archdiocese of Valencia, Spain

Mon, 04 January 2021
  Morning
    Diocese of Chur, Switzerland
    Diocese of Jujuy, Argentina
    Archdiocese of Londrina, Parana, Brazil
    Archdiocese of Rennes, France
    Apostolic Vicariate of Savannakhet, Laos
  Evening
    Diocese of Catarman, Philippines
    Archdiocese of Chattogram, Bangladesh
    Diocese of Jinja, Uganda
    Diocese of Kisii, Kenya

Tue, 05 January 2021
  Morning
    Diocese of Canelones, Uruguay
    Ruthenian Catholic Eparchy of Parma, Ohio, USA
    Military Ordinariate of Slovakia

    Ukrainian Catholic Archeparchy of Ternopil-Zboriv, Ukraine
    Diocese of Thanh Hoá, Viet Nam
  Evening
    Archdiocese of Acerenza, Italy
    Territorial Prelature of Juli, Peru
    Diocese of Sandhurst, Australia
    Diocese of Vitebsk, Belarus

Wed, 06 January 2021
  Morning
    Archdiocese of Adelaide, Australia
    Diocese of Grand-Bassam, Côte d'Ivoire
    Ukrainian Catholic Eparchy of Holy Family of London
    Diocese of Iquique, Chile
    Diocese of Ratchaburi, Thailand
  Evening
    Chaldean Catholic Eparchy of Beirut, Lebanon
    Diocese of Kahama, Tanzania
    Diocese of Latacunga, Ecuador
    Diocese of Middlesbrough, England

Thu, 07 January 2021
  Morning
    Apostolic Vicariate of Iquitos, Peru
    Territorial Prelature of Itaituba, Para, Brazil
    Diocese of Marília, Sao Paulo, Brazil
    Diocese of Santa Marta, Colombia
    Diocese of Toruń, Poland
  Evening
    Archdiocese of Benin City, Nigeria
    Diocese of Grand Falls, Newfoundland, Canada
    Diocese of Rubiataba-Mozarlândia, Goias, Brazil
    Diocese of Youngstown, Ohio, USA

Fri, 08 January 2021
  Morning
    Apostolic Prefecture of Azerbaijan
    Diocese of Bilbao, Spain
    Diocese of Dresden-Meißen, Germany
    Diocese of Lucknow, India
    Archdiocese of Singapore
  Evening
    Apostolic Vicariate of Brunei, Brunei Darussalam
    Diocese of Cartago, Costa Rica
    Diocese of Cerignola-Ascoli Satriano, Italy
    Diocese of Dubrovnik, Croatia

Sat, 09 January 2021
  Morning
    Diocese of Cubao, Philippines
    Diocese of Itanagar, India
    Archdiocese of Kota Kinabalu, Malaysia
    Diocese of Maasin, Philippines
    Syro-Malabar Catholic Eparchy of Mandya, India
  Evening
    Territorial Prelature of Cafayate, Argentina
    Diocese of Gozo, Malta
    Diocese of Legnica, Poland
    Diocese of Urgell, Spain

Sun, 10 January 2021
  Morning
    Archdiocese of Diamantina, Minas Gerais, Brazil
    Diocese of Kisantu, Democratic Republic of the Congo
    Diocese of Linz, Austria
    Archdiocese of Maceió, Alagoas, Brazil
  Evening
    Archdiocese of Agrigento, Italy
    Diocese of Lafayette in Indiana, USA
    Diocese of Reykjavik, Iceland
    Diocese of Szeged-Csanád, Hungary
Mon, 11 January 2021
  Morning
    Diocese of Abengourou, Côte d'Ivoire
    Diocese of Jiangmen, China
    Diocese of Qacha's Nek, Lesotho
    Diocese of Rožňava, Slovakia
    Diocese of Simdega, India
  Evening
    Slovakian Catholic Eparchy of Bratislava, Slovakia
    Diocese of Funchal, Portugal
    Diocese of Punto Fijo, Venezuela
    Archdiocese of Shkodrë-Pult, Albania
Tue, 12 January 2021
  Morning
    Military Ordinariate of Chile
    Archdiocese of Durban, South Africa
    Diocese of Rio Grande, Rio Grande do Sul, Brazil
    Archdiocese of Verapoly, India
    Diocese of Villa de la Concepción del Río Cuarto, Argentina
  Evening
    Archdiocese of Florianópolis, Santa Catarina, Brazil
    Diocese of Masan, South Korea
    Diocese of Oyo, Nigeria
    Diocese of Pangkalpinang, Indonesia
Wed, 13 January 2021
  Morning
    Diocese of Hyderabad in Pakistan
    Archdiocese of Otranto, Italy
    Diocese of Trenton, New Jersey, USA
    Archdiocese of Sarajevo, Bosnia and Herzegovina
    Diocese of Wa, Ghana
  Evening
    Diocese of Alto Solimões, Amazonas, Brazil
    Diocese of Baker, Oregon, USA
    Diocese of Corumbá, Mato Grosso do Sul, Brazil
    Diocese of Tursi-Lagonegro, Italy
Thu, 14 January 2021
  Morning
    Diocese of Abomey, Benin
    Armenian Catholic Apostolic Exarchate of Latin America and Mexico
    Diocese of Chiang Mai, Thailand
    Diocese of Shanba, China
    Diocese of Viedma, Argentina

Evening
  Archdiocese of Hangzhou, China
  Archdiocese of Makassar, Indonesia
  Maronite Catholic Archeparchy of Tripoli, Lebanon
  Diocese of Vélez, Colombia

Fri, 15 January 2021
  Morning
    Archdiocese of Agra, India
    Diocese of Innsbruck, Austria
    Diocese of Kolda, Senegal
    Diocese of Kongolo, Democratic Republic of the Congo
    Diocese of Sinop, Mato Grosso, Brazil
  Evening
    Chaldean Catholic Archdiocese of Baghdad, Iraq
    Diocese of Orange in California, USA
    Diocese of Osasco, Sao Paulo, Brazil
    Diocese of Vĩnh Long, Viet Nam

Sat, 16 January 2021
  Morning
    Archdiocese of Bourges, France
    Diocese of Chioggia, Italy
    Archdiocese of Eger, Hungary
    Apostolic Prefecture of Kompong-Cham, Cambodia
    Archdiocese of Visakhapatnam, India
  Evening
    Diocese of Arauca, Colombia
    Archdiocese of Monaco
    Archdiocese of Monterrey, Nuevo León, México
    Diocese of Providence, Rhode Island, USA

Sun, 17 January 2021
  Morning
    Diocese of Bata, Equatorial Guinea
    Archdiocese of Cashel and Emly, Ireland
    Diocese of Natitingou, Benin
    Diocese of Nottingham, England
    Diocese of Penonomé, Panama
  Evening
    Diocese of Cuddapah, India
    Military Ordinariate of the Dominican Republic
    Archdiocese of Nairobi, Kenya
    Archdiocese of Ozamiz, Philippines

Mon, 18 January 2021
  Morning
    Ethiopian Catholic Eparchy of Bahir Dar - Dessie, Ethiopia
    Territorial Prelature of Marawi, Philippines
    Diocese of Parintins, Amazonas, Brazil
    Diocese of San Francisco de Macorís, Dominican Republic
  Evening
    Diocese of Concepción en Paraguay
    Diocese of Kafanchan, Nigeria
    Diocese of Puerto Cabello, Venezuela
    Diocese of Santo Domingo en Ecuador

Tue, 19 January 2021
  Morning
    Apostolic Vicariate of Anatolia, Turkey

    Archdiocese of Bordeaux, France
    Diocese of Campo Limpo, Sao Paulo, Brazil
    Diocese of Ilhéus, Bahia, Brazil
    Diocese of Palmas-Francisco Beltrão, Parana, Brazil
  Evening
    Diocese of Cartago, Colombia
    Archdiocese of Detroit, Michigan, USA
    Apostolic Prefecture of Lintong, China
    Ukrainian Catholic Diocese of Wrocław-Gdańsk, Poland
Wed, 20 January 2021
  Morning
    Diocese of Auckland, New Zealand
    Diocese of Montepulciano-Chiusi-Pienza, Italy
    Diocese of Pinerolo, Italy
    Diocese of Salford, England
    Diocese of Sandakan, Malaysia
  Evening
    Archdiocese of Kalocsa-Kecskemét, Hungary
    Archdiocese of Malines-Brussels, Belgium
    Melkite Greek Catholic Eparchy of Newton, USA
    Diocese of Sekondi-Takoradi, Ghana
Thu, 21 January 2021
  Morning
    Archdiocese of Bahía Blanca, Argentina
    Diocese of Edmundston, New Brunswick, Canada
    Diocese of Passau, Germany
    Diocese of Qichun, China
    Archdiocese of Saint Andrews and Edinburgh, Scotland
  Evening
    Diocese of Araçuaí, Minas Gerais, Brazil
    Archdiocese of Avignon, France
    Diocese of Memphis, Tennessee, USA
    Diocese of Timmins, Ontario, Canada
Fri, 22 January 2021
  Morning
    Diocese of Bandung, Indonesia
    Diocese of Ipiales, Colombia
    Diocese of Kpalimé, Togo
    Diocese of Parma, Italy
    Archdiocese of Utrecht, Netherlands
  Evening
    Diocese of Ajmer, India
    Diocese of Otukpo, Nigeria
    Diocese of Punalur, India
    Archdiocese of Thare and Nonseng, Thailand
Sat, 23 January 2021
  Morning
    Armenian Catholic Ordinariate of Eastern Europe
    Diocese of Kigoma, Tanzania
    Archdiocese of Nouméa, New Caledonia
    Diocese of Portalegre-Castelo Branco, Portugal
    Diocese of Vinh, Viet Nam
  Evening
    Archdiocese of Cartagena, Colombia
    Archdiocese of Marseille, France

Diocese of Mysore, India
Diocese of Włocławek, Poland

Sun, 24 January 2021
Morning
Diocese of Abeokuta, Nigeria
Apostolic Prefecture of Ankang, China
Archdiocese of Nueva Pamplona, Colombia
Diocese of Porto Nacional, Tocatins, Brazil
Diocese of Tarbes et Lourdes, France
Evening
Diocese of Chingleput, India
Archdiocese of Gandhinagar, India
Diocese of Kamina, Democratic Republic of the Congo
Diocese of Limoeiro do Norte, Ceara, Brazil

Mon, 25 January 2021
Morning
Diocese of Acarigua-Araure, Venezuela
Diocese of Bomadi, Nigeria
Territorial Prelature of Esquel, Argentina
Coptic Catholic Eparchy of Minya, Egypt
Archdiocese of Santa Cruz de la Sierra, Bolivia
Evening
Ethiopian Catholic Archeparchy of Addis Abeba, Ethiopia
Diocese of Garzón, Colombia
Diocese of Portland, Maine, USA
Diocese of Porto Novo, Benin

Tue, 26 January 2021
Morning
Diocese of Caltanissetta, Italy
Diocese of Carora, Venezuela
Archdiocese of San Antonio, Texas, USA
Apostolic Vicariate of Tierradentro, Colombia
Evening
Diocese of Coimbatore, India
Archdiocese of Reims, France
Apostolic Prefecture of Xining, China
Apostolic Vicariate of Zamora en Ecuador

Wed, 27 January 2021
Morning
Maronite Catholic Archeparchy of Alep, Syria
Archdiocese of Juba, South Sudan
Diocese of Luçon, France
Diocese of Paracatu, Minas Gerais, Brazil
Territorial Prelature of Pompei o Beatissima Vergine Maria del Santissimo Rosario, Italy
Evening
Diocese of Cúcuta, Colombia
Territorial Prelature of Jesús María, Nayarit, México
Archdiocese of Luanda, Angola
Diocese of Salto, Uruguay

Thu, 28 January 2021
Morning
Archdiocese of Armagh, Ireland
Diocese of Goré, Chad
Diocese of Parnaíba, Piaui, Brazil
Diocese of Saltillo, Coahuila, México

 Diocese of Wuchang, China
 Evening
  Diocese of Amiens, France
  Diocese of Atambua, Indonesia
  Archdiocese of Salta, Argentina
  Archdiocese of Sherbrooke, Québec, Canada

Fri, 29 January 2021
 Morning
  Diocese of Campo Mourão, Parana, Brazil
  Diocese of Evinayong, Equatorial Guinea
  Diocese of Gualeguaychú, Argentina
  Diocese of Ponta de Pedras, Para, Brazil
  Diocese of Trujillo, Honduras
 Evening
  Diocese of Ghent, Belgium
  Diocese of Mymensingh, Bangladesh
  Diocese of Sanggau, Indonesia
  Archdiocese of São Sebastião do Rio de Janeiro, Brazil

Sat, 30 January 2021
 Morning
  Melkite Greek Catholic Apostolic Exarchate of Argentina
  Diocese of Cajamarca, Peru
  Diocese of Kikwit, Democratic Republic of the Congo
  Archdiocese of Québec, Canada
  Apostolic Vicariate of Requena, Peru
 Evening
  Archdiocese of Abidjan, Côte d'Ivoire
  Archdiocese of Catanzaro-Squillace, Italy
  Diocese of Fengxiang, China
  Armenian Catholic Eparchy of Our Lady of Nareg in Glendale, California, USA

Sun, 31 January 2021
 Morning
  Diocese of Columbus, Ohio, USA
  Diocese of Helena, Montana, USA
  Diocese of Saint-Denis-de-La Réunion
  Archdiocese of San Cristobal de la Habana, Cuba
  Diocese of Tlaxcala, México
 Evening
  Diocese of Campeche, México
  Archdiocese of Cochabamba, Bolivia
  Diocese of Matehuala, San Luís Potosí, México
  Diocese of Molfetta-Ruvo-Giovinazzo-Terlizzi, Italy

February

Mon, 01 February 2021
  Morning
    Military Ordinariate of Brazil
    Diocese of Las Vegas, Nevada, USA
    Diocese of Les Gonaïves, Haïti
    Diocese of Makurdi, Nigeria
    Archdiocese of Montes Claros, Minas Gerais, Brazil
  Evening
    Diocese of Idah, Nigeria
    Syro-Malabar Catholic Diocese of Palghat, India
    Diocese of Uijeongbu, South Korea
    Diocese of Yopal, Colombia

Tue, 02 February 2021
  Morning
    Diocese of Caldas, Colombia
    Diocese of Pistoia, Italy
    Syro-Malabar Catholic Diocese of Sagar, India
    Archdiocese of Tuguegarao, Philippines
    Diocese of Uruguaiana, Rio Grande do Sul, Brazil
  Evening
    Archdiocese of Blantyre, Malawi
    Diocese of Chipata, Zambia
    Diocese of Gregorio de Laferrere, Argentina
    Diocese of Homa Bay, Kenya

Wed, 03 February 2021
  Morning
    Diocese of Guantánamo-Baracoa, Cuba
    Diocese of Guaxupé, Minas Gerais, Brazil
    Diocese of Imus, Philippines
    Diocese of Maldonado-Punta del Este-Minas, Uruguay
    Territorial Abbey of Tŏkwon, North Korea
  Evening
    Archdiocese of Bucharest, Romania
    Archdiocese of Miami, Florida, USA
    Diocese of Mindelo, Cape Verde
    Diocese of Zomba, Malawi

Thu, 04 February 2021
  Morning
    Archdiocese of Bratislava, Slovakia
    Archdiocese of Jaro, Philippines
    Diocese of Leopoldina, Minas Gerais, Brazil
    Diocese of Limerick, Ireland
  Evening
    Diocese of Camden, New Jersey, USA
    Syro-Malabar Catholic Diocese of Kanjirapally, India
    Diocese of Kottapuram, India
    Melkite Greek Catholic Apostolic Exarchate of Venezuela

Fri, 05 February 2021
  Morning
    Diocese of Jamshedpur, India
    Diocese of Klerksdorp, South Africa
    Diocese of La Guaira, Venezuela
    Diocese of Montenegro, Rio Grande do Sul, Brazil

    Syrian Catholic Eparchy of Our Lady of Deliverance of Newark, USA
  Evening
    Diocese of Nazaré, Pernambuco, Brazil
    Diocese of Panevėžys, Lithuania
    Diocese of Piracicaba, Sao Paulo, Brazil
    Melkite Greek Catholic Archeparchy of Saïdā, Lebanon

Sat, 06 February 2021
  Morning
    Diocese of Alindao, Central African Republic
    Diocese of Imperatriz, Maranhão, Brazil
    Diocese of Kamloops, British Columbia, Canada
    Archdiocese of Malabo, Equatorial Guinea
    Diocese of Rancagua, Chile
  Evening
    Diocese of Breda, Netherlands
    Diocese of Kasana-Luweero, Uganda
    Melkite Greek Catholic Patriarchal Exarchate of Kuwait
    Albanian Catholic Apostolic Administration of Southern Albania

Sun, 07 February 2021
  Morning
    Diocese of Boma, Democratic Republic of the Congo
    Diocese of Churchill-Baie d'Hudson, Manitoba, Canada
    Diocese of Foz do Iguaçu, Parana, Brazil
    Diocese of Mati, Philippines
    Diocese of Tanjung Selor, Indonesia
  Evening
    Diocese of Criciúma, Santa Catarina, Brazil
    Diocese of Fenoarivo Atsinanana, Madagascar
    Diocese of Ningbo, China
    Diocese of Scranton, Pennsylvania, USA

Mon, 08 February 2021
  Morning
    Diocese of Baruipur, India
    Diocese of Massa Carrara-Pontremoli, Italy
    Diocese of Nardò-Gallipoli, Italy
    Archdiocese of Nyeri, Kenya
    Archdiocese of Santo Domingo, Dominican Republic
  Evening
    Diocese of Changting, China
    Diocese of Cheyenne, Wyoming, USA
    Diocese of Malolos, Philippines
    Diocese of Tarlac, Philippines

Tue, 09 February 2021
  Morning
    Syro-Malabar Catholic Eparchy of Hosur, India
    Diocese of Lanusei, Italy
    Diocese of San Nicolás de los Arroyos, Argentina
    Diocese of Srikakulam, India
    Diocese of Viana do Castelo, Portugal
  Evening
    Diocese of Awgu, Nigeria
    Diocese of Colima, México
    Apostolic Vicariate of El Petén, Guatemala
    Diocese of Lodwar, Kenya

Wed, 10 February 2021
- Morning
  - Apostolic Administration of Atyrau, Kazakhstan
  - Apostolic Exarchate of Italy for the Faithful of the Ukrainian Catholic Church
  - Diocese of Kolwezi, Democratic Republic of the Congo
  - Italo-Albanese Catholic Eparchy of Piana degli Albanesi, Italy
  - Patriarchate of West Indies, Spain
- Evening
  - Archdiocese of Lubumbashi, Democratic Republic of the Congo
  - Diocese of Pozzuoli, Italy
  - Archdiocese of São Luís do Maranhão, Brazil
  - Diocese of Tivoli, Italy

Thu, 11 February 2021
- Morning
  - Archdiocese of Agaña, Guam
  - Diocese of Bukoba, Tanzania
  - Diocese of Guntur, India
  - Diocese of Huánuco, Peru
  - Apostolic Prefecture of Xiangtan, China
- Evening
  - Archdiocese of Davao, Philippines
  - Archdiocese of Jalapa, Veracruz, México
  - Diocese of Metz, France
  - Diocese of Port-Louis, Mauritius

Fri, 12 February 2021
- Morning
  - Diocese of Anguo, China
  - Maronite Catholic Eparchy of Cairo, Egypt
  - Diocese of São Mateus, Espirito Santo, Brazil
  - Archdiocese of Zamboanga, Philippines
- Evening
  - Apostolic Prefecture of Battambang, Cambodia
  - Diocese of Enshi, China
  - Archdiocese of Piura, Peru
  - Diocese of Whitehorse, Yukon, Canada

Sat, 13 February 2021
- Morning
  - Diocese of Bayeux, France
  - Diocese of Faro, Portugal
  - Diocese of Paramaribo, Suriname, Antilles
  - Archdiocese of Port Moresby, Papua New Guinea
  - Diocese of Zhoucun, China
- Evening
  - Diocese of Almenara, Minas Gerais, Brazil
  - Diocese of Bengbu, China
  - Syro-Malabar Catholic Eparchy of Great Britain
  - Diocese of Timika, Indonesia

Sun, 14 February 2021
- Morning
  - Diocese of Ciudad Altamirano, Guerrero, México
  - Diocese of Rarotonga, Cook Islands
  - Diocese of Tricarico, Italy
  - Archdiocese of Uberaba, Minas Gerais, Brazil
  - Diocese of Umtata, South Africa

Evening
- Archdiocese of Kaifeng, China
- Diocese of Los Teques, Venezuela
- Hungarian Catholic Eparchy of Nyíregyháza, Hungary
- Maronite Catholic Eparchy of San Charbel en Buenos Aires, Argentina

Mon, 15 February 2021
Morning
- Diocese of Cametá, Para, Brazil
- Diocese of Gurk, Austria
- Diocese of Kandy, Sri Lanka
- Diocese of Nocera Inferiore-Sarno, Italy
- Archdiocese of Toronto, Ontario, Canada

Evening
- Archdiocese of Berlin, Germany
- Diocese of Ciudad Guayana, Venezuela
- Eritrean Catholic Eparchy of Segheneity, Eritrea
- Diocese of Viterbo, Italy

Tue, 16 February 2021
Morning
- Diocese of Campina Grande, Paraiba, Brazil
- Diocese of Kamyanets-Podilskyi, Ukraine
- Diocese of Kidapawan, Philippines
- Diocese of Laval, France
- Archdiocese of Warsaw, Poland

Evening
- Diocese of Hazaribag, India
- Diocese of Menongue, Angola
- Diocese of Mỹ Tho, Viet Nam
- Diocese of Trois-Rivières, Québec, Canada

Wed, 17 February 2021
Morning
- Archdiocese of Bombay, India
- Diocese of Callao, Peru
- Maronite Catholic Archdiocese of Cipro, Cyprus
- Diocese of Meerut, India
- Diocese of Puntarenas, Costa Rica

Evening
- Diocese of Alcalá de Henares, Spain
- Diocese of Kannur, India
- Diocese of Ootacamund, India
- Chaldean Catholic Eparchy of Saint Thomas the Apostle of Sydney, Australia

Thu, 18 February 2021
Morning
- Diocese of Frosinone-Veroli-Ferentino, Italy
- Diocese of Guajará-Mirim, Rondonia, Brazil
- Diocese of San Clemente a Saratov, Russian Federation
- Diocese of San Roque de Presidencia Roque Sáenz Peña, Argentina
- Diocese of Valdivia, Chile

Evening
- Diocese of Charleston, South Carolina, USA
- Diocese of Saint-Brieuc, France
- Diocese of Samoa-Pago Pago, American Samoa
- Diocese of Vijayapuram, India

Fri, 19 February 2021
　Morning
　　Diocese of Créteil, France
　　Diocese of El Tigre, Venezuela
　　Diocese of Franca, Sao Paulo, Brazil
　　Diocese of Mbaïki, Central African Republic
　　Diocese of Venado Tuerto, Argentina
　Evening
　　Diocese of Iguatu, Ceara, Brazil
　　Diocese of Mawlamyine, Myanmar
　　Diocese of Ozieri, Italy
　　Apostolic Vicariate of Tripoli, Libya

Sat, 20 February 2021
　Morning
　　Territorial Prelature of Moyobamba, Peru
　　Diocese of Sarh, Chad
　　Apostolic Prefecture of Xinjiang, China
　　Diocese of Zhengzhou, China
　Evening
　　Archdiocese of Košice, Slovakia
　　Archdiocese of Lipa, Philippines
　　Diocese of Nancheng, China
　　Diocese of Toledo, Parana, Brazil

Sun, 21 February 2021
　Morning
　　Diocese of Butuan, Philippines
　　Diocese of Chicoutimi, Québec, Canada
　　Diocese of Gokwe, Zimbabwe
　　Ukrainian Catholic Eparchy of New Westminster, Canada
　　Military Ordinariate of Peru
　Evening
　　Diocese of Aitape, Papua New Guinea
　　Diocese of Kokstad, South Africa
　　Diocese of N'Dali, Benin
　　Diocese of Yichang, China

Mon, 22 February 2021
　Morning
　　Archdiocese of Botucatu, Sao Paulo, Brazil
　　Apostolic Vicariate of Darién, Panama
　　Diocese of Kildare and Leighlin, Ireland
　　Archdiocese of Tlalnepantla, México, México
　　Diocese of Yola, Nigeria
　Evening
　　Diocese of Hà Tĩnh, Viet Nam
　　Syro-Malabar Catholic Diocese of Jagdalpur, India
　　Diocese of Limoges, France
　　Diocese of Pembroke, Ontario, Canada

Tue, 23 February 2021
　Morning
　　Diocese of Alto Valle del Río Negro, Argentina
　　Diocese of Amargosa, Bahia, Brazil
　　Diocese of Sigüenza-Guadalajara, Spain
　　Diocese of Stockton, California, USA
　　Diocese of Victoria, British Columbia, Canada

Evening
- Archdiocese of Díli, Timor-Leste
- Diocese of Ferns, Ireland
- Ukrainian Catholic Archeparchy of Ivano-Frankivsk, Ukraine
- Military Ordinariate of Uganda

Wed, 24 February 2021

Morning
- Diocese of Abakaliki, Nigeria
- Diocese of Basankusu, Democratic Republic of the Congo
- Diocese of Doruma-Dungu, Democratic Republic of the Congo
- Diocese of Galway and Kilmacduagh, Ireland
- Diocese of Patos, Paraiba, Brazil

Evening
- Ukrainian Catholic Eparchy of Edmonton, Canada
- Diocese of Rochester, New York, USA
- Diocese of Saluzzo, Italy
- Diocese of Trujillo, Venezuela

Thu, 25 February 2021

Morning
- Diocese of Aurangabad, India
- Diocese of Coronel Oviedo, Paraguay
- Diocese of Fano-Fossombrone-Cagli-Pergola, Italy
- Archdiocese of Kinshasa, Democratic Republic of the Congo
- Diocese of Santarém, Portugal

Evening
- Diocese of Kundiawa, Papua New Guinea
- Diocese of Monze, Zambia
- Diocese of Sultanpet, India
- Archdiocese of Tuam, Ireland

Fri, 26 February 2021

Morning
- Syro-Malabar Catholic Diocese of Bijnor, India
- Archdiocese of Dhaka, Bangladesh
- Diocese of San Cristóbal de La Laguna o Tenerife, Spain
- Suburbicarian See of Velletri-Segni, Italy
- Diocese of Yanggu, China

Evening
- Archdiocese of Hartford, Connecticut, USA
- Diocese of La Ceiba, Honduras
- Diocese of Mpanda, Tanzania
- Diocese of Székesfehérvár, Hungary

Sat, 27 February 2021

Morning
- Diocese of Cremona, Italy
- Diocese of Fall River, Massachusetts, USA
- Diocese of Liège, Belgium
- Archdiocese of Merauke, Indonesia
- Diocese of Palayamkottai, India

Evening
- Archdiocese of Bangkok, Thailand
- Military Ordinariate of Great Britain
- Archdiocese of New York, New York, USA
- Diocese of Owensboro, Kentucky, USA

Sun, 28 February 2021
- Morning
  - Diocese of Brejo, Maranhão, Brazil
  - Diocese of Udon Thani, Thailand
  - Apostolic Administration of Uzbekistan
  - Diocese of Yokohama, Japan
- Evening
  - Diocese of Daloa, Côte d'Ivoire
  - Diocese of Eunápolis, Bahia, Brazil
  - Diocese of Copenhagen, Denmark
  - Diocese of Laoag, Philippines

March

Mon, 01 March 2021
　Morning
　　Diocese of Alajuela, Costa Rica
　　Diocese of Bethlehem, South Africa
　　Diocese of Kalibo, Philippines
　　Archdiocese of Lahore, Pakistan
　　Archdiocese of Ranchi, India
　Evening
　　Diocese of Agats, Indonesia
　　Diocese of Albany, New York, USA
　　Diocese of Culiacán, Sinaloa, México
　　Apostolic Vicariate of Luang Prabang, Laos

Tue, 02 March 2021
　Morning
　　Diocese of Coroatá, Maranhão, Brazil
　　Apostolic Vicariate of Isiolo, Kenya
　　Diocese of Nicopoli, Bulgaria
　　Diocese of Okigwe, Nigeria
　　Diocese of Winona-Rochester, Minnesota, USA
　Evening
　　Archdiocese of Cosenza-Bisignano, Italy
　　Diocese of Romblon, Philippines
　　Archdiocese of Windhoek, Namibia
　　Diocese of Zacatecas, México

Wed, 03 March 2021
　Morning
　　Diocese of Busan, South Korea
　　Maronite Catholic Patriarchal Exarchate of Jerusalem and Palestine, Palestine
　　Diocese of Macapá, Amapa, Brazil
　　Archdiocese of Santiago de Guatemala, Guatemala
　　Diocese of Tarnów, Poland
　Evening
　　Diocese of Abancay, Peru
　　Diocese of Elphin, Ireland
　　Diocese of Pinsk, Belarus
　　Diocese of Surat Thani, Thailand

Thu, 04 March 2021
　Morning
　　Diocese of Januária, Minas Gerais, Brazil
　　Archdiocese of Madrid, Spain
　　Diocese of Nakhon Sawan, Thailand
　　Diocese of Njombe, Tanzania
　　Diocese of Ségou, Mali
　Evening
　　Diocese of Belleville, Illinois, USA
　　Diocese of Palencia, Spain
　　Diocese of Propriá, Sergipe, Brazil
　　Archdiocese of Trnava, Slovakia

Fri, 05 March 2021
　Morning
　　Ukrainian Catholic Apostolic Exarchate of Germany and Scandinavia
　　Diocese of the Canary Islands, Spain
　　Diocese of Puno, Peru

    Diocese of Würzburg, Germany
    Diocese of Xiapu, China
  Evening
    Diocese of Jacmel, Haïti
    Ukrainian Catholic Eparchy of Kolomyia, Ukraine
    Archdiocese of La Serena, Chile
    Diocese of Ngong, Kenya

Sat, 06 March 2021
  Morning
    Coptic Catholic Eparchy of Alexandria, Egypt
    Military Ordinariate of Argentina
    Archdiocese of Hyderabad, India
    Diocese of Parral, Chihuahua, México
    Archdiocese of Trujillo, Peru
  Evening
    Diocese of Garanhuns, Pernambuco, Brazil
    Diocese of Lausanne, Genève et Fribourg, Switzerland
    Diocese of Miracema do Tocantins, Brazil
    Diocese of Port Harcourt, Nigeria

Sun, 07 March 2021
  Morning
    Diocese of Alghero-Bosa, Italy
    Diocese of Balanga, Philippines
    Archdiocese of Brisbane, Australia
    Apostolic Prefecture of Jiamusi, China
    Mission Sui Iuris of Tokelau
  Evening
    Diocese of Cádiz y Ceuta, Spain
    Romanian Catholic Diocese of Cluj-Gherla, Romania
    Diocese of Santos, Sao Paulo, Brazil
    Diocese of Sion, Switzerland

Mon, 08 March 2021
  Morning
    Diocese of Buenaventura, Colombia
    Diocese of Juína, Mato Grosso, Brazil
    Maronite Catholic Eparchy of Latakia, Syria
    Diocese of Monterey in California, USA
    Territorial Abbey of Subiaco, Italy
  Evening
    Chaldean Catholic Diocese of Alquoch, Iraq
    Territorial Prelature of Chuquibambilla, Peru
    Diocese of Kagoshima, Japan
    Diocese of Quilon, India

Tue, 09 March 2021
  Morning
    Archdiocese of Madang, Papua New Guinea
    Diocese of Rayagada, India
    Diocese of Shanghai, China
    Diocese of Tete, Mozambique
  Evening
    Diocese of Antsirabé, Madagascar
    Archdiocese of Birmingham, England
    Diocese of Boise City, Idaho, USA
    Diocese of San Ignacio de Velasco, Bolivia

Wed, 10 March 2021
  Morning
    Diocese of Antigonish, Nova Scotia, Canada
    Diocese of Hvar, Croatia
    Diocese of Lins, Sao Paulo, Brazil
    Diocese of Moshi, Tanzania
    Diocese of Varaždin, Croatia
  Evening
    Archdiocese of Crotone-Santa Severina, Italy
    Diocese of Kalisz, Poland
    Diocese of Legazpi, Philippines
    Diocese of Uyo, Nigeria

Thu, 11 March 2021
  Morning
    Diocese of Bauchi, Nigeria
    Ordinariate of the Faithful of the Eastern Rites in Brazil
    Melkite Greek Catholic Patriarchal Dependent Territory of Jerusalem, Palestine
    Diocese of Konongo-Mampong, Ghana
    Territorial Prelature of Mixes, Oaxaca, México
  Evening
    Diocese of Cyangugu, Rwanda
    Archdiocese of Ispahan, Iran
    Diocese of Sale, Australia
    Mission Sui Iuris of Turks and Caicos, Antilles

Fri, 12 March 2021
  Morning
    Diocese of Bogor, Indonesia
    Diocese of Caroline Islands, Federated States of Micronesia
    Diocese of Fabriano-Matelica, Italy
    Archdiocese of San José de Costa Rica
    Archdiocese of San Juan de Puerto Rico
  Evening
    Diocese of Assisi-Nocera Umbra-Gualdo Tadino, Italy
    Territorial Prelature of Loreto, Italy
    Archdiocese of Potenza-Muro Lucano-Marsico Nuovo, Italy
    Diocese of Puqi, China

Sat, 13 March 2021
  Morning
    Diocese of Brentwood, England
    Diocese of Ciudad Valles, San Luís Potosí, México
    Diocese of Kibungo, Rwanda
    Chaldean Catholic Eparchy of Cairo, Egypt
    Diocese of Novara, Italy
  Evening
    Diocese of Luz, Minas Gerais, Brazil
    Diocese of Multan, Pakistan
    Diocese of Phú Cường, Viet Nam
    Diocese of Roseau, Dominica, Antilles

Sun, 14 March 2021
  Morning
    Diocese of Astorga, Spain
    Archdiocese of Guangzhou, China
    Diocese of Kimbe, Papua New Guinea
    Diocese of Oran, Algeria
    Archdiocese of Panamá

Evening
    Diocese of Girona, Spain
    Diocese of La Crosse, Wisconsin, USA
    Archdiocese of Pesaro, Italy
    Diocese of San Felipe, Venezuela
Mon, 15 March 2021
  Morning
    Diocese of Alagoinhas, Bahia, Brazil
    Diocese of Bunia, Democratic Republic of the Congo
    Archdiocese of Mandalay, Myanmar
    Apostolic Prefecture of Marshall Islands
    Diocese of Orlando, Florida, USA
  Evening
    Diocese of Franceville, Gabon
    Diocese of Mercedes, Uruguay
    Archdiocese of Moncton, New Brunswick, Canada
    Ukrainian Catholic Archdiocese of Przemyśl-Warszawa, Poland
Tue, 16 March 2021
  Morning
    Diocese of Cancún-Chetumal, Quintana Roo, México
    Archdiocese of Dublin, Ireland
    Diocese of Hasselt, Belgium
    Diocese of Langres, France
    Diocese of Sibu, Malaysia
  Evening
    Apostolic Vicariate of Guapi, Colombia
    Diocese of Lubbock, Texas, USA
    Apostolic Vicariate of Puerto Carreño, Colombia
    Chaldean Catholic Eparchy of Saint Thomas the Apostle of Detroit, USA
Wed, 17 March 2021
  Morning
    Diocese of Balsas, Maranhão, Brazil
    Diocese of Changzhi, China
    Diocese of Garagoa, Colombia
    Diocese of Saginaw, Michigan, USA
  Evening
    Archdiocese of Guayaquil, Ecuador
    Diocese of Jacarezinho, Parana, Brazil
    Diocese of Luebo, Democratic Republic of the Congo
    Diocese of Solsona, Spain
Thu, 18 March 2021
  Morning
    Diocese of Grand Rapids, Michigan, USA
    Archdiocese of Milwaukee, Wisconsin, USA
    Diocese of Nagoya, Japan
    Diocese of Rapid City, South Dakota, USA
    Apostolic Prefecture of Tunxi, China
  Evening
    Chaldean Catholic Archeparchy of Basra, Iraq
    Diocese of Bokungu-Ikela, Democratic Republic of the Congo
    Diocese of Goaso, Ghana
    Syrian Catholic Apostolic Exarchate of Venezuela
Fri, 19 March 2021
  Morning
    Archdiocese of Bobo-Dioulasso, Burkina Faso

    Diocese of Kengtung, Myanmar
    Diocese of Limón, Costa Rica
    Diocese of Nouakchott, Mauritania
    Diocese of Pontoise, France
  Evening
    Archdiocese of Cape Town, South Africa
    Diocese of Faisalabad, Pakistan
    Archdiocese of Glasgow, Scotland
    Diocese of Lugo, Spain

Sat, 20 March 2021
  Morning
    Diocese of Banská Bystrica, Slovakia
    Diocese of Digne, France
    Archdiocese of Palmas, Tocatins, Brazil
    Diocese of Taiohae o Tefenuaenata, French Polynesia
    Archdiocese of Washington, District of Columbia, USA
  Evening
    Maronite Catholic Eparchy of Baalbek-Deir El-Ahmar, Lebanon
    Diocese of Ekiti, Nigeria
    Archdiocese of Poitiers, France
    Diocese of Xuzhou, China

Sun, 21 March 2021
  Morning
    Mission Sui Iuris of Afghanistan
    Diocese of San Isidro, Argentina
    Diocese of Shreveport, Louisiana, USA
    Archdiocese of Tamale, Ghana
    Diocese of Weetebula, Indonesia
  Evening
    Diocese of Asansol, India
    Diocese of Digos, Philippines
    Archdiocese of Nassau, Bahamas, Antilles
    Diocese of Ponta Grossa, Parana, Brazil

Mon, 22 March 2021
  Morning
    Diocese of Jaboticabal, Sao Paulo, Brazil
    Archdiocese of Reggio Calabria-Bova, Italy
    Apostolic Prefecture of Suixian, China
    Chaldean Catholic Archdiocese of Rezayeh, Iran
    Archdiocese of Wellington, New Zealand
  Evening
    Chaldean Catholic Archeparchy of Erbil, Iraq
    Apostolic Vicariate of Awasa, Ethiopia
    Diocese of Blumenau, Santa Catarina, Brazil
    Ukrainian Catholic Eparchy of Saint Nicholas of Chicago, Illinois, USA

Tue, 23 March 2021
  Morning
    Diocese of Bùi Chu, Viet Nam
    Diocese of Caratinga, Minas Gerais, Brazil
    Diocese of Graz-Seckau, Austria
    Diocese of Kaišiadorys, Lithuania
    Diocese of Sankt Pölten, Austria
  Evening
    Archdiocese of Cebu, Philippines
    Diocese of Djibouti

Diocese of Lishui, China
　　Diocese of Tezpur, India
Wed, 24 March 2021
　Morning
　　Archdiocese of Asunción, Paraguay
　　Territorial Prelature of Huamachuco, Peru
　　Diocese of Jeonju, South Korea
　　Diocese of Port Blair, India
　　Ukrainian Catholic Eparchy of Santa María del Patrocinio en Buenos Aires, Argentina
　Evening
　　Diocese of Angers, France
　　Diocese of Brownsville, Texas, USA
　　Diocese of Colorado Springs, Colorado, USA
　　Diocese of Santiago de Cabo Verde
Thu, 25 March 2021
　Morning
　　Diocese of Ahmedabad, India
　　Diocese of Ji'an, China
　　Apostolic Vicariate of Puerto Princesa, Philippines
　　Diocese of Termoli-Larino, Italy
　Evening
　　Archdiocese of Halifax-Yarmouth, Nova Scotia, Canada
　　Territorial Prelature of Lábrea, Amazonas, Brazil
　　Archdiocese of Lecce, Italy
　　Diocese of Lucena, Philippines
Fri, 26 March 2021
　Morning
　　Archdiocese of Ancona-Osimo, Italy
　　Archdiocese of Białystok, Poland
　　Archdiocese of Kansas City in Kansas, USA
　　Diocese of Linares, Chile
　　Diocese of Morondava, Madagascar
　Evening
　　Diocese of Iaşi, Romania
　　Apostolic Vicariate of Nepal
　　Diocese of Sendai, Japan
　　Archdiocese of Taiyuan, China
Sat, 27 March 2021
　Morning
　　Diocese of Houma-Thibodaux, Louisiana, USA
　　Diocese of N'Zérékoré, Guinea
　　Romanian Catholic Eparchy of Sfântul Vasile cel Mare de Bucureşti, Romania
　　Diocese of Tianguá, Ceara, Brazil
　　Diocese of Ubon Ratchathani, Thailand
　Evening
　　Diocese of Ivrea, Italy
　　Diocese of Novaliches, Philippines
　　Diocese of Tula, Hidalgo, México
　　Diocese of Wau, South Sudan
Sun, 28 March 2021
　Morning
　　Archdiocese of Calcutta, India
　　Diocese of Itapetininga, Sao Paulo, Brazil
　　Diocese of Jashpur, India
　　Armenian Catholic Eparchy of Kamichlié, Syria

    Diocese of Łowicz, Poland
  Evening
    Archdiocese of Bamako, Mali
    Diocese of Maliana, Timor-Leste
    Ukrainian Catholic Eparchy of Sambir-Drohobych, Ukraine
    Diocese of Worcester, Massachusetts, USA

Mon, 29 March 2021
  Morning
    Diocese of Bossangoa, Central African Republic
    Diocese of Chanthaburi, Thailand
    Diocese of Ilorin, Nigeria
    Diocese of Jhansi, India
    Diocese of P'yŏng-yang, North Korea
  Evening
    Archdiocese of Daegu, South Korea
    Ruthenian Catholic Archeparchy of Pittsburgh, Pennsylvania, USA
    Diocese of Saint Thomas, American Virgin Islands, USA
    Archdiocese of Sassari, Italy

Tue, 30 March 2021
  Morning
    Diocese of Dibrugarh, India
    Apostolic Vicariate of Inírida, Colombia
    Diocese of Mondoñedo-Ferrol, Spain
    Archdiocese of Tunja, Colombia
    Diocese of Verapaz, Cobán, Guatemala
  Evening
    Diocese of Caserta, Italy
    Diocese of Lindi, Tanzania
    Diocese of Solwezi, Zambia
    Diocese of Thiès, Senegal

Wed, 31 March 2021
  Morning
    Archdiocese of Bari-Bitonto, Italy
    Diocese of Gaylord, Michigan, USA
    Diocese of Kalay, Myanmar
    Diocese of Lolo, Democratic Republic of the Congo
    Diocese of Rome, Italy
  Evening
    Diocese of Auki, Solomon Islands
    Military Ordinariate of Hungary
    Diocese of Timișoara, Romania
    Diocese of Vigevano, Italy

April

Thu, 01 April 2021
  Morning
    Diocese of Cruzeiro do Sul, Acre, Brazil
    Diocese of Formosa, Argentina
    Diocese of Salt Lake City, Utah, USA
    Diocese of Sete Lagoas, Minas Gerais, Brazil
    Diocese of Varanasi, India
  Evening
    Diocese of Potosí, Bolivia
    Diocese of Richmond, Virginia, USA
    Archdiocese of Saurimo, Angola
    Diocese of Suchitepéquez-Retalhuleu, Guatemala

Fri, 02 April 2021
  Morning
    Diocese of Kroonstad, South Africa
    Diocese of Kwito-Bié, Angola
    Archdiocese of Lingayen-Dagupan, Philippines
    Diocese of Oslo, Norway
    Archdiocese of Rossano-Cariati, Italy
  Evening
    Maronite Catholic Patriarchate of Antioch, Lebanon
    Ordinariate of the Faithful of the Eastern Rites in Argentina
    Archdiocese of Ende, Indonesia
    Archdiocese of Gagnoa, Côte d'Ivoire

Sat, 03 April 2021
  Morning
    Diocese of Ciudad Rodrigo, Spain
    Chaldean Catholic Patriarchal Dependent Territory of Jerusalem, Palestine
    Diocese of Trasfigurazione a Novosibirsk, Russian Federation
    Diocese of Zamora, Spain
  Evening
    Diocese of Kaya, Burkina Faso
    Diocese of Mar del Plata, Argentina
    Diocese of Purwokerto, Indonesia
    Slovakian Catholic Eparchy of Saints Cyril and Methodius of Toronto, Canada

Sun, 04 April 2021
  Morning
    Diocese of Hpa-an, Myanmar
    Diocese of Melipilla, Chile
    Archdiocese of Paderborn, Germany
    Archdiocese of Rosario, Argentina
    Diocese of Sumbe, Angola
  Evening
    Diocese of Barretos, Sao Paulo, Brazil
    Diocese of Galloway, Scotland
    Suburbicarian See of Ostia, Italy
    Diocese of Yamoussoukro, Côte d'Ivoire

Mon, 05 April 2021
  Morning
    Diocese of Ardagh, Ireland
    Diocese of Bafoussam, Cameroon
    Diocese of Chiang Rai, Thailand

   Diocese of Man, Côte d'Ivoire
   Diocese of Yakima, Washington, USA
  Evening
   Diocese of Afogados da Ingazeira, Pernambuco, Brazil
   Diocese of Catamarca, Argentina
   Diocese of Mbujimayi, Democratic Republic of the Congo
   Archdiocese of Seoul, South Korea

Tue, 06 April 2021
  Morning
   Archdiocese of Dodoma, Tanzania
   Diocese of Ecatepec, México, México
   Diocese of Juticalpa, Honduras
   Apostolic Vicariate of Puerto Leguízamo-Solano, Colombia
   Diocese of Zrenjanin, Serbia
  Evening
   Archdiocese of Arusha, Tanzania
   Diocese of Fajardo-Humacao, Puerto Rico
   Archdiocese of Freetown, Sierra Leone
   Diocese of Niigata, Japan

Wed, 07 April 2021
  Morning
   Diocese of Arua, Uganda
   Archdiocese of Dijon, France
   Archdiocese of Fortaleza, Ceara, Brazil
   Apostolic Vicariate of Makokou, Gabon
   Diocese of Saint-Flour, France
  Evening
   Diocese of Cachoeira do Sul, Rio Grande do Sul, Brazil
   Diocese of Dundo, Angola
   Diocese of Port Elizabeth, South Africa
   Diocese of Xuanhua, China

Thu, 08 April 2021
  Morning
   Diocese of Cienfuegos, Cuba
   Diocese of Lugazi, Uganda
   Archdiocese of Munich and Freising, Germany
   Diocese of Orléans, France
   Archdiocese of Philadelphia, Pennsylvania, USA
  Evening
   Archdiocese of Braga, Portugal
   Diocese of Honolulu, Hawaii, USA
   Archdiocese of Mwanza, Tanzania
   Archdiocese of Taunggyi, Myanmar

Fri, 09 April 2021
  Morning
   Diocese of Albenga-Imperia, Italy
   Apostolic Vicariate of Chaco Paraguayo, Paraguay
   Diocese of Ji-Paraná, Rondonia, Brazil
   Diocese of Pingliang, China
   Diocese of San Severo, Italy
  Evening
   Archdiocese of Burgos, Spain
   Diocese of Hinche, Haïti
   Archdiocese of San Juan de Cuyo, Argentina
   Diocese of São Luíz de Cáceres, Mato Grosso, Brazil

Sat, 10 April 2021
  Morning
    Archdiocese of Kraków, Poland
    Apostolic Vicariate of Mongo, Chad
    Diocese of Qingdao, China
    Diocese of Volterra, Italy
    Diocese of Xingu-Altamira, Para, Brazil
  Evening
    Diocese of Mpika, Zambia
    Ukrainian Catholic Eparchy of Saskatoon, Canada
    Diocese of Surabaya, Indonesia
    Archdiocese of Vitória da Conquista, Bahia, Brazil

Sun, 11 April 2021
  Morning
    Diocese of Anagni-Alatri, Italy
    Syrian Catholic Patriarchate of Antioch, Lebanon
    Diocese of Quilmes, Argentina
    Diocese of San Juan de los Lagos, Jalisco, México
  Evening
    Diocese of Armenia, Colombia
    Archdiocese of Nanchang, China
    Archdiocese of Santa Fe de Antioquia, Colombia
    Diocese of Yendi, Ghana

Mon, 12 April 2021
  Morning
    Diocese of Jabalpur, India
    Archdiocese of Manizales, Colombia
    Diocese of Marsabit, Kenya
    Diocese of Pueblo, Colorado, USA
    Chaldean Catholic Archdiocese of Teheran, Iran
  Evening
    Diocese of Cần Thơ, Viet Nam
    Diocese of Magangué, Colombia
    Diocese of Ogoja, Nigeria
    Archdiocese of Palembang, Indonesia

Tue, 13 April 2021
  Morning
    Diocese of David, Panama
    Diocese of Escuintla, Guatemala
    Diocese of Nevers, France
    Archdiocese of Osaka, Japan
    Diocese of Tenancingo, México, México
  Evening
    Eritrean Catholic Archeparchy of Asmara, Eritrea
    Diocese of Barra, Bahia, Brazil
    Diocese of Saitama, Japan
    Apostolic Prefecture of Western Sahara

Wed, 14 April 2021
  Morning
    Diocese of Belley-Ars, France
    Diocese of Crookston, Minnesota, USA
    Patriarchate of Jerusalem, Palestine
    Diocese of Khulna, Bangladesh
    Archdiocese of Pouso Alegre, Minas Gerais, Brazil

Evening
- Archdiocese of Bukavu, Democratic Republic of the Congo
- Archdiocese of Santiago de Cuba
- Syro-Malabar Catholic Eparchy of Shamshabad, India
- Archdiocese of Vaduz, Liechtenstein

Thu, 15 April 2021
Morning
- Diocese of Calgary, Alberta, Canada
- Diocese of Novo Hamburgo, Rio Grande do Sul, Brazil
- Diocese of Pagadian, Philippines
- Mission Sui Iuris of Saint Helena, Ascension and Tristan da Cunha
- Diocese of Tehuantepec, Oaxaca, México

Evening
- Diocese of Beauvais, France
- Diocese of Chosica, Peru
- Diocese of Esteli, Nicaragua
- Diocese of San Jose, Philippines

Fri, 16 April 2021
Morning
- Diocese of Albacete, Spain
- Diocese of Bougainville, Papua New Guinea
- Archdiocese of Kupang, Indonesia
- Italo-Albanese Catholic Territorial Abbey of Santa Maria di Grottaferrata, Italy
- Diocese of Valle de Chalco, México, México

Evening
- Diocese of Huarí, Peru
- Diocese of Masbate, Philippines
- Diocese of San Pablo, Philippines
- Diocese of Shimoga, India

Sat, 17 April 2021
Morning
- Diocese of Acerra, Italy
- Military Ordinariate of Australia
- Archdiocese of Gorizia, Italy
- Diocese of Netzahualcóyotl, México, México
- Diocese of Vijayawada, India

Evening
- Diocese of Hsinchu, Taiwan
- Diocese of Pescia, Italy
- Diocese of San José del Guaviare, Colombia
- Diocese of Santa Rosa de Copán, Honduras

Sun, 18 April 2021
Morning
- Archdiocese of Cardiff, Wales
- Diocese of Juigalpa, Nicaragua
- Diocese of Killaloe, Ireland
- Archdiocese of Madurai, India
- Diocese of Morogoro, Tanzania

Evening
- Archdiocese of Jos, Nigeria
- Archdiocese of Cologne, Germany
- Apostolic Vicariate of Méndez, Ecuador
- Diocese of San Diego, California, USA

Mon, 19 April 2021
- Morning
  - Diocese of Bắc Ninh, Viet Nam
  - Archdiocese of Cuzco, Peru
  - Diocese of Iba, Philippines
  - Archdiocese of Montréal, Québec, Canada
- Evening
  - Diocese of Cruz del Eje, Argentina
  - Archdiocese of Lublin, Poland
  - Military Ordinariate of Portugal
  - Diocese of Santo Ângelo, Rio Grande do Sul, Brazil

Tue, 20 April 2021
- Morning
  - Diocese of Araçatuba, Sao Paulo, Brazil
  - Diocese of Fontibón, Colombia
  - Diocese of Kohima, India
  - Romanian Catholic Diocese of Oradea Mare, Romania
  - Diocese of Picos, Piaui, Brazil
- Evening
  - Archdiocese of Córdoba, Argentina
  - Archdiocese of Kunming, China
  - Diocese of Obala, Cameroon
  - Diocese of São João da Boa Vista, Sao Paulo, Brazil

Wed, 21 April 2021
- Morning
  - Archdiocese of Auch, France
  - Diocese of Daru-Kiunga, Papua New Guinea
  - Syro-Malabar Catholic Eparchy of Ramanathapuram, India
  - Apostolic Vicariate of San Ramón, Peru
  - Diocese of Umuahia, Nigeria
- Evening
  - Diocese of Des Moines, Iowa, USA
  - Ukrainian Catholic Archiepiscopal Exarchate of Donets'k, Ukraine
  - Archdiocese of Kaunas, Lithuania
  - Archdiocese of Udine, Italy

Thu, 22 April 2021
- Morning
  - Apostolic Vicariate of Gambella, Ethiopia
  - Archdiocese of Malanje, Angola
  - Diocese of Oita, Japan
  - Diocese of Pittsburgh, Pennsylvania, USA
  - Territorial Abbey of Santissima Trinità di Cava de' Tirreni, Italy
- Evening
  - Diocese of Aachen, Germany
  - Diocese of Kumba, Cameroon
  - Diocese of Siedlce, Poland
  - Diocese of Trivento, Italy

Fri, 23 April 2021
- Morning
  - Diocese of Jinzhou, China
  - Archdiocese of Mariana, Minas Gerais, Brazil
  - Diocese of Nacala, Mozambique
  - Diocese of Norwich, Connecticut, USA
  - Diocese of Tumaco, Colombia

Evening
- Diocese of Badulla, Sri Lanka
- Diocese of Fresno, California, USA
- Diocese of Jaén, Spain
- Diocese of La Vega, Dominican Republic

Sat, 24 April 2021
Morning
- Diocese of Gaspé, Québec, Canada
- Diocese of Governador Valadares, Minas Gerais, Brazil
- Diocese of Santa Ana, El Salvador
- Diocese of Sololá-Chimaltenango, Guatemala
- Diocese of Subotica, Serbia

Evening
- Territorial Prelature of Batanes, Philippines
- Diocese of El Vigia-San Carlos del Zulia, Venezuela
- Diocese of Jining, China
- Diocese of Oyem, Gabon

Sun, 25 April 2021
Morning
- Military Ordinariate of Croatia
- Armenian Catholic Ordinariate of Greece
- Diocese of Itabira-Fabriciano, Minas Gerais, Brazil
- Diocese of Kotido, Uganda
- Diocese of Ventimiglia-San Remo, Italy

Evening
- Syro-Malabar Catholic Diocese of Gorakhpur, India
- Diocese of Grodno, Belarus
- Diocese of Livramento de Nossa Senhora, Bahia, Brazil
- Maronite Catholic Eparchy of Nuestra Señora de los Mártires del Libano en México

Mon, 26 April 2021
Morning
- Archdiocese of Belém do Pará, Brazil
- Diocese of Hiroshima, Japan
- Diocese of Kara, Togo
- Diocese of Lincoln, Nebraska, USA
- Diocese of Valle de la Pascua, Venezuela

Evening
- Diocese of Avellaneda-Lanús, Argentina
- Diocese of Goroka, Papua New Guinea
- Diocese of Mannar, Sri Lanka
- Archdiocese of Olomouc, Czech Republic

Tue, 27 April 2021
Morning
- Military Ordinariate of Austria
- Archdiocese of Guwahati, India
- Diocese of Huaraz, Peru
- Archdiocese of Luxembourg
- Diocese of San Juan Bautista de Calama, Chile

Evening
- Diocese of Casale Monferrato, Italy
- Diocese of Kole, Democratic Republic of the Congo
- Archdiocese of Lucca, Italy
- Diocese of Salina, Kansas, USA

Wed, 28 April 2021
- Morning
  - Archdiocese of Maria Santissima in Astana, Kazakhstan
  - Archdiocese of Tarragona, Spain
  - Diocese of Tuxtepec, Oaxaca, México
  - Patriarchate of Venice, Italy
- Evening
  - Diocese of Krishnagar, India
  - Archdiocese of L'Aquila, Italy
  - Archdiocese of Paris, France
  - Diocese of Saint-Hyacinthe, Québec, Canada

Thu, 29 April 2021
- Morning
  - Diocese of Cajazeiras, Paraiba, Brazil
  - Diocese of Kaga-Bandoro, Central African Republic
  - Diocese of Machiques, Venezuela
  - Diocese of Menorca, Spain
  - Military Ordinariate of Poland
- Evening
  - Archdiocese of Montpellier, France
  - Diocese of Nkayi, Republic of the Congo
  - Archdiocese of Portoviejo, Ecuador
  - Archdiocese of São Paulo, Brazil

Fri, 30 April 2021
- Morning
  - Diocese of Baní, Dominican Republic
  - Diocese of Datong, China
  - Diocese of Khammam, India
  - Diocese of Santa Maria de Los Ángeles, Chile
  - Archdiocese of Valencia en Venezuela
- Evening
  - Diocese of Bayonne, France
  - Diocese of Limburg, Germany
  - Diocese of Nebbi, Uganda
  - Archdiocese of Santarém, Para, Brazil

May

Sat, 01 May 2021
  Morning
    Mission Sui Iuris of Cayman Islands, Antilles
    Diocese of De Aar, South Africa
    Apostolic Prefecture of Jian'ou, China
    Diocese of Sokodé, Togo
    Syro-Malankara Catholic Archeparchy of Trivandrum, India
  Evening
    Diocese of Kabwe, Zambia
    Apostolic Vicariate of Pando, Bolivia
    Diocese of Santo Amaro, Sao Paulo, Brazil
    Diocese of Sindhudurg, India

Sun, 02 May 2021
  Morning
    Apostolic Vicariate of Aysén, Chile
    Diocese of Eichstätt, Germany
    Diocese of Hanyang, China
    Diocese of Oria, Italy
    Diocese of Tagbilaran, Philippines
  Evening
    Diocese of Banja Luka, Bosnia and Herzegovina
    Syro-Malabar Catholic Diocese of Belthangady, India
    Archdiocese of Hà Nội, Viet Nam
    Diocese of Palmerston North, New Zealand

Mon, 03 May 2021
  Morning
    Archdiocese of Corfù, Zante e Cefalonia, Greece
    Diocese of Goiás, Brazil
    Archdiocese of Paraná, Argentina
    Diocese of Terrassa, Spain
    Diocese of Verdun, France
  Evening
    Diocese of Bydgoszcz, Poland
    Syrian Catholic Archeparchy of Hassaké-Nisibi, Syria
    Diocese of Vila Real, Portugal
    Archdiocese of Yaoundé, Cameroon

Tue, 04 May 2021
  Morning
    Diocese of Anuradhapura, Sri Lanka
    Diocese of Fréjus-Toulon, France
    Archdiocese of Kuching, Malaysia
    Archdiocese of Rouen, France
    Ukrainian Catholic Eparchy of Toronto, Canada
  Evening
    Diocese of Benguela, Angola
    Diocese of Evansville, Indiana, USA
    Diocese of Iglesias, Italy
    Diocese of Teixeira de Freitas-Caravelas, Bahia, Brazil

Wed, 05 May 2021
  Morning
    Diocese of Ajaccio, France
    Diocese of Bondo, Democratic Republic of the Congo

  Archdiocese of Cumaná, Venezuela
  Diocese of Ekwulobia, Nigeria
  Archdiocese of Goa e Damão, India
 Evening
  Diocese of Alife-Caiazzo, Italy
  Diocese of Huesca, Spain
  Diocese of Melo, Uruguay
  Diocese of Xiangyang, China

Thu, 06 May 2021
 Morning
  Diocese of Bacolod, Philippines
  Diocese of Civita Castellana, Italy
  Diocese of Mahagi-Nioka, Democratic Republic of the Congo
  Diocese of Rafaela, Argentina
 Evening
  Diocese of Livorno, Italy
  Diocese of Ruy Barbosa, Bahia, Brazil
  Ukrainian Catholic Eparchy of Stamford, USA
  Diocese of Steubenville, Ohio, USA

Fri, 07 May 2021
 Morning
  Archdiocese of Hankow, China
  Military Ordinariate of Indonesia
  Diocese of Lashio, Myanmar
  Diocese of Marabá, Para, Brazil
  Diocese of Maradi, Niger
 Evening
  Syrian Catholic Archeparchy of Mossul, Iraq
  Archdiocese of Strasbourg, France
  Diocese of Torreón, Coahuila, México
  Diocese of Townsville, Australia

Sat, 08 May 2021
 Morning
  Chaldean Catholic Diocese of Amadiyah and Zaku, Iraq
  Archdiocese of Caracas, Santiago de Venezuela
  Diocese of Kharkiv-Zaporizhia, Ukraine
  Diocese of Santa Rosa de Lima, Guatemala
  Diocese of Tonga
 Evening
  Diocese of Clogher, Ireland
  Diocese of Drohiczyn, Poland
  Maronite Catholic Eparchy of Our Lady of Lebanon of Los Angeles, California, USA
  Diocese of Rieti, Italy

Sun, 09 May 2021
 Morning
  Diocese of Ambanja, Madagascar
  Diocese of Blois, France
  Diocese of Ngaoundéré, Cameroon
  Archdiocese of Prague, Czech Republic
  Diocese of Saint Petersburg, Florida, USA
 Evening
  Territorial Prelature of Infanta, Philippines
  Archdiocese of Niterói, Rio de Janeiro, Brazil
  Maronite Catholic Eparchy of Saint Maron of Sydney, Australia
  Archdiocese of Salzburg, Austria

Mon, 10 May 2021
- Morning
  - Territorial Prelature of Ayaviri, Peru
  - Archdiocese of Calabozo, Venezuela
  - Diocese of Görlitz, Germany
  - Diocese of Mahenge, Tanzania
  - Archdiocese of Ouagadougou, Burkina Faso
- Evening
  - Diocese of Allentown, Pennsylvania, USA
  - Diocese of Mbulu, Tanzania
  - Diocese of Port Pirie, Australia
  - Diocese of Vellore, India

Tue, 11 May 2021
- Morning
  - Diocese of Coutances, France
  - Diocese of Koforidua, Ghana
  - Diocese of Lamezia Terme, Italy
  - Diocese of Trapani, Italy
  - Apostolic Prefecture of Yiduxian, China
- Evening
  - Diocese of Aberdeen, Scotland
  - Diocese of Dapaong, Togo
  - Diocese of Malakal, South Sudan
  - Diocese of Szombathely, Hungary

Wed, 12 May 2021
- Morning
  - Apostolic Vicariate of Caroní, Venezuela
  - Archdiocese of Lima, Peru
  - Diocese of Meaux, France
  - Archdiocese of Sucre, Bolivia
  - Diocese of Xuân Lộc, Viet Nam
- Evening
  - Archdiocese of Capua, Italy
  - Diocese of Città di Castello, Italy
  - Diocese of Huajuapan de León, Oaxaca, México
  - Military Ordinariate of the Netherlands

Thu, 13 May 2021
- Morning
  - Diocese of Chulucanas, Peru
  - Diocese of Đà Nẵng, Viet Nam
  - Apostolic Prefecture of Lingling, China
  - Romanian Catholic Diocese of Maramureş, Romania
  - Diocese of Raleigh, North Carolina, USA
- Evening
  - Archdiocese of Atlanta, Georgia, USA
  - Territorial Abbey of Maria Einsiedeln, Switzerland
  - Archdiocese of Seville, Spain
  - Archdiocese of Vercelli, Italy

Fri, 14 May 2021
- Morning
  - Archdiocese of Barcelona, Spain
  - Diocese of Cayenne, French Guyana, Antilles
  - Diocese of Lira, Uganda
  - Diocese of Polokwane, South Africa

Evening
- Diocese of Arezzo-Cortona-Sansepolcro, Italy
- Archdiocese of Kananga, Democratic Republic of the Congo
- Maronite Catholic Eparchy of Nossa Senhora do Líbano em São Paulo, Sao Paulo, Brazil
- Diocese of Udaipur, India

Sat, 15 May 2021

Morning
- Archdiocese of Malta
- Diocese of Patos de Minas, Minas Gerais, Brazil
- Diocese of Saint John, New Brunswick, Canada
- Syro-Malabar Catholic Eparchy of Saint Thomas the Apostle of Melbourne, Australia
- Syrian Catholic Patriarchal Exarchate of Turkey

Evening
- Diocese of Inhambane, Mozambique
- Diocese of Ischia, Italy
- Diocese of Nnewi, Nigeria
- Diocese of Nyahururu, Kenya

Sun, 16 May 2021

Morning
- Diocese of Ijebu-Ode, Nigeria
- Diocese of Lexington, Kentucky, USA
- Archdiocese of Mérida, Venezuela
- Archdiocese of Perugia-Città della Pieve, Italy
- Apostolic Vicariate of Puyo, Ecuador

Evening
- Diocese of Chengdu, China
- Diocese of Kotor, Montenegro
- Diocese of León, Spain
- Archdiocese of Ljubljana, Slovenia

Mon, 17 May 2021

Morning
- Diocese of Alaminos, Philippines
- Diocese of Hamhŭng, North Korea
- Archdiocese of Quito, Ecuador
- Syro-Malabar Catholic Diocese of Satna, India
- Diocese of Sora-Cassino-Aquino-Pontecorvo, Italy

Evening
- Diocese of Achonry, Ireland
- Diocese of Fushun, China
- Diocese of Gliwice, Poland
- Diocese of San Giuseppe a Irkutsk, Russian Federation

Tue, 18 May 2021

Morning
- Diocese of Caxias do Sul, Rio Grande do Sul, Brazil
- Archdiocese of Changsha, China
- Archdiocese of Conakry, Guinea
- Hungarian Catholic Archdiocese of Hajdúdorog, Hungary
- Diocese of Merlo-Moreno, Argentina

Evening
- Diocese of Mileto-Nicotera-Tropea, Italy
- Diocese of Sangmélima, Cameroon
- Diocese of Tempio-Ampurias, Italy
- Territorial Prelature of Yauyos, Peru

Wed, 19 May 2021
- Morning
  - Diocese of Carcassonne et Narbonne, France
  - Diocese of Ełk, Poland
  - Diocese of Humaitá, Amazonas, Brazil
  - Diocese of Linares, Nuevo León, México
  - Diocese of Takamatsu, Japan
- Evening
  - Archdiocese of Campo Grande, Mato Grosso do Sul, Brazil
  - Diocese of Guarda, Portugal
  - Syro-Malabar Catholic Eparchy of Mississauga
  - Diocese of Serrinha, Bahia, Brazil

Thu, 20 May 2021
- Morning
  - Melkite Greek Catholic Patriarchate of Antioch, Syria
  - Apostolic Administration of Caucaso, Armenia
  - Diocese of Fairbanks, Alaska, USA
  - Diocese of Fiesole, Italy
  - Archdiocese of Santiago de Chile
- Evening
  - Archdiocese of Morelia, Michoacán, México
  - Archdiocese of Pondicherry and Cuddalore, India
  - Diocese of Saint George's in Grenada, Antilles
  - Diocese of San Miniato, Italy

Fri, 21 May 2021
- Morning
  - Diocese of Chiclayo, Peru
  - Diocese of Ciudad Quesada, Costa Rica
  - Diocese of Mamfe, Cameroon
  - Archdiocese of Papeete, French Polynesia
  - Diocese of Vitoria, Spain
- Evening
  - Diocese of Chimbote, Peru
  - Diocese of Cuneo, Italy
  - Diocese of Lurín, Peru
  - Syro-Malankara Catholic Eparchy of Parassala, India

Sat, 22 May 2021
- Morning
  - Diocese of Amos, Québec, Canada
  - Ukrainian Catholic Eparchy of Chernivtsi, Ukraine
  - Diocese of Dromore, Ireland
  - Diocese of East Anglia, England
  - Archdiocese of Mount Hagen, Papua New Guinea
- Evening
  - Diocese of Kalemie-Kirungu, Democratic Republic of the Congo
  - Archdiocese of Paraíba, Brazil
  - Diocese of Reconquista, Argentina
  - Diocese of Soroti, Uganda

Alphabetical List

22	Apr	2021	Aachen (Diocese), Germany
11	Dec	2020	Aba (Diocese), Nigeria
20	Sep	2020	Abaetetuba (Diocese), Para, Brazil
24	Feb	2021	Abakaliki (Diocese), Nigeria
03	Mar	2021	Abancay (Diocese), Peru
11	Jan	2021	Abengourou (Diocese), Côte d'Ivoire
24	Jan	2021	Abeokuta (Diocese), Nigeria
11	May	2021	Aberdeen (Diocese), Scotland, Great Britain
30	Jan	2021	Abidjan (Archdiocese), Côte d'Ivoire
14	Jan	2021	Abomey (Diocese), Benin
28	Nov	2020	Abuja (Archdiocese), Nigeria
27	Jul	2020	Abu Qurqas (Coptic) (Eparchy), Egypt
18	Nov	2020	Acapulco (Archdiocese), Guerrero, México
25	Jan	2021	Acarigua-Araure (Diocese), Venezuela
19	Jul	2020	Accra (Archdiocese), Ghana
05	Jan	2021	Acerenza (Archdiocese), Italy
17	Apr	2021	Acerra (Diocese), Italy
17	May	2021	Achonry (Diocese), Ireland
22	Oct	2020	Acireale (Diocese), Italy
24	Nov	2020	Acqui (Diocese), Italy
25	Jan	2021	Addis Abeba (Ethiopian) (Archeparchy), Ethiopia
06	Jan	2021	Adelaide (Archdiocese), Australia
03	Aug	2020	Adigrat (Ethiopian) (Eparchy), Ethiopia
10	Jun	2020	Adilabad (Syro-Malabar) (Diocese), India
17	Aug	2020	Adria-Rovigo (Diocese), Italy
21	Mar	2021	Afghanistan (Mission Sui Iuris)
05	Apr	2021	Afogados da Ingazeira (Diocese), Pernambuco, Brazil
11	Feb	2021	Agaña (Archdiocese), Guam, Pacific (Oceania)
22	Nov	2020	Agartala (Diocese), India
01	Mar	2021	Agats (Diocese), Indonesia
05	Jun	2020	Agboville (Diocese), Côte d'Ivoire
27	Sep	2020	Agen (Diocese), France
15	Jan	2021	Agra (Archdiocese), India
10	Jan	2021	Agrigento (Archdiocese), Italy
06	Jun	2020	Aguarico (Vicariate Apostolic), Ecuador
06	Dec	2020	Aguascalientes (Diocese), México
14	Nov	2020	Ahiara (Diocese), Nigeria
25	Mar	2021	Ahmedabad (Diocese), India
06	Dec	2020	Ahwaz (Chaldean) (Archeparchy), Iran
03	Nov	2020	Aiquile (Territorial Prelature), Bolivia
12	Aug	2020	Aire et Dax (Diocese), France
21	Feb	2021	Aitape (Diocese), Papua New Guinea

30	Oct	2020	Aix (-Arles) (Archdiocese), France
11	Jun	2020	Aizawl (Diocese), India
05	May	2021	Ajaccio (Diocese), France
22	Jan	2021	Ajmer (Diocese), India
24	Dec	2020	Akka [San Giovanni d'Acri; Tolemaide] (Melkite Greek) (Archeparchy), Israel
15	Mar	2021	Alagoinhas (Diocese), Bahia, Brazil
01	Mar	2021	Alajuela (Diocese), Costa Rica
17	May	2021	Alaminos (Diocese), Philippines
12	Nov	2020	Alba (Pompea) (Diocese), Italy
16	Apr	2021	Albacete (Diocese), Spain
04	Jun	2020	Alba Iulia (Archdiocese), Romania
05	Oct	2020	Albano (Suburbicarian See), Italy
01	Mar	2021	Albany (Diocese), New York, USA
09	Apr	2021	Albenga-Imperia (Diocese), Italy
15	Jul	2020	Albi (-Castres-Lavaur) (Archdiocese), France
17	Feb	2021	Alcalá de Henares (Diocese), Spain
22	Aug	2020	Alep [Beroea, Halab] (Armenian) (Archeparchy), Syria
13	Nov	2020	Alep [Beroea, Halab] (Vicariate Apostolic), Syria
27	Jan	2021	Alep [Beroea, Halab] (Maronite) (Archeparchy), Syria
03	Jan	2021	Alep [Beroea, Halab] (Chaldean) (Eparchy), Syria
23	Jun	2020	Alep [Beroea, Halab] (Melkite Greek) (Archdiocese), Syria
30	Jun	2020	Alep [Beroea, Halab] (Syrian) (Archeparchy), Syria
31	Dec	2020	Alessandria (della Paglia) (Diocese), Italy
16	Nov	2020	Ales-Terralba (Diocese), Italy
02	Dec	2020	Alexandria (Diocese), Louisiana, USA
06	Mar	2021	Alexandria {Alessandria} (Coptic) (Eparchy), Egypt
16	Sep	2020	Alexandria {Alessandria} (Coptic) (Patriarchate), Egypt
01	Jun	2020	Alexandria of Egypt {Alessandria di Egitto} (-Eliopoli di Egitto-Port-Said) (Vicariate
20	Jun	2020	Alger (Archdiocese), Algeria
07	Mar	2021	Alghero-Bosa (Diocese), Italy
05	May	2021	Alife-Caiazzo (Diocese), Italy
06	Feb	2021	Alindao (Diocese), Central African Republic
18	Nov	2020	Aliwal (Diocese), South Africa
17	Aug	2020	Allahabad (Diocese), India
10	May	2021	Allentown (Diocese), Pennsylvania, USA
22	Jun	2020	Alleppey (Diocese), India
13	Feb	2021	Almenara (Diocese), Minas Gerais, Brazil
06	Oct	2020	Almería (Diocese), Spain
25	Jun	2020	Alotau-Sideia (Diocese), Papua New Guinea
08	Mar	2021	Alquoch (Chaldean) (Diocese), Iraq
05	Oct	2020	Altamura-Gravina-Acquaviva delle Fonti (Diocese), Italy
20	Aug	2020	Altoona-Johnstown (Diocese), Pennsylvania, USA
13	Jan	2021	Alto Solimões (Diocese), Amazonas, Brazil
23	Feb	2021	Alto Valle del Río Negro (Diocese), Argentina

09	Jun	2020	Alto Xingu-Tucumã (Territorial Prelature), Para, Brazil
08	May	2021	Amadiyah and Zaku (Chaldean) (Diocese), Iraq
16	Nov	2020	Amalfi-Cava de' Tirreni (Archdiocese), Italy
23	Feb	2021	Amargosa (Diocese), Bahia, Brazil
18	Dec	2020	Amarillo (Diocese), Texas, USA
09	May	2021	Ambanja (Diocese), Madagascar
26	Oct	2020	Ambato (Diocese), Ecuador
09	Oct	2020	Ambatondrazaka (Diocese), Madagascar
11	Sep	2020	Ambikapur (Diocese), India
06	Aug	2020	Amboina (Diocese), Indonesia
27	Jun	2020	Ambositra (Diocese), Madagascar
14	Jan	2021	America Latina e Messico {Latin America and Mexico} (Armenian) (Apostolic
28	Jan	2021	Amiens (Diocese), France
22	May	2021	Amos (Diocese), Québec, Canada
15	Oct	2020	Amparo (Diocese), Sao Paulo, Brazil
26	Nov	2020	Amravati (Diocese), India
11	Apr	2021	Anagni-Alatri (Diocese), Italy
14	Jun	2020	Anápolis (Diocese), Goias, Brazil
19	Jan	2021	Anatolia (Vicariate Apostolic), Turkey
29	Jul	2020	Añatuya (Diocese), Argentina
03	Nov	2020	Anchorage-Juneau (Archdiocese), Alaska, USA
26	Mar	2021	Ancona-Osimo (Archdiocese), Italy
09	Oct	2020	Andong (Diocese), Korea (South)
18	Sep	2020	Andria (Diocese), Italy
19	Nov	2020	Aného (Diocese), Togo
24	Mar	2021	Angers (Diocese), France
09	Oct	2020	Angoulême (Diocese), France
22	Dec	2020	Angra (Diocese), Portugal
12	Feb	2021	Anguo [Ankwo] (Diocese), China
24	Jan	2021	Ankang [Hinganfu] (Prefecture Apostolic), China
30	Oct	2020	Anlong [Lanlung] (Diocese), China
25	Oct	2020	Annecy (Diocese), France
31	May	2020	Anqing [Anking, Huai-ning] (Archdiocese), China
21	Sep	2020	Anse-à-Veau et Miragoâne (Diocese), Haïti
13	Jun	2020	Antananarivo (Archdiocese), Madagascar
12	Jun	2020	Antélias (Maronite) (Archeparchy), Lebanon
14	Jun	2020	Antequera, Oaxaca (Archdiocese), México
10	Mar	2021	Antigonish (Diocese), Nova Scotia, Canada
02	Apr	2021	Antiochia {Antioch} (Maronite) (Patriarchate), Lebanon
20	May	2021	Antiochia {Antioch} (Melkite Greek) (Patriarchate), Syria
11	Apr	2021	Antiochia {Antioch} (Syrian) (Patriarchate), Lebanon
25	Oct	2020	Antipolo (Diocese), Philippines
03	Jul	2020	Antofagasta (Archdiocese), Chile
09	Mar	2021	Antsirabé (Diocese), Madagascar

28	Dec	2020	Antsiranana (Archdiocese), Madagascar
10	Jul	2020	Antwerpen {Antwerp} (Diocese), Belgium
04	May	2021	Anuradhapura (Diocese), Sri Lanka
15	Nov	2020	Aosta (Diocese), Italy
20	Oct	2020	Aparecida (Archdiocese), Sao Paulo, Brazil
23	Dec	2020	Apartadó (Diocese), Colombia
14	Jul	2020	Apatzingán (Diocese), Michoacán, México
19	Oct	2020	Apucarana (Diocese), Parana, Brazil
09	Jun	2020	Aqrā {Akra} (Chaldean) (Diocese), Iraq
02	Jul	2020	Aracajú (Archdiocese), Sergipe, Brazil
20	Apr	2021	Araçatuba (Diocese), Sao Paulo, Brazil
21	Jan	2021	Araçuaí (Arassuaí) (Diocese), Minas Gerais, Brazil
16	Jan	2021	Arauca (Diocese), Colombia
22	Mar	2021	Arbil {Erbil} (Chaldean) (Archeparchy), Iraq
11	Dec	2020	Archipelago of the Comores (Vicariate Apostolic)
05	Apr	2021	Ardagh (and Clonmacnois) (Diocese), Ireland
16	Nov	2020	Arecibo (Diocese), Puerto Rico
16	Jul	2020	Arequipa (Archdiocese), Peru
14	May	2021	Arezzo-Cortona-Sansepolcro (Diocese), Italy
30	Jan	2021	Argentina (Melkite Greek) (Apostolic Exarchate)
06	Mar	2021	Argentina, Military (Military Ordinariate)
02	Apr	2021	Argentina, Faithful of the Eastern Rites (Ordinariate)
24	Jun	2020	Argyll and The Isles (Diocese), Scotland, Great Britain
07	Sep	2020	Ariano Irpino-Lacedonia (Diocese), Italy
26	Jul	2020	Arlington (Diocese), Virginia, USA
28	Jan	2021	Armagh (Archdiocese), Ireland
11	Apr	2021	Armenia (Diocese), Colombia
24	Dec	2020	Armidale (Diocese), Australia
21	Sep	2020	Arras (-Boulogne-Saint-Omer) (Diocese), France
07	Apr	2021	Arua (Diocese), Uganda
23	Dec	2020	Arundel and Brighton (Diocese), England, Great Britain
06	Apr	2021	Arusha (Archdiocese), Tanzania
21	Mar	2021	Asansol (Diocese), India
10	Jul	2020	Ascoli Piceno (Diocese), Italy
13	Apr	2021	Asmara (Eritrean) (Archeparchy), Eritrea
31	Oct	2020	Assis (Diocese), Sao Paulo, Brazil
12	Mar	2021	Assisi-Nocera Umbra-Gualdo Tadino (Diocese), Italy
21	Jul	2020	Assiut {Lycopolis} (Coptic) (Eparchy), Egypt
10	Sep	2020	Asti (Diocese), Italy
14	Mar	2021	Astorga (Diocese), Spain
24	Mar	2021	Asunción (Archdiocese), Paraguay
02	Oct	2020	Atakpamé (Diocese), Togo
28	Jan	2021	Atambua (Diocese), Indonesia
04	Jun	2020	Athēnai {Athens} (Archdiocese), Greece

02	Aug	2020	Atlacomulco (Diocese), México, México
13	May	2021	Atlanta (Archdiocese), Georgia, USA
10	Feb	2021	Atyrau (Apostolic Administration), Kazakhstan
21	Apr	2021	Auch (-Condom-Lectoure-Lombez) (Archdiocese), France
30	Jul	2020	Auchi (Diocese), Nigeria
20	Jan	2021	Auckland (Diocese), New Zealand
26	Sep	2020	Augsburg (Diocese), Germany
31	Mar	2021	Auki (Diocese), Solomon Islands
25	Feb	2021	Aurangabad (Diocese), India
05	Dec	2020	Austin (Diocese), Texas, USA
17	Apr	2021	Australia, Military (Military Ordinariate)
08	Jul	2020	Austria, Faithful of Eastern Rites (Ordinariate)
27	Apr	2021	Austria, Military (Military Ordinariate)
30	Jul	2020	Autlán (Diocese), Jalisco, México
10	Nov	2020	Autun (-Châlon-sur-Saône-Mâcon-Cluny) (Diocese), France
24	Dec	2020	Aveiro (Diocese), Portugal
26	Apr	2021	Avellaneda-Lanús (Diocese), Argentina
09	Nov	2020	Avellino (Diocese), Italy
20	Jun	2020	Aversa (Diocese), Italy
06	Jun	2020	Avezzano (Diocese), Italy
21	Jan	2021	Avignon (Archdiocese), France
25	Sep	2020	Ávila (Diocese), Spain
22	Mar	2021	Awasa (Vicariate Apostolic), Ethiopia
09	Feb	2021	Awgu (Diocese), Nigeria
03	Jan	2021	Awka (Diocese), Nigeria
15	Jun	2020	Ayacucho o Huamanga (Archdiocese), Peru
10	May	2021	Ayaviri (Territorial Prelature), Peru
02	May	2021	Aysén (Vicariate Apostolic), Chile
13	Dec	2020	Azcapotzalco (Diocese), México, México
08	Jan	2021	Azerbaijan (Prefecture Apostolic)
24	Dec	2020	Azogues (Diocese), Ecuador
08	Jun	2020	Azul (Diocese), Argentina
24	Nov	2020	Baalbek (Melkite Greek) (Archeparchy), Lebanon
20	Mar	2021	Baalbek-Deir El-Ahmar (Maronite) (Eparchy), Lebanon
27	Sep	2020	Babahoyo (Diocese), Ecuador
14	Sep	2020	Babylon {Babilonia} (Chaldean) (Patriarchate), Iraq
03	Aug	2020	Bacabal (Diocese), Maranhão, Brazil
19	Apr	2021	Bắc Ninh (Diocese), Viet Nam
06	May	2021	Bacolod (Diocese), Philippines
23	Apr	2021	Badulla (Diocese), Sri Lanka
05	Jul	2020	Bafang (Diocese), Cameroon
18	Oct	2020	Bafatá (Diocese), Guinea-Bissau
30	Jul	2020	Bafia (Diocese), Cameroon
05	Apr	2021	Bafoussam (Diocese), Cameroon

30	Aug	2020	Bagdogra (Diocese), India
05	Oct	2020	Bagé (Diocese), Rio Grande do Sul, Brazil
23	Jun	2020	Baghdad (Archdiocese), Iraq
19	Aug	2020	Baghdad (Armenian) (Archeparchy), Iraq
15	Jan	2021	Baghdad (Chaldean) (Archdiocese), Iraq
14	Jul	2020	Baghdad (Syrian) (Archeparchy), Iraq
16	Nov	2020	Baguio (Diocese), Philippines
21	Jan	2021	Bahía Blanca (Archdiocese), Argentina
18	Jan	2021	Bahir Dar - Dessie (Ethiopian) (Eparchy), Ethiopia
27	Nov	2020	Baie-Comeau (Diocese), Québec, Canada
13	Jan	2021	Baker (Diocese), Oregon, USA
07	Mar	2021	Balanga (Diocese), Philippines
18	Jun	2020	Balasore (Diocese), India
29	Oct	2020	Ballarat (Diocese), Australia
17	Mar	2021	Balsas (Diocese), Maranhão, Brazil
25	Jun	2020	Baltimore (Archdiocese), Maryland, USA
28	Mar	2021	Bamako (Archdiocese), Mali
11	Dec	2020	Bambari (Diocese), Central African Republic
14	Oct	2020	Bamberg (Archdiocese), Germany
25	Nov	2020	Bamenda (Archdiocese), Cameroon
22	Jan	2021	Bandung (Diocese), Indonesia
28	Nov	2020	Banfora (Diocese), Burkina Faso
20	Aug	2020	Bangalore (Archdiocese), India
04	Aug	2020	Bangassou (Diocese), Central African Republic
27	Feb	2021	Bangkok (Archdiocese), Thailand
27	Oct	2020	Bangued (Diocese), Philippines
25	Jul	2020	Bangui (Archdiocese), Central African Republic
30	Apr	2021	Baní (Diocese), Dominican Republic
31	May	2020	Bāniyās {Cesarea di Filippo; Paneade} (Melkite Greek) (Archeparchy), Lebanon
02	May	2021	Banja Luka (Diocese), Bosnia and Herzegovina
03	Jan	2021	Banjarmasin (Diocese), Indonesia
30	Nov	2020	Banjul (Diocese), Gambia
22	Oct	2020	Banmaw (Diocese), Myanmar
21	Nov	2020	Ban Mê Thuột (Diocese), Viet Nam
20	Mar	2021	Banská Bystrica (Diocese), Slovakia
31	Jul	2020	Baoding [Paoting, Ching-Yüan] (Diocese), China
28	Sep	2020	Baojing [Paoking, Shaoyang] (Prefecture Apostolic), China
26	Aug	2020	Bar (Antivari) (Archdiocese), Montenegro
10	Nov	2020	Barahona (Diocese), Dominican Republic
07	Jul	2020	Barbastro-Monzón (Diocese), Spain
15	Dec	2020	Barcelona (Diocese), Venezuela
14	May	2021	Barcelona (Archdiocese), Spain
17	Sep	2020	Bareilly (Diocese), India
02	Jun	2020	Barentu (Eritrean) (Eparchy), Eritrea

11	Jun	2020	Bà Rịa (Diocese), Viet Nam
31	Mar	2021	Bari-Bitonto (Archdiocese), Italy
07	Jun	2020	Barinas (Diocese), Venezuela
06	Oct	2020	Barishal (Diocese), Bangladesh
23	Aug	2020	Baroda (Diocese), India
26	Sep	2020	Barquisimeto (Archdiocese), Venezuela
13	Apr	2021	Barra (do Rio Grande) (Diocese), Bahia, Brazil
06	Jul	2020	Barra do Garças (Diocese), Mato Grosso, Brazil
30	Aug	2020	Barra do Piraí-Volta Redonda (Diocese), Rio de Janeiro, Brazil
12	Jul	2020	Barrancabermeja (Diocese), Colombia
09	Sep	2020	Barranquilla (Archdiocese), Colombia
30	Jun	2020	Barreiras (Diocese), Bahia, Brazil
04	Apr	2021	Barretos (Diocese), Sao Paulo, Brazil
08	Feb	2021	Baruipur (Diocese), India
24	Feb	2021	Basankusu (Diocese), Congo (Dem. Rep.)
31	Dec	2020	Basel {Bâle, Basilea} (Diocese), Switzerland
09	Jul	2020	Basse-Terre (et Pointe-à-Pitre) (Diocese), Guadeloupe, Antilles
18	Mar	2021	Bassorah {Basra} (Chaldean) (Archeparchy), Iraq
28	Dec	2020	Bassorah e Golfo (Syrian) (Patriarchal Exarchate), Iraq
17	Jan	2021	Bata (Diocese), Equatorial Guinea
24	Apr	2021	Batanes (Territorial Prelature), Philippines
18	Nov	2020	Bathurst (Diocese), Australia
07	Nov	2020	Bathurst in Canada (Diocese), New Brunswick
12	Dec	2020	Baton Rouge (Diocese), Louisiana, USA
04	Nov	2020	Batouri (Diocese), Cameroon
14	Oct	2020	Batrun (Maronite) (Eparchy), Lebanon
12	Feb	2021	Battambang (Prefecture Apostolic), Cambodia
13	Oct	2020	Battery (Bathery) (Syro-Malankara) (Eparchy), India
01	Dec	2020	Batticaloa (Diocese), Sri Lanka
05	Aug	2020	Baucau (Diocese), Timor-Leste
11	Mar	2021	Bauchi (Diocese), Nigeria
28	Sep	2020	Bauru (Diocese), Sao Paulo, Brazil
13	Feb	2021	Bayeux (-Lisieux) (Diocese), France
08	Jul	2020	Bayombong (Diocese), Philippines
30	Apr	2021	Bayonne (-Lescar e Oloron) (Diocese), France
13	Aug	2020	Beata Maria Vergine Assunta in Strumica-Skopje (Macedonian) (Eparchy)
27	Sep	2020	Beaumont (Diocese), Texas, USA
15	Apr	2021	Beauvais (-Noyon-Senlis) (Diocese), France
25	Aug	2020	Beihai [Pakhoi] (Diocese), China
16	Oct	2020	Beijing [Peking] (Archdiocese), China
25	Dec	2020	Beira (Archdiocese), Mozambique
06	Jul	2020	Beirut {Bairut} (Syrian) (Eparchy), Lebanon
31	Oct	2020	Beirut {Bairut} (Armenian) (Archdiocese), Lebanon
06	Jan	2021	Beirut {Bairut} (Chaldean) (Eparchy), Lebanon

27	Nov	2020	Beirut {Bairut} (Vicariate Apostolic), Lebanon
06	Sep	2020	Beirut {Bairut} (Maronite) (Archeparchy), Lebanon
01	Oct	2020	Beirut and Jbeil {Bairut e Gibail} (Melkite Greek) (Archdiocese), Lebanon
06	Jun	2020	Beja (Diocese), Portugal
26	Apr	2021	Belém do Pará (Archdiocese), Brazil
14	Aug	2020	Belfort-Montbéliard (Diocese), France
02	Oct	2020	Belgaum (Diocese), India
08	Aug	2020	Belgium, Military (Military Ordinariate)
02	Aug	2020	Belize City-Belmopan (Diocese), Belize, Antilles
27	Dec	2020	Bellary (Diocese), India
04	Mar	2021	Belleville (Diocese), Illinois, USA
14	Apr	2021	Belley-Ars (Diocese), France
11	Oct	2020	Belluno-Feltre (Diocese), Italy
14	Dec	2020	Belo Horizonte (Archdiocese), Minas Gerais, Brazil
02	May	2021	Belthangady (Syro-Malabar) (Diocese), India
15	Nov	2020	Benevento (Archdiocese), Italy
13	Feb	2021	Bengbu [Pengpu, Peng-Fou] (Diocese), China
02	Jul	2020	Benghazi (Vicariate Apostolic), Libya
04	May	2021	Benguela (Diocese), Angola
07	Jan	2021	Benin City (Archdiocese), Nigeria
24	Jun	2020	Benjamín Aceval (Diocese), Paraguay
20	Dec	2020	Beograd (-Smederevo) (Archdiocese), Serbia
04	Sep	2020	Berbérati (Diocese), Central African Republic
18	Jul	2020	Bereina (Diocese), Papua New Guinea
07	Aug	2020	Bergamo (Diocese), Italy
24	Jul	2020	Berhampur (Diocese), India
15	Feb	2021	Berlin (Archdiocese), Germany
18	Oct	2020	Bertoua (Archdiocese), Cameroon
22	Oct	2020	Besançon (Archdiocese), France
01	Mar	2021	Bethlehem (Diocese), South Africa
12	Jun	2020	Bettiah (Diocese), India
05	Nov	2020	Bhadravathi (Syro-Malabar) (Eparchy), India
23	Dec	2020	Bhagalpur (Diocese), India
27	Jul	2020	Bhopal (Archdiocese), India
26	Mar	2021	Białystok (Archdiocese), Poland
04	Jul	2020	Biella (Diocese), Italy
12	Nov	2020	Bielsko-Żywiec (Diocese), Poland
26	Feb	2021	Bijnor (Syro-Malabar) (Diocese), India
08	Jan	2021	Bilbao (Diocese), Spain
25	Jun	2020	Biloxi (Diocese), Mississippi, USA
07	Oct	2020	Birmingham (Diocese), Alabama, USA
09	Mar	2021	Birmingham (Archdiocese), England, Great Britain
10	Sep	2020	Bismarck (Diocese), North Dakota, USA
27	Jul	2020	Bissau (Diocese), Guinea-Bissau

26	Aug	2020	Bjelovar-Križevci (Diocese), Croatia
02	Feb	2021	Blantyre (Archdiocese), Malawi
13	Jul	2020	Bloemfontein (Archdiocese), South Africa
09	May	2021	Blois (Diocese), France
28	Aug	2020	Bluefields (Diocese), Nicaragua
22	Mar	2021	Blumenau (Diocese), Santa Catarina, Brazil
27	Oct	2020	Bo (Diocese), Sierra Leone
11	Nov	2020	Boac (Diocese), Philippines
19	Mar	2021	Bobo-Dioulasso (Archdiocese), Burkina Faso
27	Oct	2020	Bocas del Toro (Territorial Prelature), Panama
12	Mar	2021	Bogor (Diocese), Indonesia
11	Jul	2020	Bogotá (Archdiocese), Colombia
09	Mar	2021	Boise City (Diocese), Idaho, USA
18	Mar	2021	Bokungu-Ikela (Diocese), Congo (Dem. Rep.)
04	Nov	2020	Bolivia, Military (Military Ordinariate)
21	Oct	2020	Bologna (Archdiocese), Italy
25	Oct	2020	Bolzano-Bressanone {Bozen-Brixen} (Diocese), Italy
07	Feb	2021	Boma (Diocese), Congo (Dem. Rep.)
25	Jan	2021	Bomadi (Diocese), Nigeria
17	Feb	2021	Bombay (Archdiocese), India
08	Sep	2020	Bom Jesus da Lapa (Diocese), Bahia, Brazil
05	Jul	2020	Bom Jesus do Gurguéia (Diocese), Piaui, Brazil
05	May	2021	Bondo (Diocese), Congo (Dem. Rep.)
23	Jun	2020	Bondoukou (Diocese), Côte d'Ivoire
08	Jun	2020	Bonfim (Diocese), Bahia, Brazil
25	Sep	2020	Bongaigaon (Diocese), India
07	Jul	2020	Bontoc-Lagawe (Vicariate Apostolic), Philippines
26	Jun	2020	Borba (Territorial Prelature), Amazonas, Brazil
19	Jan	2021	Bordeaux (-Bazas) (Archdiocese), France
19	Nov	2020	Borongan (Diocese), Philippines
29	Nov	2020	Bosnia and Herzegovina, Military (Military Ordinariate)
01	Dec	2020	Bosra e Haūrān (Melkite Greek) (Archdiocese), Syria
29	Mar	2021	Bossangoa (Diocese), Central African Republic
27	Sep	2020	Boston (Archdiocese), Massachusetts, USA
22	Feb	2021	Botucatu (Archdiocese), Sao Paulo, Brazil
10	Dec	2020	Bouaké (Archdiocese), Côte d'Ivoire
21	Jun	2020	Bouar (Diocese), Central African Republic
16	Apr	2021	Bougainville (Diocese), Papua New Guinea
16	Jan	2021	Bourges (Archdiocese), France
08	Apr	2021	Braga (Archdiocese), Portugal
10	Dec	2020	Bragança do Pará (Diocese), Brazil
01	Jul	2020	Bragança-Miranda (Diocese), Portugal
13	Sep	2020	Bragança Paulista (Diocese), Sao Paulo, Brazil
21	Aug	2020	Brasília (Archdiocese), Distrito Federal, Brazil

04	Feb	2021	Bratislava (Archdiocese), Slovakia
11	Jan	2021	Bratislava (Slovakian) (Eparchy), Slovakia
01	Feb	2021	Brazil, Military (Military Ordinariate)
11	Mar	2021	Brazil, Faithful of the Eastern Rites (Ordinariate)
25	Jul	2020	Brazzaville (Archdiocese), Congo
06	Feb	2021	Breda (Diocese), Netherlands
28	Feb	2021	Brejo (Diocese), Maranhão, Brazil
13	Mar	2021	Brentwood (Diocese), England, Great Britain
03	Jun	2020	Brescia (Diocese), Italy
03	Nov	2020	Bridgeport (Diocese), Connecticut, USA
25	Nov	2020	Bridgetown (Diocese), Barbados, Antilles
21	Jun	2020	Brindisi-Ostuni (Archdiocese), Italy
07	Mar	2021	Brisbane (Archdiocese), Australia
15	Jul	2020	Brno (Diocese), Czech Republic
12	Jul	2020	Broken Bay (Diocese), Australia
25	Jun	2020	Brooklyn (Diocese), New York, USA
26	Aug	2020	Broome (Diocese), Australia
24	Mar	2021	Brownsville (Diocese), Texas, USA
13	Jul	2020	Brugge {Bruges} (Diocese), Belgium
08	Jan	2021	Brunei (Vicariate Apostolic), Brunei Darussalam
06	Aug	2020	Bubanza (Diocese), Burundi
08	Jul	2020	Bucaramanga (Archdiocese), Colombia
03	Feb	2021	Bucarest {Bucureşti} (Archdiocese), Romania
19	Jun	2020	Buchach {Bučač} (Ukrainian) (Eparchy), Ukraine
30	Nov	2020	Budjala (Diocese), Congo (Dem. Rep.)
11	Aug	2020	Buéa (Diocese), Cameroon
08	Mar	2021	Buenaventura (Diocese), Colombia
11	Jun	2020	Buenos Aires (Archdiocese), Argentina
02	Sep	2020	Buffalo (Diocese), New York, USA
11	Aug	2020	Buga (Diocese), Colombia
23	Mar	2021	Bùi Chu (Diocese), Viet Nam
10	Oct	2020	Bujumbura (Archdiocese), Burundi
14	Apr	2021	Bukavu (Archdiocese), Congo (Dem. Rep.)
11	Feb	2021	Bukoba (Diocese), Tanzania
28	Nov	2020	Bulawayo (Archdiocese), Zimbabwe
30	Jun	2020	Bunbury (Diocese), Australia
03	Sep	2020	Bunda (Diocese), Tanzania
26	Jun	2020	Bungoma (Diocese), Kenya
15	Mar	2021	Bunia (Diocese), Congo (Dem. Rep.)
09	Apr	2021	Burgos (Archdiocese), Spain
07	Oct	2020	Burlington (Diocese), Vermont, USA
01	Dec	2020	Bururi (Diocese), Burundi
03	Mar	2021	Busan {Pusan} (Diocese), Korea (South)
01	Aug	2020	Buta (Diocese), Congo (Dem. Rep.)

23	Jun	2020	Butare (Diocese), Rwanda
27	Aug	2020	Butembo-Beni (Diocese), Congo (Dem. Rep.)
21	Feb	2021	Butuan (Diocese), Philippines
13	Oct	2020	Buxar (Diocese), India
03	May	2021	Bydgoszcz (Diocese), Poland
29	Jul	2020	Byumba (Diocese), Rwanda
14	Nov	2020	Caacupé (Diocese), Paraguay
02	Jul	2020	Cabanatuan (Diocese), Philippines
17	Jun	2020	Cabimas (Diocese), Venezuela
04	Dec	2020	Cabinda (Diocese), Angola
29	Dec	2020	Caçador (Diocese), Santa Catarina, Brazil
31	Dec	2020	Caceres (Nueva Caceres) (Archdiocese), Philippines
07	Apr	2021	Cachoeira do Sul (Diocese), Rio Grande do Sul, Brazil
25	Dec	2020	Cachoeiro do Itapemirim (Diocese), Espirito Santo, Brazil
07	Mar	2021	Cádiz y Ceuta (Diocese), Spain
26	Oct	2020	Caetité (Diocese), Bahia, Brazil
09	Jan	2021	Cafayate (Territorial Prelature), Argentina
26	Dec	2020	Cagayan de Oro (Archdiocese), Philippines
27	Aug	2020	Cagliari (Archdiocese), Italy
29	Sep	2020	Caguas (Diocese), Puerto Rico
21	Jul	2020	Cahors (Diocese), France
16	Jul	2020	Caicó (Diocese), Rio Grande do Norte, Brazil
15	Jul	2020	Cairns (Diocese), Australia
30	Jan	2021	Cajamarca (Diocese), Peru
29	Apr	2021	Cajazeiras (Diocese), Paraiba, Brazil
20	Dec	2020	Calabar (Archdiocese), Nigeria
10	May	2021	Calabozo (Archdiocese), Venezuela
19	Sep	2020	Calahorra y La Calzada-Logroño (Diocese), Spain
03	Nov	2020	Calapan (Vicariate Apostolic), Philippines
12	Sep	2020	Calbayog (Diocese), Philippines
28	Mar	2021	Calcutta (Archdiocese), India
02	Feb	2021	Caldas (Diocese), Colombia
15	Apr	2021	Calgary (Diocese), Alberta, Canada
25	Aug	2020	Cali (Archdiocese), Colombia
17	Jun	2020	Calicut (Diocese), India
17	Feb	2021	Callao (Diocese), Peru
04	Oct	2020	Caltagirone (Diocese), Italy
26	Jan	2021	Caltanissetta (Diocese), Italy
05	Dec	2020	Camaçari (Diocese), Bahia, Brazil
11	Oct	2020	Camagüey (Archdiocese), Cuba
15	Jun	2020	Cambrai (Archdiocese), France
04	Feb	2021	Camden (Diocese), New Jersey, USA
21	Oct	2020	Camerino-San Severino Marche (Archdiocese), Italy
15	Feb	2021	Cametá (Diocese), Para, Brazil

21	Jun	2020	Camiri (Vicariate Apostolic), Bolivia
19	Sep	2020	Campanha (Diocese), Minas Gerais, Brazil
31	Jan	2021	Campeche (Diocese), México
16	Feb	2021	Campina Grande (Diocese), Paraiba, Brazil
31	Oct	2020	Campinas (Archdiocese), Sao Paulo, Brazil
27	Dec	2020	Campobasso-Boiano (Archdiocese), Italy
19	May	2021	Campo Grande (Archdiocese), Mato Grosso do Sul, Brazil
19	Jan	2021	Campo Limpo (Diocese), Sao Paulo, Brazil
25	Dec	2020	Campo Maior (Diocese), Piaui, Brazil
29	Jan	2021	Campo Mourão (Diocese), Parana, Brazil
11	Jul	2020	Campos (Diocese), Rio de Janeiro, Brazil
04	Dec	2020	Canada (Syrian) (Apostolic Exarchate)
26	Nov	2020	Canada, Military (Military Ordinariate)
01	Jan	2021	Canberra-Goulburn (Archdiocese), Australia
16	Mar	2021	Cancún-Chetumal (Diocese), Quintana Roo, México
05	Jan	2021	Canelones (Diocese), Uruguay
12	Apr	2021	Cần Thơ (Diocese), Viet Nam
15	Jul	2020	Caozhou/Heze [Tsaochow] (Diocese), China
22	Aug	2020	Cape Coast (Archdiocese), Ghana
18	Dec	2020	Cape Palmas (Diocese), Liberia
19	Mar	2021	Cape Town {Kaapstad} (Archdiocese), South Africa
14	Jul	2020	Cap-Haïtien (Archdiocese), Haïti
12	Aug	2020	Capiz (Archdiocese), Philippines
12	May	2021	Capua (Archdiocese), Italy
12	Sep	2020	Carabayllo (Diocese), Peru
08	May	2021	Caracas, Santiago de Venezuela (Archdiocese)
08	Dec	2020	Caraguatatuba (Diocese), Sao Paulo, Brazil
28	Nov	2020	Carapeguá (Diocese), Paraguay
23	Mar	2021	Caratinga (Diocese), Minas Gerais, Brazil
04	Dec	2020	Caravelí (Territorial Prelature), Peru
19	May	2021	Carcassonne et Narbonne (Diocese), France
18	Apr	2021	Cardiff (Archdiocese), Wales, Great Britain
08	Oct	2020	Carolina (Diocese), Maranhão, Brazil
12	Mar	2021	Caroline Islands (Diocese), Federated States of Micronesia, Pacific (Oceania)
12	May	2021	Caroní (Vicariate Apostolic), Venezuela
26	Jan	2021	Carora (Diocese), Venezuela
05	Nov	2020	Carpi (Diocese), Italy
02	Jul	2020	Cartagena (en España) (Diocese)
23	Jan	2021	Cartagena (Archdiocese), Colombia
08	Jan	2021	Cartago (Diocese), Costa Rica
19	Jan	2021	Cartago (Diocese), Colombia
21	Nov	2020	Caruaru (Diocese), Pernambuco, Brazil
19	Oct	2020	Carúpano (Diocese), Venezuela
27	Apr	2021	Casale Monferrato (Diocese), Italy

06	Dec	2020	Cascavel (Archdiocese), Parana, Brazil
30	Mar	2021	Caserta (Diocese), Italy
17	Jan	2021	Cashel and Emly (Archdiocese), Ireland
26	Aug	2020	Cassano all'Jonio (Diocese), Italy
31	Jul	2020	Castanhal (Diocese), Para, Brazil
02	Jan	2021	Castellaneta (Diocese), Italy
05	Dec	2020	Castries (Archdiocese), Saint Lucia, Antilles
05	Apr	2021	Catamarca (Diocese), Argentina
23	Sep	2020	Catanduva (Diocese), Sao Paulo, Brazil
07	Dec	2020	Catania (Archdiocese), Italy
30	Jan	2021	Catanzaro-Squillace (Archdiocese), Italy
04	Jan	2021	Catarman (Diocese), Philippines
20	May	2021	Caucaso (Apostolic Administration), Armenia
13	Jun	2020	Caxias do Maranhão (Diocese), Brazil
18	May	2021	Caxias do Sul (Diocese), Rio Grande do Sul, Brazil
21	Dec	2020	Caxito (Diocese), Angola
14	May	2021	Cayenne (Cajenna) (Diocese), French Guyana, Antilles
01	May	2021	Cayman Islands (Mission Sui Iuris), Antilles
23	Mar	2021	Cebu (Archdiocese), Philippines
18	Aug	2020	Cefalù (Diocese), Italy
17	Aug	2020	Celaya (Diocese), Guanajuato, México
20	Jul	2020	Celje (Diocese), Slovenia
08	Jan	2021	Cerignola-Ascoli Satriano (Diocese), Italy
24	Aug	2020	Cerreto Sannita-Telese-Sant'Agata de' Goti (Diocese), Italy
25	Dec	2020	Cesena-Sarsina (Diocese), Italy
04	Nov	2020	České Budějovice {Budweis} (Diocese), Czech Republic
25	Dec	2020	Chachapoyas (Diocese), Peru
09	Apr	2021	Chaco Paraguayo (Vicariate Apostolic), Paraguay
17	Nov	2020	The Chair of Saint Peter (Personal Ordinariate), USA
23	Jul	2020	Chalan Kanoa (Diocese), Northern Mariana Islands, Pacific (Oceania)
29	Aug	2020	Chalatenango (Diocese), El Salvador
15	Jun	2020	Châlons (Diocese), France
26	Dec	2020	Chambéry (-Saint-Jean-de-Maurienne-Tarentaise) (Archdiocese), France
29	Aug	2020	Chanda (Syro-Malabar) (Eparchy), India
17	Dec	2020	Changanacherry (Syro-Malabar) (Archeparchy), India
02	Jan	2021	Changde [Changteh] (Diocese), China
18	May	2021	Changsha [Changsha] (Archdiocese), China
08	Feb	2021	Changting [Tingchow] (Diocese), China
17	Mar	2021	Changzhi [Luan] (Diocese), China
29	Mar	2021	Chanthaburi (Diocese), Thailand
10	Jun	2020	Chapecó (Diocese), Santa Catarina, Brazil
18	Feb	2021	Charleston (Diocese), South Carolina, USA
26	Sep	2020	Charlotte (Diocese), North Carolina, USA
16	Jun	2020	Charlottetown (Diocese), Prince Edward Island, Canada

23	Dec	2020	Chartres (Diocese), France
26	Aug	2020	Chascomús (Diocese), Argentina
04	Jan	2021	Chattogram (Archdiocese), Bangladesh
07	Aug	2020	Cheju (Diocese), Korea (South)
22	Jun	2020	Chengde (Diocese), China
16	May	2021	Chengdu [Chengtu] (Diocese), China
02	Jun	2020	Cheongju {Ch'ongju} (Diocese), Korea (South)
22	May	2021	Chernivtsi (Ukrainian) (Eparchy), Ukraine
08	Feb	2021	Cheyenne (Diocese), Wyoming, USA
14	Jan	2021	Chiang Mai (Diocese), Thailand
05	Apr	2021	Chiang Rai (Diocese), Thailand
13	Aug	2020	Chiavari (Diocese), Italy
26	Nov	2020	Chicago (Archdiocese), Illinois, USA
21	May	2021	Chiclayo (Diocese), Peru
21	Feb	2021	Chicoutimi (Diocese), Québec, Canada
08	Sep	2020	Chieti-Vasto (Archdiocese), Italy
17	Sep	2020	Chifeng [Chihfeng] (Diocese), China
25	Jun	2020	Chihuahua (Archdiocese), México
13	Oct	2020	Chikmagalur (Diocese), India
19	Sep	2020	Chikwawa (Diocese), Malawi
05	Jul	2020	Chilaw (Diocese), Sri Lanka
12	Jan	2021	Chile, Military (Military Ordinariate)
10	Jun	2020	Chilpancingo-Chilapa (Diocese), Guerrero, México
21	May	2021	Chimbote (Diocese), Peru
14	Oct	2020	Chimoio (Diocese), Mozambique
24	Jan	2021	Chingleput (Diocese), India
29	Aug	2020	Chinhoyi (Diocese), Zimbabwe
16	Jan	2021	Chioggia (Diocese), Italy
16	Jul	2020	Chios (Scio) (Diocese), Greece
02	Feb	2021	Chipata (Diocese), Zambia
20	Nov	2020	Chiquinquirá (Diocese), Colombia
04	Jun	2020	Chişinău (Diocese), Moldova
21	Oct	2020	Chitré (Diocese), Panama
06	Aug	2020	Choluteca (Diocese), Honduras
02	Jun	2020	Chongqing [Chungking] (Archdiocese), China
15	Apr	2021	Chosica (Diocese), Peru
14	Aug	2020	Chota (Territorial Prelature), Peru
26	Oct	2020	Christchurch (Diocese), New Zealand
13	May	2021	Chulucanas (Diocese), Peru
30	Sep	2020	Ch'unch'ŏn (Diocese), Korea (South)
28	Jun	2020	Chuquibamba (Territorial Prelature), Peru
08	Mar	2021	Chuquibambilla (Territorial Prelature), Peru
04	Jan	2021	Chur (Diocese), Switzerland
07	Feb	2021	Churchill-Baie d'Hudson (Diocese), Manitoba, Canada

08	Sep	2020	Ciego de Ávila (Diocese), Cuba
08	Apr	2021	Cienfuegos (Diocese), Cuba
24	Jul	2020	Cilicia (Armenian) (Patriarchate), Lebanon
05	Jul	2020	Cincinnati (Archdiocese), Ohio, USA
17	Feb	2021	Cipro (Maronite) (Archdiocese), Cyprus
12	May	2021	Città di Castello (Diocese), Italy
14	Feb	2021	Ciudad Altamirano (Diocese), Guerrero, México
27	Dec	2020	Ciudad Bolívar (Archdiocese), Venezuela
15	Sep	2020	Ciudad del Este (Diocese), Paraguay
15	Feb	2021	Ciudad Guayana (Diocese), Venezuela
15	Dec	2020	Ciudad Guzmán (Diocese), Jalisco, México
22	Nov	2020	Ciudad Juárez (Diocese), Chihuahua, México
17	Jul	2020	Ciudad Lázaro Cárdenas (Diocese), Michoacán, México
08	Jun	2020	Ciudad Obregón (Diocese), Sonora, México
21	May	2021	Ciudad Quesada (Diocese), Costa Rica
07	Sep	2020	Ciudad Real (Diocese), Spain
03	Apr	2021	Ciudad Rodrigo (Diocese), Spain
13	Mar	2021	Ciudad Valles (Diocese), San Luís Potosí, México
24	Sep	2020	Ciudad Victoria (Diocese), Tamaulipas, México
06	May	2021	Civita Castellana (Diocese), Italy
26	Sep	2020	Civitavecchia-Tarquinia (Diocese), Italy
01	Oct	2020	Clermont (Archdiocese), France
15	Sep	2020	Cleveland (Diocese), Ohio, USA
01	Jan	2021	Clifton (Diocese), England, Great Britain
08	May	2021	Clogher (Diocese), Ireland
17	Jun	2020	Clonfert (Diocese), Ireland
30	Jun	2020	Cloyne (Diocese), Ireland
07	Mar	2021	Cluj-Gherla (Romanian) (Diocese), Romania
03	Jul	2020	Coari (Diocese), Amazonas, Brazil
28	Dec	2020	Coatzacoalcos (Diocese), Veracruz, México
31	Jan	2021	Cochabamba (Archdiocese), Bolivia
16	Dec	2020	Cochin (Diocese), India
26	Jan	2021	Coimbatore (Diocese), India
06	Aug	2020	Coimbra (Diocese), Portugal
15	Jun	2020	Colatina (Diocese), Espirito Santo, Brazil
09	Feb	2021	Colima (Diocese), México
12	Jul	2020	Colombia (Maronite) (Apostolic Exarchate)
02	Sep	2020	Colombia, Military (Military Ordinariate)
27	Jun	2020	Colombo (Archdiocese), Sri Lanka
11	Sep	2020	Colón-Kuna Yala (Diocese), Panama
24	Mar	2021	Colorado Springs (Diocese), Colorado, USA
31	Jan	2021	Columbus (Diocese), Ohio, USA
29	Jun	2020	Comayagua (Diocese), Honduras
28	Oct	2020	Como (Diocese), Italy

07	Nov	2020	Comodoro Rivadavia (Diocese), Argentina
18	May	2021	Conakry {Konakry} (Archdiocese), Guinea
04	Dec	2020	Concepción (Santissima Concezione) (Archdiocese), Chile
15	Jul	2020	Concepción (Diocese), Argentina
18	Jan	2021	Concepción (Santissima Concezione) en Paraguay (Diocese)
31	Aug	2020	Concordia (Diocese), Argentina
26	Nov	2020	Concordia-Pordenone (Diocese), Italy
03	Nov	2020	Constantine (-Hippone) (Diocese), Algeria
29	Sep	2020	Conversano-Monopoli (Diocese), Italy
07	Jul	2020	Copiapó (Diocese), Chile
06	Oct	2020	Córdoba (Diocese), Veracruz, México
29	Jun	2020	Córdoba (Diocese), Spain
20	Apr	2021	Córdoba (Archdiocese), Argentina
03	May	2021	Corfù, Zante e Cefalonia (Archdiocese), Greece
09	Oct	2020	Coria-Cáceres (Diocese), Spain
21	Nov	2020	Cork and Ross (Diocese), Ireland
25	Jul	2020	Cornélio Procópio (Diocese), Parana, Brazil
30	Oct	2020	Corner Brook and Labrador (Diocese), Newfoundland, Canada
27	Jul	2020	Coro (Archdiocese), Venezuela
02	Mar	2021	Coroatá (Diocese), Maranhão, Brazil
13	Sep	2020	Corocoro (Territorial Prelature), Bolivia
13	Nov	2020	Coroico (Diocese), Bolivia
25	Feb	2021	Coronel Oviedo (Diocese), Paraguay
07	Dec	2020	Corpus Christi (Diocese), Texas, USA
15	Dec	2020	Corrientes (Archdiocese), Argentina
13	Jan	2021	Corumbá (Diocese), Mato Grosso do Sul, Brazil
02	Mar	2021	Cosenza-Bisignano (Archdiocese), Italy
05	Oct	2020	Cotabato (Archdiocese), Philippines
28	Dec	2020	Cotonou (Archdiocese), Benin
11	May	2021	Coutances (-Avranches) (Diocese), France
23	Nov	2020	Covington (Diocese), Kentucky, USA
12	Oct	2020	Coxim (Diocese), Mato Grosso do Sul, Brazil
15	Jun	2020	Crateús (Diocese), Ceara, Brazil
05	Oct	2020	Crato (Diocese), Ceara, Brazil
12	Jun	2020	Crema (Diocese), Italy
27	Feb	2021	Cremona (Diocese), Italy
05	Jul	2020	Crete {Candia} (Diocese), Greece
19	Feb	2021	Créteil (Diocese), France
07	Feb	2021	Criciúma (Diocese), Santa Catarina, Brazil
30	Sep	2020	Cristalândia (Diocese), Goias, Brazil
25	Apr	2021	Croatia, Military (Military Ordinariate)
14	Apr	2021	Crookston (Diocese), Minnesota, USA
10	Mar	2021	Crotone-Santa Severina (Archdiocese), Italy
29	Jul	2020	Cruz Alta (Diocese), Rio Grande do Sul, Brazil

04	Nov	2020	Cruz das Almas (Diocese), Bahia, Brazil
19	Apr	2021	Cruz del Eje (Diocese), Argentina
01	Apr	2021	Cruzeiro do Sul (Diocese), Acre, Brazil
15	Nov	2020	Cuauhtémoc-Madera (Diocese), Chihuahua, México
12	Oct	2020	Cuautitlán (Diocese), México, México
09	Jan	2021	Cubao (Diocese), Philippines
27	Jan	2021	Cúcuta (Diocese), Colombia
17	Jan	2021	Cuddapah (Diocese), India
11	Nov	2020	Cuenca (Archdiocese), Ecuador
02	Dec	2020	Cuenca (Diocese), Spain
08	Oct	2020	Cuernavaca (Diocese), Morelos, México
11	Jul	2020	Cuiabá (Archdiocese), Mato Grosso, Brazil
01	Mar	2021	Culiacán (Diocese), Sinaloa, México
05	May	2021	Cumaná (Archdiocese), Venezuela
21	May	2021	Cuneo (Diocese), Italy
21	Jun	2020	Curitiba (Archdiocese), Parana, Brazil
25	Aug	2020	Cuttack-Bhubaneswar (Archdiocese), India
19	Apr	2021	Cuzco (Archdiocese), Peru
11	Mar	2021	Cyangugu (Diocese), Rwanda
17	Oct	2020	Czech Republic (Ruthenian) (Apostolic Exarchate)
09	Aug	2020	Częstochowa (Archdiocese), Poland
29	Mar	2021	Daegu {Taegu} (Archdiocese), Korea (South)
04	Sep	2020	Daejeon {Taejon} (Diocese), Korea (South)
25	Sep	2020	Daet (Diocese), Philippines
20	Aug	2020	Dakar (Archdiocese), Senegal
14	Dec	2020	Đakovo-Osijek (Archdiocese), Croatia
23	Oct	2020	Đà Lạt (Diocese), Viet Nam
26	Aug	2020	Dali [Tali] (Diocese), China
08	Nov	2020	Dallas (Diocese), Texas, USA
28	Feb	2021	Daloa (Diocese), Côte d'Ivoire
27	Dec	2020	Daltonganj (Diocese), India
11	Nov	2020	Damas (Armenian) (Patriarchal Exarchate), Syria
20	Jul	2020	Damas (Maronite) (Archeparchy), Syria
21	Oct	2020	Damas (Melkite Greek) (Archdiocese), Syria
07	Jun	2020	Damas (Syrian) (Archdiocese), Syria
11	Nov	2020	Daming [Taming] (Diocese), China
08	Nov	2020	Damongo (Diocese), Ghana
13	May	2021	Đà Nẵng (Diocese), Viet Nam
24	Aug	2020	Danlí (Diocese), Honduras
11	May	2021	Dapaong (Diocese), Togo
07	Aug	2020	Dar-es-Salaam (Archdiocese), Tanzania
22	Feb	2021	Darién (Vicariate Apostolic), Panama
19	Jun	2020	Darjeeling (Diocese), India
21	Apr	2021	Daru-Kiunga (Diocese), Papua New Guinea

12	Dec	2020	Darwin (Diocese), Australia
20	Dec	2020	Dassa-Zoumé (Diocese), Benin
30	Apr	2021	Datong [Tatung] (Diocese), China
11	Feb	2021	Davao (Archdiocese), Philippines
03	Jan	2021	Davenport (Diocese), Iowa, USA
13	Apr	2021	David (Diocese), Panama
01	May	2021	De Aar (Diocese), South Africa
01	Oct	2020	Deán Funes (Territorial Prelature), Argentina
24	Sep	2020	Debrecen-Nyíregyháza (Diocese), Hungary
15	Nov	2020	Dédougou (Diocese), Burkina Faso
18	Jul	2020	Dedza (Diocese), Malawi
29	Dec	2020	Delhi (Archdiocese), India
11	Jun	2020	Denpasar (Diocese), Indonesia
04	Aug	2020	Denver (Archdiocese), Colorado, USA
16	Nov	2020	Derna (Vicariate Apostolic), Libya
26	Jun	2020	Derry (Diocese), Ireland
21	Apr	2021	Des Moines (Diocese), Iowa, USA
19	Jan	2021	Detroit (Archdiocese), Michigan, USA
05	Mar	2021	Deutschland und Skandinavien {Germany and Scandinavia} (Ukrainian) (Apostolic
26	Feb	2021	Dhaka (Archdiocese), Bangladesh
08	Aug	2020	Dharmapuri (Diocese), India
10	Jan	2021	Diamantina (Archdiocese), Minas Gerais, Brazil
28	Nov	2020	Diamantino (Diocese), Mato Grosso, Brazil
04	Sep	2020	Diarbekir (Amida) (Chaldean) (Archeparchy), Turkey
30	Mar	2021	Dibrugarh (Diocese), India
23	Jul	2020	Diébougou (Diocese), Burkina Faso
20	Mar	2021	Digne (-Riez-Sisteron) (Diocese), France
21	Mar	2021	Digos (Diocese), Philippines
07	Apr	2021	Dijon (Archdiocese), France
23	Feb	2021	Díli (Archdiocese), Timor-Leste
28	Nov	2020	Dinajpur (Diocese), Bangladesh
14	Jul	2020	Dindigul (Diocese), India
16	Dec	2020	Diphu (Diocese), India
11	Nov	2020	Dipolog (Diocese), Philippines
23	Jul	2020	Divinópolis (Diocese), Minas Gerais, Brazil
23	Mar	2021	Djibouti (Diocese)
10	Jul	2020	Djougou (Diocese), Benin
01	Sep	2020	Doba (Diocese), Chad
25	Jul	2020	Dodge City (Diocese), Kansas, USA
06	Apr	2021	Dodoma (Archdiocese), Tanzania
28	Jun	2020	Dolisie (Diocese), Congo
17	Jan	2021	Dominican Republic, Military (Military Ordinariate)
21	Apr	2021	Donets'k (Ukrainian) (Archiepiscopal Exarchate), Ukraine
21	Aug	2020	Donkorkrom (Vicariate Apostolic), Ghana

19	Jul	2020	Dori (Diocese), Burkina Faso
24	Feb	2021	Doruma-Dungu (Diocese), Congo (Dem. Rep.)
16	Jul	2020	Douala (Archdiocese), Cameroon
13	Sep	2020	Doumé-Abong' Mbang (Diocese), Cameroon
18	Dec	2020	Dourados (Diocese), Mato Grosso do Sul, Brazil
07	Dec	2020	Down and Connor (Diocese), Ireland
08	Jan	2021	Dresden-Meißen (Meissen) (Diocese), Germany
08	May	2021	Drohiczyn (Diocese), Poland
22	May	2021	Dromore (Diocese), Ireland
16	Mar	2021	Dublin (Archdiocese), Ireland
08	Jan	2021	Dubrovnik (Ragusa) (Diocese), Croatia
14	Sep	2020	Dubuque (Archdiocese), Iowa, USA
10	Oct	2020	Duitama-Sogamoso (Diocese), Colombia
09	Dec	2020	Duluth (Diocese), Minnesota, USA
24	Sep	2020	Dumaguete (Diocese), Philippines
19	Nov	2020	Dumka (Diocese), India
29	Nov	2020	Dundee (Diocese), South Africa
07	Apr	2021	Dundo (Diocese), Angola
18	Oct	2020	Dunedin (Diocese), New Zealand
13	Dec	2020	Dunkeld (Diocese), Scotland, Great Britain
03	Jul	2020	Duque de Caxias (Diocese), Rio de Janeiro, Brazil
19	Aug	2020	Durango (Archdiocese), México
12	Jan	2021	Durban (Archdiocese), South Africa
22	May	2021	East Anglia (Diocese), England, Great Britain
23	Jan	2021	Eastern Europe {Europa Orientale} (Armenian) (Ordinariate)
06	Sep	2020	East Indies (Patriarchate), India
26	Dec	2020	Ebebiyin (Diocese), Equatorial Guinea
27	Aug	2020	Ebolowa (Diocese), Cameroon
06	Apr	2021	Ecatepec (Diocese), México, México
28	Jun	2020	Ecuador, Military (Military Ordinariate)
09	Jul	2020	Edéa (Diocese), Cameroon
29	Aug	2020	Edmonton (Archdiocese), Alberta, Canada
24	Feb	2021	Edmonton (Ukrainian) (Eparchy), Canada
21	Jan	2021	Edmundston (Diocese), New Brunswick, Canada
16	Jan	2021	Eger (Archdiocese), Hungary
02	Oct	2020	Egypt, Sudan, and South Sudan (Melkite Greek) (Patriarchal Dependent Territory)
02	May	2021	Eichstätt (Diocese), Germany
06	Jun	2020	Eisenstadt (Diocese), Austria
20	Mar	2021	Ekiti (Diocese), Nigeria
05	May	2021	Ekwulobia (Diocese), Nigeria
07	Oct	2020	El Alto (Diocese), Bolivia
12	Jul	2020	El Banco (Diocese), Colombia
11	Nov	2020	El Beni o Beni (Vicariate Apostolic), Bolivia
26	Jun	2020	Elbląg (Diocese), Poland

12	Oct	2020	Eldoret (Diocese), Kenya
19	May	2021	Ełk (Diocese), Poland
30	Dec	2020	El Obeid (Diocese), Sudan
17	Nov	2020	El Paso (Diocese), Texas, USA
09	Feb	2021	El Petén (Vicariate Apostolic), Guatemala
03	Mar	2021	Elphin (Diocese), Ireland
26	Jun	2020	El Salto (Territorial Prelature), Durango, México
14	Jun	2020	El Salvador, Military (Military Ordinariate)
19	Feb	2021	El Tigre (Diocese), Venezuela
09	Sep	2020	Eluru (Diocese), India
24	Apr	2021	El Vigia-San Carlos del Zulia (Diocese), Venezuela
10	Nov	2020	Embu (Diocese), Kenya
03	Aug	2020	Emdeber (Ethiopian) (Eparchy), Ethiopia
12	Sep	2020	Encarnación (Diocese), Paraguay
02	Apr	2021	Ende (Archdiocese), Indonesia
29	Nov	2020	Engativá (Diocese), Colombia
24	Dec	2020	Ensenada (Diocese), Baja California Norte, México
12	Feb	2021	Enshi [Shihnan] (Diocese), China
16	Aug	2020	Enugu (Diocese), Nigeria
23	Jul	2020	Erexim (Diocese), Rio Grande do Sul, Brazil
02	Jan	2021	Erfurt (Diocese), Germany
16	Oct	2020	Erie (Diocese), Pennsylvania, USA
09	Aug	2020	Ernakulam-Angamaly (Syro-Malabar) (Archdiocese), India
13	Apr	2021	Escuintla (Diocese), Guatemala
10	Jul	2020	Eséka (Diocese), Cameroon
17	Dec	2020	Eshowe (Diocese), South Africa
16	Aug	2020	Esmeraldas (Vicariate Apostolic), Ecuador
13	Nov	2020	Espinal (Diocese), Colombia
25	Jan	2021	Esquel (Territorial Prelature), Argentina
11	Aug	2020	Essen (Diocese), Germany
24	Jun	2020	Estância (Diocese), Sergipe, Brazil
15	Apr	2021	Esteli (Diocese), Nicaragua
20	Sep	2020	Estonia (Apostolic Administration)
03	Oct	2020	Esztergom-Budapest (Archdiocese), Hungary
28	Feb	2021	Eunápolis (Diocese), Bahia, Brazil
04	May	2021	Evansville (Diocese), Indiana, USA
29	Jan	2021	Evinayong (Diocese), Equatorial Guinea
08	Aug	2020	Évora (Archdiocese), Portugal
06	Nov	2020	Evreux (Diocese), France
06	Jul	2020	Evry-Corbeil-Essonnes (Diocese), France
12	Mar	2021	Fabriano-Matelica (Diocese), Italy
14	Sep	2020	Facatativá (Diocese), Colombia
29	Jul	2020	Fada N'Gourma (Diocese), Burkina Faso
14	Nov	2020	Faenza-Modigliana (Diocese), Italy

22	Aug	2020	Făgăraş şi Alba Iulia (Romanian) (Archdiocese), Romania
20	May	2021	Fairbanks (Diocese), Alaska, USA
19	Mar	2021	Faisalabad (Diocese), Pakistan
06	Apr	2021	Fajardo-Humacao (Diocese), Puerto Rico
30	Dec	2020	Falkland Islands o Malvinas (Prefecture Apostolic)
27	Feb	2021	Fall River (Diocese), Massachusetts, USA
25	Feb	2021	Fano-Fossombrone-Cagli-Pergola (Diocese), Italy
09	Aug	2020	Farafangana (Diocese), Madagascar
07	Aug	2020	Fargo (Diocese), North Dakota, USA
26	Sep	2020	Faridabad (Syro-Malabar) (Eparchy), India
13	Feb	2021	Faro {Algarve} (Diocese), Portugal
18	Jun	2020	Feira de Santana (Archdiocese), Bahia, Brazil
10	Oct	2020	Feldkirch (Diocese), Austria
30	Jan	2021	Fengxiang [Fengsiang] (Diocese), China
07	Feb	2021	Fenoarivo Atsinanana (Diocese), Madagascar
29	Jul	2020	Fenyang [Fenyang] (Diocese), China
27	Oct	2020	Fermo (Archdiocese), Italy
23	Feb	2021	Ferns (Diocese), Ireland
19	Sep	2020	Ferrara-Comacchio (Archdiocese), Italy
07	Sep	2020	Fianarantsoa (Archdiocese), Madagascar
28	Dec	2020	Fidenza (Diocese), Italy
20	May	2021	Fiesole (Diocese), Italy
03	Jun	2020	Firenze {Florence} (Archdiocese), Italy
24	Aug	2020	Florencia (Archdiocese), Colombia
22	Dec	2020	Floresta (Diocese), Pernambuco, Brazil
27	Aug	2020	Floriano (Diocese), Piaui, Brazil
12	Jan	2021	Florianópolis (Archdiocese), Santa Catarina, Brazil
28	Jul	2020	Florida (Diocese), Uruguay
01	Jul	2020	Foggia-Bovino (Archdiocese), Italy
24	Oct	2020	Foligno (Diocese), Italy
20	Apr	2021	Fontibón (Diocese), Colombia
02	Dec	2020	Forli-Bertinoro (Diocese), Italy
06	Oct	2020	Formosa (Diocese), Goias, Brazil
01	Apr	2021	Formosa (Diocese), Argentina
07	Apr	2021	Fortaleza (Archdiocese), Ceara, Brazil
01	Aug	2020	Fort-de-France (e Saint Pierre) (Archdiocese), Martinique, Antilles
09	Nov	2020	Fort-Liberté (Diocese), Haïti
09	Aug	2020	Fort Portal (Diocese), Uganda
12	Oct	2020	Fort Wayne-South Bend (Diocese), Indiana, USA
15	Dec	2020	Fort Worth (Diocese), Texas, USA
05	Nov	2020	Fossano (Diocese), Italy
07	Feb	2021	Foz do Iguaçu (Diocese), Parana, Brazil
19	Feb	2021	Franca (Diocese), Sao Paulo, Brazil
28	Dec	2020	France, Military (Military Ordinariate)

31	Jul	2020	France, Faithful of Eastern Rites (Ordinariate)
15	Mar	2021	Franceville (Diocese), Gabon
02	Dec	2020	Francistown (Diocese), Botswana
31	May	2020	Frascati (Suburbicarian See), Italy
23	Sep	2020	Frederico Westphalen (Diocese), Rio Grande do Sul, Brazil
06	Apr	2021	Freetown (Archdiocese), Sierra Leone
18	Jul	2020	Freiburg im Breisgau (Archdiocese), Germany
04	May	2021	Fréjus-Toulon (Diocese), France
23	Apr	2021	Fresno (Diocese), California, USA
18	Feb	2021	Frosinone-Veroli-Ferentino (Diocese), Italy
15	Oct	2020	Fukuoka (Diocese), Japan
20	Sep	2020	Fulda (Diocese), Germany
20	Oct	2020	Funafuti (Mission Sui Iuris), Tuvalu, Pacific (Oceania)
11	Jan	2021	Funchal (Diocese), Portugal
17	May	2021	Fushun [Fushun] (Diocese), China
16	Jun	2020	Fuzhou [Foochow] (Archdiocese), China
01	Oct	2020	Gaborone (Diocese), Botswana
13	Oct	2020	Gaeta (Archdiocese), Italy
02	Apr	2021	Gagnoa (Archdiocese), Côte d'Ivoire
19	Sep	2020	Galápagos (Vicariate Apostolic), Ecuador
13	Jun	2020	Galle (Diocese), Sri Lanka
04	Apr	2021	Galloway (Diocese), Scotland, Great Britain
18	Jul	2020	Gallup (Diocese), New Mexico, USA
06	Nov	2020	Galveston-Houston (Archdiocese), Texas, USA
24	Feb	2021	Galway and Kilmacduagh (Diocese), Ireland
22	Apr	2021	Gambella (Vicariate Apostolic), Ethiopia
08	Oct	2020	Gamboma (Diocese), Congo
24	Jan	2021	Gandhinagar (Archdiocese), India
07	Oct	2020	Ganzhou [Kanchow] (Diocese), China
05	Sep	2020	Gaoua (Diocese), Burkina Faso
04	Aug	2020	Gap (-Embrun) (Diocese), France
17	Mar	2021	Garagoa (Diocese), Colombia
06	Mar	2021	Garanhuns (Diocese), Pernambuco, Brazil
03	Jan	2021	Garissa (Diocese), Kenya
30	Jun	2020	Garoua (Archdiocese), Cameroon
28	Aug	2020	Gary (Diocese), Indiana, USA
25	Jan	2021	Garzón (Diocese), Colombia
24	Apr	2021	Gaspé (Diocese), Québec, Canada
27	Jun	2020	Gatineau (Archdiocese), Québec, Canada
31	Mar	2021	Gaylord (Diocese), Michigan, USA
04	Jun	2020	Gbarnga (Diocese), Liberia
27	Sep	2020	Gboko (Diocese), Nigeria
25	Dec	2020	Gdańsk (Archdiocese), Poland
18	Jul	2020	Geita (Diocese), Tanzania

16	Dec	2020	Genova {Genoa} (Archdiocese), Italy
29	Jan	2021	Gent {Ghent, Gand} (Diocese), Belgium
31	Jul	2020	Georgetown (Diocese), Guyana, Antilles
28	Oct	2020	Geraldton (Diocese), Australia
02	Jan	2021	Germany, Military (Military Ordinariate)
31	Jul	2020	Getafe (Diocese), Spain
26	Nov	2020	Gibraltar (Diocese)
18	Sep	2020	Gikongoro (Diocese), Rwanda
17	Oct	2020	Girardot (Diocese), Colombia
06	Aug	2020	Girardota (Diocese), Colombia
14	Mar	2021	Girona (Diocese), Spain
17	Nov	2020	Gitega (Archdiocese), Burundi
21	Aug	2020	Gizo (Diocese), Solomon Islands
19	Mar	2021	Glasgow (Archdiocese), Scotland, Great Britain
17	May	2021	Gliwice (Diocese), Poland
16	Oct	2020	Gniezno (Archdiocese), Poland
05	May	2021	Goa e Damão (Archdiocese), India
18	Mar	2021	Goaso (Diocese), Ghana
10	Aug	2020	Goiânia (Archdiocese), Goias, Brazil
03	May	2021	Goiás (Diocese), Brazil
21	Feb	2021	Gokwe (Diocese), Zimbabwe
22	Dec	2020	Goma (Diocese), Congo (Dem. Rep.)
03	Sep	2020	Gómez Palacio (Diocese), Durango, México
25	Apr	2021	Gorakhpur (Syro-Malabar) (Diocese), India
28	Jan	2021	Goré (Diocese), Chad
17	Apr	2021	Gorizia (Archdiocese), Italy
10	May	2021	Görlitz (Diocese), Germany
26	Apr	2021	Goroka (Diocese), Papua New Guinea
08	Sep	2020	Gospić-Senj (Diocese), Croatia
24	Apr	2021	Governador Valadares (Diocese), Minas Gerais, Brazil
23	Dec	2020	Goya (Diocese), Argentina
09	Jan	2021	Gozo (Diocese), Malta
15	Nov	2020	Grajaú (Diocese), Maranhão, Brazil
23	Oct	2020	Granada (Diocese), Nicaragua
13	Oct	2020	Granada (Archdiocese), Spain
13	Jul	2020	Granada en Colombia (Diocese)
06	Jan	2021	Grand-Bassam (Diocese), Côte d'Ivoire
07	Jan	2021	Grand Falls (Diocese), Newfoundland, Canada
18	Jun	2020	Grand Island (Diocese), Nebraska, USA
18	Mar	2021	Grand Rapids (Diocese), Michigan, USA
23	Mar	2021	Graz-Seckau (Diocese), Austria
13	Feb	2021	Great Britain (Syro-Malabar) (Eparchy)
27	Feb	2021	Great Britain, Military (Military Ordinariate)
11	Oct	2020	Great Falls-Billings (Diocese), Montana, USA

25	Apr	2021	Greece (Armenian) (Ordinariate)
05	Dec	2020	Greece (Greek) (Apostolic Exarchate)
22	Dec	2020	Green Bay (Diocese), Wisconsin, USA
25	Nov	2020	Greensburg (Diocese), Pennsylvania, USA
02	Feb	2021	Gregorio de Laferrere (Diocese), Argentina
01	Jun	2020	Grenoble-Vienne (Diocese), France
25	Apr	2021	Grodno (Diocese), Belarus
09	Aug	2020	Groningen-Leeuwarden (Diocese), Netherlands
26	Oct	2020	Grosseto (Diocese), Italy
27	Jun	2020	Grouard-McLennan (Archdiocese), Alberta, Canada
12	Nov	2020	Guadalajara (Archdiocese), Jalisco, México
18	Aug	2020	Guadix (Diocese), Spain
18	Feb	2021	Guajará-Mirim (Diocese), Rondonia, Brazil
29	Jan	2021	Gualeguaychú (Diocese), Argentina
19	Jun	2020	Guanare (Diocese), Venezuela
14	Mar	2021	Guangzhou [Canton] (Archdiocese), China
14	Sep	2020	Guanhães (Diocese), Minas Gerais, Brazil
03	Feb	2021	Guantánamo-Baracoa (Diocese), Cuba
16	Mar	2021	Guapi (Vicariate Apostolic), Colombia
22	Jul	2020	Guarabira (Diocese), Paraiba, Brazil
06	Oct	2020	Guaranda (Diocese), Ecuador
25	Jul	2020	Guarapuava (Diocese), Parana, Brazil
19	May	2021	Guarda (Diocese), Portugal
14	Jun	2020	Guarenas (Diocese), Venezuela
19	Sep	2020	Guarulhos (Diocese), Sao Paulo, Brazil
21	Sep	2020	Guasdualito (Diocese), Venezuela
03	Feb	2021	Guaxupé (Diocese), Minas Gerais, Brazil
17	Mar	2021	Guayaquil (Archdiocese), Ecuador
07	Jun	2020	Gubbio (Diocese), Italy
15	Nov	2020	Guilin [Kweilin] (Prefecture Apostolic), China
13	Jul	2020	Guiyang [Kweyang] (Archdiocese), China
03	Oct	2020	Guizeh (Coptic) (Eparchy), Egypt
09	Jun	2020	Gulbarga (Diocese), India
23	Nov	2020	Gulu (Archdiocese), Uganda
02	Oct	2020	Gumaca (Diocese), Philippines
03	Sep	2020	Gumla (Diocese), India
11	Feb	2021	Guntur (Diocese), India
15	Feb	2021	Gurk (Diocese), Austria
12	Sep	2020	Gurué (Diocese), Mozambique
27	Apr	2021	Guwahati (Archdiocese), India
27	Nov	2020	Gwalior (Diocese), India
27	Jul	2020	Gwangju (Archdiocese), Korea (South)
19	Jun	2020	Gweru (Diocese), Zimbabwe
03	Dec	2020	Győr (Raab) (Diocese), Hungary

06	Jun	2020	Haarlem-Amsterdam (Diocese), Netherlands
11	Sep	2020	Hadiab-Erbil (Syrian) (Archeparchy), Iraq
13	Oct	2020	Haifa and the Holy Land {Haifa e Terra Santa} (Maronite) (Archeparchy), Israel
09	Nov	2020	Haimen [Haimen] (Diocese), China
12	Dec	2020	Hainan [Hainan] (Prefecture Apostolic), China
08	Aug	2020	Hải Phòng (Diocese), Viet Nam
14	Nov	2020	Haizhou [Haichow, Donghai, Tunghai] (Prefecture Apostolic), China
18	May	2021	Hajdúdorog (Hungarian) (Archdiocese), Hungary
11	Nov	2020	Hakha (Diocese), Myanmar
25	Mar	2021	Halifax-Yarmouth (Archdiocese), Nova Scotia, Canada
03	Jan	2021	Hallam (Diocese), England, Great Britain
23	Sep	2020	Hamburg (Archdiocese), Germany
17	May	2021	Hamhŭng (Diocese), Korea (North)
01	Oct	2020	Hamilton (Diocese), Ontario, Canada
16	Sep	2020	Hamilton in Bermuda (Diocese), Antilles
30	Nov	2020	Hamilton in New Zealand (Diocese)
14	Jan	2021	Hangzhou [Hangchow] (Archdiocese), China
07	May	2021	Hankow [Hankou] (Archdiocese), China
02	May	2021	Hà Nội (Archdiocese), Viet Nam
02	May	2021	Hanyang [Hanyang] (Diocese), China
25	Dec	2020	Hanzhong [Hanchung] (Diocese), China
27	Aug	2020	Harar (Vicariate Apostolic), Ethiopia
19	Dec	2020	Harare (Archdiocese), Zimbabwe
19	Oct	2020	Harbin [Harbin] (Russian) (Apostolic Exarchate), China
12	Jun	2020	Harbin [Harbin] (Apostolic Administration), China
02	Dec	2020	Harrisburg (Diocese), Pennsylvania, USA
26	Feb	2021	Hartford (Archdiocese), Connecticut, USA
03	May	2021	Hassaké-Nisibi (Syrian) (Archeparchy), Syria
16	Mar	2021	Hasselt (Diocese), Belgium
22	Feb	2021	Hà Tĩnh (Diocese), Viet Nam
16	Feb	2021	Hazaribag (Diocese), India
17	Sep	2020	Hearst-Moosonee (Diocese), Ontario, Canada
31	Jan	2021	Helena (Diocese), Montana, USA
02	Jul	2020	Helsinki (Diocese), Finland
07	Aug	2020	Hengyang [Hengchow] (Diocese), China
14	Nov	2020	Hermosillo (Archdiocese), Sonora, México
09	Nov	2020	Hexham and Newcastle (Diocese), England, Great Britain
02	Jun	2020	Hildesheim (Diocese), Germany
09	Apr	2021	Hinche (Diocese), Haïti
26	Apr	2021	Hiroshima (Diocese), Japan
03	Jun	2020	Ho (Diocese), Ghana
09	Oct	2020	Hobart (Archdiocese), Australia
15	Nov	2020	Hohhot [Suiyüan] (Archdiocese), China
11	Aug	2020	Hoima (Diocese), Uganda

26	Jun	2020	Holguín (Diocese), Cuba
06	Jan	2021	Holy Family of London (Ukrainian) (Eparchy)
03	Jun	2020	Holy Protection of Mary of Phoenix (Ruthenian) (Eparchy), Arizona, USA
02	Feb	2021	Homa Bay (Diocese), Kenya
04	Dec	2020	Homs (-Hama-Jabrud) (Melkite Greek) (Archdiocese), Syria
23	Dec	2020	Homs (-Hama-Nabk) (Syrian) (Archdiocese), Syria
05	Dec	2020	Hongdong [Hungtung] (Diocese), China
18	Sep	2020	Hong Kong [Xianggang] (Diocese), China
21	Dec	2020	Honiara (Archdiocese), Solomon Islands
08	Apr	2021	Honolulu (Diocese), Hawaii, USA
27	Nov	2020	Hosanna (Vicariate Apostolic), Ethiopia
09	Feb	2021	Hosur (Syro-Malabar) (Eparchy), India
27	Mar	2021	Houma-Thibodaux (Diocese), Louisiana, USA
04	Apr	2021	Hpa-an (Diocese), Myanmar
20	Jun	2020	Hradec Králové (Diocese), Czech Republic
17	Apr	2021	Hsinchu (Diocese), Taiwan
27	Dec	2020	Huacho (Diocese), Peru
12	May	2021	Huajuapan de León (Diocese), Oaxaca, México
24	Mar	2021	Huamachuco (Territorial Prelature), Peru
31	Dec	2020	Huambo (Archdiocese), Angola
07	Jun	2020	Huancavélica (Diocese), Peru
06	Dec	2020	Huancayo (Archdiocese), Peru
11	Feb	2021	Huánuco (Diocese), Peru
27	Apr	2021	Huaraz (Diocese), Peru
16	Apr	2021	Huarí (Diocese), Peru
10	Sep	2020	Huautla (Territorial Prelature), Oaxaca, México
21	Oct	2020	Hué (Archdiocese), Viet Nam
22	Jun	2020	Huehuetenango (Diocese), Guatemala
05	Jun	2020	Huejutla (Diocese), Hidalgo, México
01	Sep	2020	Huelva (Diocese), Spain
05	May	2021	Huesca (Diocese), Spain
20	Nov	2020	Humahuaca (Territorial Prelature), Argentina
19	May	2021	Humaitá (Diocese), Amazonas, Brazil
31	Mar	2021	Hungary, Military (Military Ordinariate)
11	Dec	2020	Hưng Hóa (Diocese), Viet Nam
10	Mar	2021	Hvar (-Brac e Vis) (Diocese), Croatia
14	Jul	2020	Hwalien (Diocese), Taiwan
17	Sep	2020	Hwange (Diocese), Zimbabwe
06	Mar	2021	Hyderabad (Archdiocese), India
13	Jan	2021	Hyderabad in Pakistan (Diocese)
26	Mar	2021	Iaşi (Diocese), Romania
19	Apr	2021	Iba (Diocese), Philippines
23	Aug	2020	Ibadan (Archdiocese), Nigeria
19	Jun	2020	Ibagué (Archdiocese), Colombia

27	Dec	2020	Ibarra (Diocese), Ecuador
03	Jan	2021	Ibiza (Diocese), Spain
31	Oct	2020	Ica (Diocese), Peru
01	Feb	2021	Idah (Diocese), Nigeria
24	Oct	2020	Idiofa (Diocese), Congo (Dem. Rep.)
29	Sep	2020	Idukki (Syro-Malabar) (Eparchy), India
01	Dec	2020	Ifakara (Diocese), Tanzania
04	May	2021	Iglesias (Diocese), Italy
19	Feb	2021	Iguatu (Diocese), Ceara, Brazil
09	Dec	2020	Ihosy (Diocese), Madagascar
16	May	2021	Ijebu-Ode (Diocese), Nigeria
27	Oct	2020	Ikot Ekpene (Diocese), Nigeria
06	Oct	2020	Ilagan (Diocese), Philippines
19	Jan	2021	Ilhéus (Diocese), Bahia, Brazil
02	Dec	2020	Iligan (Diocese), Philippines
18	Jul	2020	Illapel (Territorial Prelature), Chile
29	Mar	2021	Ilorin (Diocese), Nigeria
02	Nov	2020	Imaculada Conceição in Prudentópolis (Ukrainian) (Eparchy), Brazil
20	Sep	2020	Imola (Diocese), Italy
06	Feb	2021	Imperatriz (Diocese), Maranhão, Brazil
12	Nov	2020	Impfondo (Diocese), Congo
17	Aug	2020	Imphal (Archdiocese), India
03	Feb	2021	Imus (Diocese), Philippines
23	Sep	2020	Incheon {Inch'on} (Diocese), Korea (South)
02	Sep	2020	Indianapolis (Archdiocese), Indiana, USA
07	May	2021	Indonesia, Military (Military Ordinariate)
30	Dec	2020	Indore (Diocese), India
09	May	2021	Infanta (Territorial Prelature), Philippines
23	Sep	2020	Ingwavuma (Vicariate Apostolic), South Africa
15	May	2021	Inhambane (Diocese), Mozambique
30	Mar	2021	Inírida (Vicariate Apostolic), Colombia
15	Jan	2021	Innsbruck (Diocese), Austria
14	Jun	2020	Inongo (Diocese), Congo (Dem. Rep.)
06	Dec	2020	Ipameri (Diocese), Goias, Brazil
22	Jan	2021	Ipiales (Diocese), Colombia
21	Jul	2020	Ipil (Diocese), Philippines
06	Jan	2021	Iquique (Diocese), Chile
07	Jan	2021	Iquitos (Vicariate Apostolic), Peru
10	Jun	2020	Irapuato (Diocese), Guanajuato, México
23	Nov	2020	Iraq (Melkite Greek) (Patriarchal Exarchate)
02	Sep	2020	Irecê (Diocese), Bahia, Brazil
08	Aug	2020	Iringa (Diocese), Tanzania
17	Jun	2020	Irinjalakuda (Syro-Malabar) (Diocese), India
17	Sep	2020	Isabela (Territorial Prelature), Philippines

28	Jul	2020	Isangi (Diocese), Congo (Dem. Rep.)
15	May	2021	Ischia (Diocese), Italy
06	Sep	2020	Isernia-Venafro (Diocese), Italy
02	Mar	2021	Isiolo (Vicariate Apostolic), Kenya
12	Nov	2020	Isiro-Niangara (Diocese), Congo (Dem. Rep.)
10	Dec	2020	Iskanderiya {Alexandria} (Armenian) (Eparchy), Egypt
29	Jun	2020	Islamabad-Rawalpindi (Diocese), Pakistan
05	Mar	2021	Islas Canarias {Canary Islands} (Diocese), Spain
27	Nov	2020	Ismayliah (Coptic) (Eparchy), Egypt
15	Aug	2020	Ispahan {Esfáan} (Armenian) (Eparchy), Iran
11	Mar	2021	Ispahan (Archdiocese), Iran
09	Oct	2020	Issele-Uku (Diocese), Nigeria
20	Nov	2020	Istanbul (Armenian) (Archeparchy), Turkey
13	Sep	2020	Istanbul (Constantinople) (Greek) (Apostolic Exarchate), Turkey
21	Dec	2020	Istanbul (Vicariate Apostolic), Turkey
08	Jun	2020	Istmina-Tadó (Diocese), Colombia
25	Apr	2021	Itabira-Fabriciano (Diocese), Minas Gerais, Brazil
30	Oct	2020	Itabuna (Diocese), Bahia, Brazil
17	Nov	2020	Itacoatiara (Territorial Prelature), Amazonas, Brazil
24	Dec	2020	Itaguaí (Diocese), Rio de Janeiro, Brazil
07	Jan	2021	Itaituba (Territorial Prelature), Para, Brazil
10	Feb	2021	Italy, Faithful of the Ukrainian Catholic Church (Ukrainian) (Apostolic Exarchate)
13	Oct	2020	Italy, Military (Military Ordinariate)
09	Jan	2021	Itanagar (Diocese), India
28	Mar	2021	Itapetininga (Diocese), Sao Paulo, Brazil
20	Jul	2020	Itapeva (Diocese), Sao Paulo, Brazil
28	Sep	2020	Itapipoca (Diocese), Ceara, Brazil
02	Dec	2020	Ituiutaba (Diocese), Minas Gerais, Brazil
05	Sep	2020	Itumbiara (Diocese), Goias, Brazil
23	Feb	2021	Ivano-Frankivsk [Stanislaviv] (Ukrainian) (Archeparchy), Ukraine
27	Mar	2021	Ivrea (Diocese), Italy
09	Nov	2020	Izabal (Vicariate Apostolic), Guatemala
18	Aug	2020	Izcalli (Diocese), México, México
31	Dec	2020	Izmir (Smirne) (Archdiocese), Turkey
24	Nov	2020	Iztapalapa (Diocese), México, México
12	Apr	2021	Jabalpur (Diocese), India
22	Mar	2021	Jaboticabal (Diocese), Sao Paulo, Brazil
03	Oct	2020	Jaca (Diocese), Spain
17	Mar	2021	Jacarezinho (Diocese), Parana, Brazil
17	Aug	2020	Jackson (Diocese), Mississippi, USA
05	Mar	2021	Jacmel (Diocese), Haïti
23	Apr	2021	Jaén (Diocese), Spain
16	Aug	2020	Jaén en Peru o San Francisco Javier (Vicariate Apostolic)
25	Sep	2020	Jaffna (Diocese), Sri Lanka

22	Feb	2021	Jagdalpur (Syro-Malabar) (Diocese), India
11	Jun	2020	Jaipur (Diocese), India
17	Jul	2020	Jakarta (Archdiocese), Indonesia
11	Feb	2021	Jalapa (Xalapa) (Archdiocese), Veracruz, México
25	Aug	2020	Jalapa (Diocese), Guatemala
04	Jul	2020	Jales (Diocese), Sao Paulo, Brazil
13	Dec	2020	Jalingo (Diocese), Nigeria
28	Oct	2020	Jalpaiguri (Diocese), India
01	Nov	2020	Jammu-Srinagar (Diocese), India
05	Feb	2021	Jamshedpur (Diocese), India
13	Nov	2020	Janaúba (Diocese), Minas Gerais, Brazil
04	Mar	2021	Januária (Diocese), Minas Gerais, Brazil
24	Aug	2020	Jardim (Diocese), Mato Grosso do Sul, Brazil
04	Feb	2021	Jaro (Archdiocese), Philippines
28	Mar	2021	Jashpur (Diocese), India
19	Dec	2020	Jasikan (Diocese), Ghana
21	Jun	2020	Jataí (Diocese), Goias, Brazil
01	Jul	2020	Jayapura (Diocese), Indonesia
13	Dec	2020	Jbeil {Byblos} (Maronite) (Eparchy), Lebanon
08	Sep	2020	Jefferson City (Diocese), Missouri, USA
14	Nov	2020	Jelgava (Diocese), Latvia
24	Mar	2021	Jeonju {Chonju, Jeon Ju} (Diocese), Korea (South)
03	Oct	2020	Jequié (Diocese), Bahia, Brazil
08	Dec	2020	Jérémie (Diocese), Haïti
16	Dec	2020	Jerez de la Frontera (Diocese), Spain
19	Aug	2020	Jericó (Diocese), Colombia
14	Apr	2021	Jerusalem {Gerusalemme} (Patriarchate), Palestine
04	Jul	2020	Jerusalem {Gerusalemme} (Syrian) (Patriarchal Exarchate), Palestine
03	Apr	2021	Jerusalem (Chaldean) (Patriarchal Dependent Territory), Palestine
11	Mar	2021	Jerusalem {Gerusalemme} (Melkite Greek) (Patriarchal Dependent Territory),
12	Aug	2020	Jerusalem and Amman {Gerusalemme e Amman} (Armenian) (Patriarchal Exarchate),
03	Mar	2021	Jerusalem and Palestine {Gerusalemme e Palestina} (Maronite) (Patriarchal Exarchate),
02	Aug	2020	Jesi (Diocese), Italy
27	Jan	2021	Jesús María (del Nayar) (Territorial Prelature), Nayarit, México
07	Nov	2020	Jhabua (Diocese), India
29	Mar	2021	Jhansi (Diocese), India
07	Mar	2021	Jiamusi [Kiamusze] (Prefecture Apostolic), China
25	Mar	2021	Ji'an [Kian] (Diocese), China
11	Jan	2021	Jiangmen [Kongmoon] (Diocese), China
01	May	2021	Jian'ou [Kienow, Kienning] (Prefecture Apostolic), China
16	Sep	2020	Jilin [Kirin] (Diocese), China
22	Dec	2020	Jimma-Bonga (Vicariate Apostolic), Ethiopia
17	Aug	2020	Jinan [Tsinan] (Archdiocese), China
14	Jul	2020	Jingxian [Kinghsien] (Diocese), China

24	Apr	2021	Jining [Tsining] (Diocese), China
04	Jan	2021	Jinja (Diocese), Uganda
07	Oct	2020	Jinotega (Diocese), Nicaragua
23	Apr	2021	Jinzhou [Jehol] (Diocese), China
09	Apr	2021	Ji-Paraná (Diocese), Rondonia, Brazil
27	Nov	2020	Jixian [Weihwei] (Diocese), China
11	Sep	2020	Joaçaba (Diocese), Santa Catarina, Brazil
01	Jun	2020	Johannesburg (Archdiocese), South Africa
25	Aug	2020	Joinville (Diocese), Santa Catarina, Brazil
26	Jul	2020	Joliet in Illinois (Diocese), USA
30	Oct	2020	Joliette (Diocese), Québec, Canada
12	Dec	2020	Jolo (Vicariate Apostolic), Philippines
21	Dec	2020	Jordan (Chaldean) (Patriarchal Dependent Territory)
08	Nov	2020	Jordan {Giordania} (Maronite) (Patriarchal Exarchate)
18	Apr	2021	Jos (Archdiocese), Nigeria
18	Aug	2020	Joubbé, Sarba e Jounieh (Maronite) (Eparchy), Lebanon
21	Sep	2020	Jowai (Diocese), India
02	Jan	2021	Juazeiro (Diocese), Bahia, Brazil
27	Jan	2021	Juba (Archdiocese), South Sudan
18	Apr	2021	Juigalpa (Diocese), Nicaragua
08	Mar	2021	Juína (Diocese), Mato Grosso, Brazil
09	Nov	2020	Juiz de Fora (Archdiocese), Minas Gerais, Brazil
04	Jan	2021	Jujuy (Diocese), Argentina
05	Jan	2021	Juli (Territorial Prelature), Peru
14	Aug	2020	Jullundur (Diocese), India
13	Oct	2020	Jundiaí (Diocese), Sao Paulo, Brazil
06	Apr	2021	Juticalpa (Diocese), Honduras
02	Jan	2021	Kabale (Diocese), Uganda
16	Dec	2020	Kabankalan (Diocese), Philippines
22	Dec	2020	Kabgayi (Diocese), Rwanda
09	Oct	2020	Kabinda (Diocese), Congo (Dem. Rep.)
01	May	2021	Kabwe (Diocese), Zambia
17	Dec	2020	Kaduna (Archdiocese), Nigeria
18	Jan	2021	Kafanchan (Diocese), Nigeria
29	Apr	2021	Kaga-Bandoro (Diocese), Central African Republic
08	Mar	2021	Kagoshima (Diocese), Japan
06	Jan	2021	Kahama (Diocese), Tanzania
14	Feb	2021	Kaifeng [Kaifeng] (Archdiocese), China
23	Mar	2021	Kaišiadorys (Diocese), Lithuania
05	Aug	2020	Kakamega (Diocese), Kenya
22	Sep	2020	Kalamazoo (Diocese), Michigan, USA
31	Mar	2021	Kalay (Diocese), Myanmar
22	May	2021	Kalemie-Kirungu (Diocese), Congo (Dem. Rep.)
01	Mar	2021	Kalibo (Diocese), Philippines

10	Mar	2021	Kalisz (Diocese), Poland
20	Jan	2021	Kalocsa-Kecskemét (Archdiocese), Hungary
29	Dec	2020	Kalookan (Diocese), Philippines
03	Dec	2020	Kalyan (Syro-Malabar) (Diocese), India
28	Mar	2021	Kamichlié (Armenian) (Eparchy), Syria
24	Jan	2021	Kamina (Diocese), Congo (Dem. Rep.)
06	Feb	2021	Kamloops (Diocese), British Columbia, Canada
02	Aug	2020	Kampala (Archdiocese), Uganda
16	Feb	2021	Kamyanets-Podilskyi (Diocese), Ukraine
04	Oct	2020	Kamyanets-Podilskyi (Ukrainian) (Eparchy), Ukraine
14	May	2021	Kananga (Archdiocese), Congo (Dem. Rep.)
07	Dec	2020	Kandi (Diocese), Benin
15	Feb	2021	Kandy (Diocese), Sri Lanka
10	Aug	2020	Kangding [Kangting] (Diocese), China
04	Feb	2021	Kanjirapally (Syro-Malabar) (Diocese), India
07	Aug	2020	Kankan (Diocese), Guinea
17	Feb	2021	Kannur (Diocese), India
04	Dec	2020	Kano (Diocese), Nigeria
26	Mar	2021	Kansas City in Kansas (Archdiocese), USA
06	Jul	2020	Kansas City-Saint Joseph (Diocese), Missouri, USA
15	Jul	2020	Kaohsiung (Diocese), Taiwan
14	Aug	2020	Kaolack (Diocese), Senegal
22	Dec	2020	Kaposvár (Diocese), Hungary
26	Apr	2021	Kara (Diocese), Togo
07	Sep	2020	Karachi (Archdiocese), Pakistan
22	Jun	2020	Karaganda (Diocese), Kazakhstan
10	Sep	2020	Karonga (Diocese), Malawi
19	Oct	2020	Karwar (Diocese), India
30	Dec	2020	Kasama (Archdiocese), Zambia
06	Feb	2021	Kasana-Luweero (Diocese), Uganda
06	Aug	2020	Kasese (Diocese), Uganda
14	Dec	2020	Kasongo (Diocese), Congo (Dem. Rep.)
27	Dec	2020	Katiola (Diocese), Côte d'Ivoire
30	Aug	2020	Katowice (Archdiocese), Poland
26	Dec	2020	Katsina-Ala (Diocese), Nigeria
21	Apr	2021	Kaunas (Archdiocese), Lithuania
08	Nov	2020	Kavieng (Diocese), Papua New Guinea
03	Apr	2021	Kaya (Diocese), Burkina Faso
02	Nov	2020	Kayanga (Diocese), Tanzania
24	Dec	2020	Kayes (Diocese), Mali
26	Jun	2020	Kazakhstan and Central Asia, Faithful of the Byzantine Rite (Apostolic
13	Sep	2020	Keetmanshoop (Diocese), Namibia
28	Aug	2020	Keewatin-Le Pas (Archdiocese), Manitoba, Canada
08	Jun	2020	Keimoes-Upington (Diocese), South Africa

29	Dec	2020	Kenema (Diocese), Sierra Leone
25	Sep	2020	Kenge (Diocese), Congo (Dem. Rep.)
19	Mar	2021	Kengtung (Diocese), Myanmar
09	Jun	2020	Keningau (Diocese), Malaysia
16	Oct	2020	Kenya, Military (Military Ordinariate)
11	Oct	2020	Kerema (Diocese), Papua New Guinea
29	Dec	2020	Keren (Eritrean) (Eparchy), Eritrea
20	Jul	2020	Kericho (Diocese), Kenya
20	Dec	2020	Kerkūk (Chaldean) (Archdiocese), Iraq
06	Jul	2020	Kerry (Diocese), Ireland
06	Dec	2020	Keta-Akatsi (Diocese), Ghana
18	Oct	2020	Ketapang (Diocese), Indonesia
30	Apr	2021	Khammam (Diocese), India
04	Oct	2020	Khandwa (Diocese), India
22	Nov	2020	Kharkiv (Ukrainian) (Archiepiscopal Exarchate), Ukraine
08	May	2021	Kharkiv-Zaporizhia (Diocese), Ukraine
09	Sep	2020	Khartoum (Archdiocese), Sudan
14	Apr	2021	Khulna (Diocese), Bangladesh
18	Oct	2020	Khunti (Diocese), India
22	Oct	2020	Kiayi (Diocese), Taiwan
13	Mar	2021	Kibungo (Diocese), Rwanda
16	Feb	2021	Kidapawan (Diocese), Philippines
14	Jul	2020	Kielce (Diocese), Poland
21	Jul	2020	Kigali (Archdiocese), Rwanda
23	Jan	2021	Kigoma (Diocese), Tanzania
30	Jan	2021	Kikwit (Diocese), Congo (Dem. Rep.)
22	Feb	2021	Kildare and Leighlin (Diocese), Ireland
08	Oct	2020	Killala (Diocese), Ireland
18	Apr	2021	Killaloe (Diocese), Ireland
10	Sep	2020	Kilmore (Diocese), Ireland
17	Jul	2020	Kilwa-Kasenga (Diocese), Congo (Dem. Rep.)
14	Mar	2021	Kimbe (Diocese), Papua New Guinea
15	Oct	2020	Kimberley (Diocese), South Africa
25	Sep	2020	Kindu (Diocese), Congo (Dem. Rep.)
17	Sep	2020	Kingston (Archdiocese), Ontario, Canada
20	Aug	2020	Kingston in Jamaica (Archdiocese), Antilles
10	Nov	2020	Kingstown (Diocese), Saint Vincent and Grenadines, Antilles
12	Jun	2020	Kinkala (Diocese), Congo
25	Feb	2021	Kinshasa (Archdiocese), Congo (Dem. Rep.)
13	Aug	2020	Kisangani (Archdiocese), Congo (Dem. Rep.)
10	Jan	2021	Kisantu (Diocese), Congo (Dem. Rep.)
04	Jan	2021	Kisii (Diocese), Kenya
11	Jun	2020	Kisumu (Archdiocese), Kenya
07	Nov	2020	Kitale (Diocese), Kenya

07	Jun	2020	Kitui (Diocese), Kenya
14	Sep	2020	Kiyinda-Mityana (Diocese), Uganda
05	Feb	2021	Klerksdorp (Diocese), South Africa
01	Aug	2020	Knoxville (Diocese), Tennessee, USA
28	Feb	2021	København {Copenhagen} (Diocese), Denmark
11	May	2021	Koforidua (Diocese), Ghana
20	Apr	2021	Kohima (Diocese), India
21	Feb	2021	Kokstad (Diocese), South Africa
15	Jan	2021	Kolda (Diocese), Senegal
27	Apr	2021	Kole (Diocese), Congo (Dem. Rep.)
18	Apr	2021	Köln {Cologne} (Archdiocese), Germany
05	Mar	2021	Kolomyia (Ukrainian) (Eparchy), Ukraine
10	Feb	2021	Kolwezi (Diocese), Congo (Dem. Rep.)
16	Jan	2021	Kompong-Cham (Prefecture Apostolic), Cambodia
19	Jun	2020	Kondoa (Diocese), Tanzania
15	Jan	2021	Kongolo (Diocese), Congo (Dem. Rep.)
11	Mar	2021	Konongo-Mampong (Diocese), Ghana
01	Oct	2020	Kontagora (Diocese), Nigeria
28	Oct	2020	Kontum (Diocese), Viet Nam
09	Dec	2020	Koper (Diocese), Slovenia
29	Oct	2020	Korea, Military (Military Ordinariate)
19	Aug	2020	Korhogo (Archdiocese), Côte d'Ivoire
02	Aug	2020	Košice (Slovakian) (Eparchy), Slovakia
20	Feb	2021	Košice (Archdiocese), Slovakia
05	Dec	2020	Koszalin-Kołobrzeg (Diocese), Poland
09	Jan	2021	Kota Kinabalu (Archdiocese), Malaysia
29	Dec	2020	Kothamangalam (Syro-Malabar) (Diocese), India
25	Apr	2021	Kotido (Diocese), Uganda
16	May	2021	Kotor (Cattaro) (Diocese), Montenegro
04	Feb	2021	Kottapuram (Diocese), India
06	Nov	2020	Kottar (Diocese), India
01	Nov	2020	Kottayam (Syro-Malabar) (Archeparchy), India
03	Sep	2020	Koudougou (Diocese), Burkina Faso
06	Nov	2020	Koupéla (Archdiocese), Burkina Faso
22	Jan	2021	Kpalimé (Diocese), Togo
10	Apr	2021	Kraków {Cracow} (Archdiocese), Poland
21	Nov	2020	Kribi (Diocese), Cameroon
28	Apr	2021	Krishnagar (Diocese), India
22	Sep	2020	Križevci (Kreutz) (Križevci) (Diocese), Croatia
04	Jul	2020	Krk (Veglia) (Diocese), Croatia
02	Apr	2021	Kroonstad (Diocese), South Africa
08	Oct	2020	Krym (Ukrainian) (Archiepiscopal Exarchate), Ukraine
12	Sep	2020	Kuala Lumpur (Archdiocese), Malaysia
04	May	2021	Kuching (Archdiocese), Malaysia

02	Oct	2020	Kumasi (Archdiocese), Ghana
22	Apr	2021	Kumba (Diocese), Cameroon
02	Nov	2020	Kumbakonam (Diocese), India
28	Dec	2020	Kumbo (Diocese), Cameroon
25	Feb	2021	Kundiawa (Diocese), Papua New Guinea
20	Apr	2021	Kunming [Kunming] (Archdiocese), China
16	Apr	2021	Kupang (Archdiocese), Indonesia
24	Dec	2020	Kurnool (Diocese), India
22	Sep	2020	Kurunegala (Diocese), Sri Lanka
06	Feb	2021	Kuwait (Melkite Greek) (Patriarchal Exarchate)
23	Dec	2020	Kuzhithurai (Diocese), India
02	Apr	2021	Kwito-Bié (Diocese), Angola
29	Oct	2020	Kyiv-Halyč {Kiev-Galicia} (Ukrainian) (Archeparchy), Ukraine
01	Jan	2021	Kyiv-Zhytomyr (Diocese), Ukraine
23	Aug	2020	Kyōto (Diocese), Japan
29	Oct	2020	Kyrgyzstan (Apostolic Administration)
25	Mar	2021	Lábrea (Territorial Prelature), Amazonas, Brazil
26	Feb	2021	La Ceiba (Diocese), Honduras
14	Mar	2021	La Crosse (Diocese), Wisconsin, USA
04	Aug	2020	La Dorada-Guaduas (Diocese), Colombia
07	Jun	2020	Lae (Diocese), Papua New Guinea
27	Sep	2020	Lafayette (Diocese), Louisiana, USA
10	Jan	2021	Lafayette in Indiana (Diocese), USA
29	Dec	2020	Lafia (Diocese), Nigeria
30	Dec	2020	Lages (Diocese), Santa Catarina, Brazil
23	Sep	2020	Laghouat (Diocese), Algeria
04	Sep	2020	Lagos (Archdiocese), Nigeria
05	Feb	2021	La Guaira (Diocese), Venezuela
01	Mar	2021	Lahore (Archdiocese), Pakistan
10	Oct	2020	Lai (Diocese), Chad
02	Jan	2021	Lake Charles (Diocese), Louisiana, USA
09	Aug	2020	Lamego (Diocese), Portugal
11	May	2021	Lamezia Terme (Diocese), Italy
09	Dec	2020	Lancaster (Diocese), England, Great Britain
19	Nov	2020	Lanciano-Ortona (Archdiocese), Italy
16	Mar	2021	Langres (Diocese), France
23	Nov	2020	Lạng Sơn et Cao Bằng (Diocese), Viet Nam
31	Dec	2020	Lansing (Diocese), Michigan, USA
09	Feb	2021	Lanusei (Diocese), Italy
04	Oct	2020	Lanzhou [Lanchow] (Archdiocese), China
28	Feb	2021	Laoag (Diocese), Philippines
06	Aug	2020	Laohekou [Laohokow] (Diocese), China
18	Oct	2020	La Paz (Archdiocese), Bolivia
07	Nov	2020	La Paz en la Baja California Sur (Diocese), México

23	Jul	2020	La Plata (Archdiocese), Argentina
28	Apr	2021	L'Aquila (Archdiocese), Italy
10	Aug	2020	Larantuka (Diocese), Indonesia
28	Jun	2020	Laredo (Diocese), Texas, USA
18	Jun	2020	La Rioja (Diocese), Argentina
19	Sep	2020	La Rochelle (-Saintes) (Diocese), France
26	Jul	2020	Las Cruces (Diocese), New Mexico, USA
05	Mar	2021	La Serena (Archdiocese), Chile
07	May	2021	Lashio (Diocese), Myanmar
10	Aug	2020	La Spezia-Sarzana-Brugnato (Diocese), Italy
01	Feb	2021	Las Vegas (Diocese), Nevada, USA
06	Jan	2021	Latacunga (Diocese), Ecuador
28	Aug	2020	Latina-Terracina-Sezze-Priverno (Diocese), Italy
08	Mar	2021	Lattaquié {Laodicea} (Maronite) (Eparchy), Syria
16	Aug	2020	Lattaquié {Laodicea} (Melkite Greek) (Archeparchy), Syria
06	Mar	2021	Lausanne, Genève et Fribourg (Freiburg) (Diocese), Switzerland
16	Feb	2021	Laval (Diocese), France
23	Apr	2021	La Vega (Diocese), Dominican Republic
13	Mar	2021	Le Caire {Cairo} (Chaldean) (Eparchy), Egypt
12	Feb	2021	Le Caire {Cairo} (Maronite) (Eparchy), Egypt
03	Jun	2020	Le Caire {Cairo} (Syrian) (Eparchy), Egypt
25	Mar	2021	Lecce (Archdiocese), Italy
31	Jul	2020	Leeds (Diocese), England, Great Britain
10	Mar	2021	Legazpi (Diocese), Philippines
09	Jan	2021	Legnica (Diocese), Poland
17	Dec	2020	Le Havre (Diocese), France
01	Oct	2020	Leiria-Fátima (Diocese), Portugal
18	Nov	2020	Le Mans (Diocese), France
06	Nov	2020	León (Archdiocese), Guanajuato, México
16	May	2021	León (Diocese), Spain
10	Jun	2020	León en Nicaragua (Diocese)
04	Feb	2021	Leopoldina (Diocese), Minas Gerais, Brazil
22	Jun	2020	Le Puy-en-Velay (Diocese), France
01	Sep	2020	Leribe (Diocese), Lesotho
20	Sep	2020	Les Cayes (Diocese), Haïti
01	Feb	2021	Les Gonaïves (Diocese), Haïti
30	Jun	2020	Leshan [Kiating] (Diocese), China
16	Oct	2020	Leticia (Vicariate Apostolic), Colombia
16	May	2021	Lexington (Diocese), Kentucky, USA
30	Jun	2020	Lezhë {Lesh, Alessio} (Diocese), Albania
01	Aug	2020	Líbano-Honda (Diocese), Colombia
11	Jul	2020	Libmanan (Diocese), Philippines
07	Jul	2020	Libreville (Archdiocese), Gabon
19	Jun	2020	Lichinga (Diocese), Mozambique

27	Feb	2021	Liège (Luik, Lüttich) (Diocese), Belgium
17	Dec	2020	Liepāja (Diocese), Latvia
02	Jul	2020	Lille (Archdiocese), France
02	Jul	2020	Lilongwe (Archdiocese), Malawi
12	May	2021	Lima (Archdiocese), Peru
30	Apr	2021	Limburg (Diocese), Germany
19	Aug	2020	Limeira (Diocese), Sao Paulo, Brazil
04	Feb	2021	Limerick (Diocese), Ireland
24	Jan	2021	Limoeiro do Norte (Diocese), Ceara, Brazil
22	Feb	2021	Limoges (Diocese), France
19	Mar	2021	Limón (Diocese), Costa Rica
19	May	2021	Linares (Diocese), Nuevo León, México
26	Mar	2021	Linares (Diocese), Chile
26	Apr	2021	Lincoln (Diocese), Nebraska, USA
30	Mar	2021	Lindi (Diocese), Tanzania
02	Apr	2021	Lingayen-Dagupan (Archdiocese), Philippines
13	May	2021	Lingling [Yungchow] (Prefecture Apostolic), China
05	Jun	2020	Linhai [Taichow] (Diocese), China
14	Dec	2020	Linqing [Lintsing] (Prefecture Apostolic), China
10	Mar	2021	Lins (Diocese), Sao Paulo, Brazil
19	Jan	2021	Lintong [Lintung] (Prefecture Apostolic), China
03	Nov	2020	Linyi [Ichow] (Diocese), China
10	Jan	2021	Linz (Diocese), Austria
20	Feb	2021	Lipa (Archdiocese), Philippines
14	May	2021	Lira (Diocese), Uganda
08	Jun	2020	Lisala (Diocese), Congo (Dem. Rep.)
24	Jul	2020	Lisboa {Lisbon} (Patriarchate), Portugal
23	Mar	2021	Lishui [Lishui] (Diocese), China
11	Aug	2020	Lismore (Diocese), Australia
24	Jun	2020	Lithuania, Military (Military Ordinariate)
25	Oct	2020	Litoměřice (Diocese), Czech Republic
25	Nov	2020	Little Rock (Diocese), Arkansas, USA
28	Jun	2020	Liverpool (Archdiocese), England, Great Britain
24	Oct	2020	Livingstone (Diocese), Zambia
06	May	2021	Livorno (Diocese), Italy
25	Apr	2021	Livramento de Nossa Senhora (Diocese), Bahia, Brazil
15	Oct	2020	Lixian [Lichow] (Prefecture Apostolic), China
16	May	2021	Ljubljana (Archdiocese), Slovenia
21	Jul	2020	Lleida (Diocese), Spain
07	Jul	2020	Locri-Gerace (-Santa Maria di Polsi) (Diocese), Italy
24	Nov	2020	Lodi (Diocese), Italy
09	Feb	2021	Lodwar (Diocese), Kenya
17	Dec	2020	Łódź (Archdiocese), Poland
08	Jul	2020	Loikaw (Diocese), Myanmar

09	Nov	2020	Loja (Diocese), Ecuador
05	Aug	2020	Lokoja (Diocese), Nigeria
25	Jul	2020	Lokossa (Diocese), Benin
31	Mar	2021	Lolo (Diocese), Congo (Dem. Rep.)
18	Sep	2020	Lomas de Zamora (Diocese), Argentina
27	Jun	2020	Lomé (Archdiocese), Togo
03	Dec	2020	Łomża (Diocese), Poland
02	Nov	2020	London (Diocese), Ontario, Canada
04	Jan	2021	Londrina (Archdiocese), Parana, Brazil
29	Nov	2020	Long Xuyên (Diocese), Viet Nam
18	Sep	2020	Lorena (Diocese), Sao Paulo, Brazil
12	Mar	2021	Loreto (Territorial Prelature), Italy
07	Dec	2020	Los Altos, Quetzaltenango-Totonicapán (Archdiocese), Guatemala
04	Nov	2020	Los Angeles (Archdiocese), California, USA
14	Feb	2021	Los Teques (Diocese), Venezuela
21	Jun	2020	Louisville (Archdiocese), Kentucky, USA
28	Mar	2021	Łowicz (Diocese), Poland
27	Jan	2021	Luanda (Archdiocese), Angola
01	Mar	2021	Luang Prabang (Vicariate Apostolic), Laos
03	Dec	2020	Lubango (Archdiocese), Angola
16	Mar	2021	Lubbock (Diocese), Texas, USA
19	Apr	2021	Lublin (Archdiocese), Poland
10	Feb	2021	Lubumbashi (Archdiocese), Congo (Dem. Rep.)
27	Apr	2021	Lucca (Archdiocese), Italy
25	Mar	2021	Lucena (Diocese), Philippines
05	Jul	2020	Lucera-Troia (Diocese), Italy
08	Jan	2021	Lucknow (Diocese), India
27	Jan	2021	Luçon (Diocese), France
17	Mar	2021	Luebo (Diocese), Congo (Dem. Rep.)
06	Dec	2020	Lugano (Diocese), Switzerland
08	Apr	2021	Lugazi (Diocese), Uganda
19	Mar	2021	Lugo (Diocese), Spain
13	Aug	2020	Lugoj (Romanian) (Diocese), Romania
20	Dec	2020	Luiza (Diocese), Congo (Dem. Rep.)
26	Oct	2020	Lungro degli Italo-Albanesi (Italo-Albanese) (Eparchy), Italy
10	Dec	2020	Luoyang [Loyang] (Diocese), China
21	Jul	2020	Luqsor {Tebe} (Coptic) (Eparchy), Egypt
21	May	2021	Lurín (Diocese), Peru
14	Oct	2020	Lusaka (Archdiocese), Zambia
26	Sep	2020	Lutsk (Diocese), Ukraine
16	Oct	2020	Lutsk (Ukrainian) (Archiepiscopal Exarchate), Ukraine
27	Apr	2021	Luxembourg (Archdiocese)
13	Mar	2021	Luz (Diocese), Minas Gerais, Brazil
03	Dec	2020	Luziânia (Diocese), Goias, Brazil

06	Oct	2020	Lviv (Armenian) (Archeparchy), Ukraine
10	Jul	2020	Lviv (Ukrainian) (Archeparchy), Ukraine
29	Jul	2020	Lviv (Archdiocese), Ukraine
21	Jul	2020	Lwena (Diocese), Angola
28	Jun	2020	Lyon (Archdiocese), France
09	Jan	2021	Maasin (Diocese), Philippines
03	Mar	2021	Macapá (Diocese), Amapa, Brazil
14	Aug	2020	Macau (Diocese), China
10	Jan	2021	Maceió (Archdiocese), Alagoas, Brazil
26	Jul	2020	Macerata-Tolentino-Recanati-Cingoli-Treia (Diocese), Italy
10	Dec	2020	Machakos (Diocese), Kenya
06	Jun	2020	Machala (Diocese), Ecuador
29	Apr	2021	Machiques (Diocese), Venezuela
15	Aug	2020	Mackenzie-Fort Smith (Diocese), Northwest Territories, Canada
09	Mar	2021	Madang (Archdiocese), Papua New Guinea
28	Sep	2020	Madison (Diocese), Wisconsin, USA
08	Sep	2020	Madras and Mylapore (Meliapor) (Archdiocese), India
24	Nov	2020	Madre di Dio a Mosca (Moscow) (Archdiocese), Russian Federation
04	Mar	2021	Madrid (Archdiocese), Spain
18	Apr	2021	Madurai (Archdiocese), India
12	Apr	2021	Magangué (Diocese), Colombia
22	Nov	2020	Magdeburg (Diocese), Germany
06	May	2021	Mahagi-Nioka (Diocese), Congo (Dem. Rep.)
06	Sep	2020	Mahajanga (Diocese), Madagascar
10	May	2021	Mahenge (Diocese), Tanzania
14	Aug	2020	Maiduguri (Diocese), Nigeria
30	Nov	2020	Maintirano (Diocese), Madagascar
31	Aug	2020	Mainz (Diocese), Germany
30	Sep	2020	Maitland-Newcastle (Diocese), Australia
14	Jan	2021	Makassar (Archdiocese), Indonesia
11	Oct	2020	Makeni (Diocese), Sierra Leone
07	Apr	2021	Makokou (Vicariate Apostolic), Gabon
01	Feb	2021	Makurdi (Diocese), Nigeria
06	Feb	2021	Malabo (Archdiocese), Equatorial Guinea
29	Jun	2020	Málaga (Diocese), Spain
25	Oct	2020	Málaga-Soatá (Diocese), Colombia
11	May	2021	Malakal (Diocese), South Sudan
04	Aug	2020	Malang (Diocese), Indonesia
22	Apr	2021	Malanje (Archdiocese), Angola
05	Nov	2020	Malaybalay (Diocese), Philippines
03	Feb	2021	Maldonado-Punta del Este-Minas (Diocese), Uruguay
28	Mar	2021	Maliana (Diocese), Timor-Leste
29	Jun	2020	Malindi (Diocese), Kenya
02	Sep	2020	Mallorca (Diocese), Spain

08	Feb	2021	Malolos (Diocese), Philippines
15	May	2021	Malta (Archdiocese)
21	May	2021	Mamfe (Diocese), Cameroon
05	Apr	2021	Man (Diocese), Côte d'Ivoire
05	Oct	2020	Manado (Diocese), Indonesia
19	Jun	2020	Managua (Archdiocese), Nicaragua
28	Jul	2020	Mananjary (Diocese), Madagascar
12	Jul	2020	Mananthavady (Syro-Malabar) (Eparchy), India
30	Nov	2020	Manaus (Archdiocese), Amazonas, Brazil
07	Oct	2020	Manchester (Diocese), New Hampshire, USA
15	Mar	2021	Mandalay (Archdiocese), Myanmar
20	Aug	2020	Mandeville (Diocese), Jamaica, Antilles
09	Jan	2021	Mandya (Syro-Malabar) (Eparchy), India
08	Jul	2020	Manfredonia-Vieste-San Giovanni Rotondo (Archdiocese), Italy
02	Dec	2020	Manga (Diocese), Burkina Faso
16	Nov	2020	Mangalore (Diocese), India
23	Jun	2020	Mangochi (Diocese), Malawi
04	Nov	2020	Manila (Archdiocese), Philippines
12	Apr	2021	Manizales (Archdiocese), Colombia
26	Apr	2021	Mannar (Diocese), Sri Lanka
15	Sep	2020	Manokwari-Sorong (Diocese), Indonesia
12	Dec	2020	Manono (Diocese), Congo (Dem. Rep.)
31	Aug	2020	Mansa (Diocese), Zambia
07	Aug	2020	Mantova (Diocese), Italy
02	Jun	2020	Manzini (Diocese), Swaziland
09	Sep	2020	Mao-Monte Cristi (Diocese), Dominican Republic
07	Jul	2020	Maputo (Archdiocese), Mozambique
07	May	2021	Marabá (Diocese), Para, Brazil
27	Nov	2020	Maracaibo (Archdiocese), Venezuela
19	Jul	2020	Maracay (Diocese), Venezuela
24	Aug	2020	Mar Addai of Toronto (Chaldean) (Eparchy), Canada
07	May	2021	Maradi (Diocese), Niger
13	Sep	2020	Marajó (Territorial Prelature), Para, Brazil
08	Sep	2020	Maralal (Diocese), Kenya
13	May	2021	Maramureş (Romanian) (Diocese), Romania
18	Jan	2021	Marawi (Territorial Prelature), Philippines
12	Jun	2020	Marbel (Diocese), Philippines
03	Apr	2021	Mar del Plata (Diocese), Argentina
01	Sep	2020	Margarita (Diocese), Venezuela
13	May	2021	Maria Einsiedeln (Territorial Abbey), Switzerland
23	Apr	2021	Mariana (Archdiocese), Minas Gerais, Brazil
14	Aug	2020	Mariannhill (Diocese), South Africa
28	Apr	2021	Maria Santissima in Astana (Archdiocese), Kazakhstan
10	Nov	2020	Maribor (Archdiocese), Slovenia

07	Jan	2021	Marília (Diocese), Sao Paulo, Brazil
14	Jun	2020	Maringá (Archdiocese), Parana, Brazil
16	Jun	2020	Maroua-Mokolo (Diocese), Cameroon
16	Aug	2020	Marquette (Diocese), Michigan, USA
12	Apr	2021	Marsabit (Diocese), Kenya
23	Jan	2021	Marseille (Archdiocese), France
15	Mar	2021	Marshall Islands (Prefecture Apostolic), Pacific (Oceania)
30	Jul	2020	Marthandom (Syro-Malankara) (Eparchy), India
12	Aug	2020	Masaka (Diocese), Uganda
12	Jan	2021	Masan (Diocese), Korea (South)
16	Apr	2021	Masbate (Diocese), Philippines
01	Sep	2020	Maseru (Archdiocese), Lesotho
08	Feb	2021	Massa Carrara-Pontremoli (Diocese), Italy
19	Aug	2020	Massa Marittima-Piombino (Diocese), Italy
18	Nov	2020	Masvingo (Diocese), Zimbabwe
11	Aug	2020	Matadi (Diocese), Congo (Dem. Rep.)
08	Dec	2020	Matagalpa (Diocese), Nicaragua
22	Sep	2020	Matamoros (Diocese), Tamaulipas, México
21	Oct	2020	Matanzas (Diocese), Cuba
31	Jan	2021	Matehuala (Diocese), San Luís Potosí, México
19	Nov	2020	Matera-Irsina (Archdiocese), Italy
07	Feb	2021	Mati (Diocese), Philippines
12	Jul	2020	Maturín (Diocese), Venezuela
09	Jul	2020	Maumere (Diocese), Indonesia
08	Nov	2020	Mavelikara (Syro-Malankara) (Eparchy), India
19	Feb	2021	Mawlamyine (Diocese), Myanmar
27	Nov	2020	Mayagüez (Diocese), Puerto Rico
10	Jun	2020	Mazara del Vallo (Diocese), Italy
12	Jul	2020	Mazatlán (Diocese), Sinaloa, México
19	Feb	2021	Mbaïki (Diocese), Central African Republic
04	Dec	2020	Mbalmayo (Diocese), Cameroon
11	Nov	2020	Mbandaka-Bikoro (Archdiocese), Congo (Dem. Rep.)
16	Dec	2020	Mbanza Congo (Diocese), Angola
19	Dec	2020	Mbarara (Archdiocese), Uganda
01	Nov	2020	Mbeya (Archdiocese), Tanzania
29	Sep	2020	Mbinga (Diocese), Tanzania
05	Apr	2021	Mbujimayi (Diocese), Congo (Dem. Rep.)
10	May	2021	Mbulu (Diocese), Tanzania
31	Aug	2020	Meath (Diocese), Ireland
12	May	2021	Meaux (Diocese), France
20	Jan	2021	Mechelen-Brussel {Malines-Brussels} (Archdiocese), Belgium
24	Jul	2020	Medan (Archdiocese), Indonesia
02	Jun	2020	Medellín (Archdiocese), Colombia
17	Feb	2021	Meerut (Diocese), India

08	Oct	2020	Meixian [Kaying] (Diocese), China
12	Oct	2020	Meki (Vicariate Apostolic), Ethiopia
27	Aug	2020	Melaka-Johor (Diocese), Malaysia
21	Nov	2020	Melbourne (Archdiocese), Australia
20	Jul	2020	Melfi-Rapolla-Venosa (Diocese), Italy
04	Apr	2021	Melipilla (Diocese), Chile
05	May	2021	Melo (Diocese), Uruguay
21	Jan	2021	Memphis (Diocese), Tennessee, USA
30	Oct	2020	Mende (Diocese), France
18	Apr	2021	Méndez (Vicariate Apostolic), Ecuador
26	Jun	2020	Mendi (Diocese), Papua New Guinea
24	Oct	2020	Mendoza (Archdiocese), Argentina
09	Dec	2020	Menevia (Diocese), Wales, Great Britain
16	Feb	2021	Menongue (Diocese), Angola
29	Apr	2021	Menorca (Diocese), Spain
27	Feb	2021	Merauke (Archdiocese), Indonesia
15	Mar	2021	Mercedes (Diocese), Uruguay
23	Jun	2020	Mercedes-Luján (Archdiocese), Argentina
16	May	2021	Mérida (Archdiocese), Venezuela
02	Oct	2020	Mérida-Badajoz (Archdiocese), Spain
18	May	2021	Merlo-Moreno (Diocese), Argentina
20	Jul	2020	Meru (Diocese), Kenya
18	Aug	2020	Messina-Lipari-Santa Lucia del Mela (Archdiocese), Italy
25	Jun	2020	Metuchen (Diocese), New Jersey, USA
11	Feb	2021	Metz (Diocese), France
24	Jun	2020	Mexicali (Diocese), Baja California Norte, México
15	Oct	2020	México (Archdiocese), Federal District
03	Feb	2021	Miami (Archdiocese), Florida, USA
18	Oct	2020	Miao (Diocese), India
05	Jun	2020	Miarinarivo (Diocese), Madagascar
06	Jan	2021	Middlesbrough (Diocese), England, Great Britain
15	Sep	2020	Milano {Milan} (Archdiocese), Italy
18	May	2021	Mileto-Nicotera-Tropea (Diocese), Italy
18	Mar	2021	Milwaukee (Archdiocese), Wisconsin, USA
03	Feb	2021	Mindelo (Diocese), Cape Verde
20	Nov	2020	Minna (Diocese), Nigeria
27	Oct	2020	Minsk-Mohilev (Archdiocese), Belarus
25	Jan	2021	Minya {Ermopoli Maggiore; Minieh} (Coptic) (Eparchy), Egypt
06	Mar	2021	Miracema do Tocantins (Diocese), Brazil
12	Jul	2020	Miri (Diocese), Malaysia
19	Dec	2020	Miskolc (Hungarian) (Eparchy), Hungary
23	Jul	2020	Mission de France o Pontigny (Territorial Prelature), France
19	May	2021	Mississauga (Syro-Malabar) (Eparchy)
26	Oct	2020	Misurata (Prefecture Apostolic), Libya

23	Oct	2020	Mitú (Vicariate Apostolic), Colombia
11	Mar	2021	Mixes (Territorial Prelature), Oaxaca, México
16	Oct	2020	Mobile (Archdiocese), Alabama, USA
19	Dec	2020	Mocoa-Sibundoy (Diocese), Colombia
11	Oct	2020	Modena-Nonantola (Archdiocese), Italy
10	Aug	2020	Mogadiscio (Diocese), Somalia
12	Dec	2020	Mogi das Cruzes (Diocese), Sao Paulo, Brazil
11	Jun	2020	Mohale's Hoek (Diocese), Lesotho
03	Sep	2020	Molegbe (Diocese), Congo (Dem. Rep.)
31	Jan	2021	Molfetta-Ruvo-Giovinazzo-Terlizzi (Diocese), Italy
20	Nov	2020	Mombasa (Archdiocese), Kenya
16	Jan	2021	Monaco (Archdiocese)
15	Mar	2021	Moncton (Archdiocese), New Brunswick, Canada
30	Mar	2021	Mondoñedo-Ferrol (Diocese), Spain
12	Oct	2020	Mondovi (Diocese), Italy
10	Apr	2021	Mongo (Vicariate Apostolic), Chad
11	Jun	2020	Mongomo (Diocese), Equatorial Guinea
20	Sep	2020	Mongu (Diocese), Zambia
09	Aug	2020	Monreale (Archdiocese), Italy
07	Aug	2020	Monrovia (Archdiocese), Liberia
25	Aug	2020	Montauban (Diocese), France
16	Jul	2020	Montecassino (Territorial Abbey), Italy
14	Aug	2020	Montego Bay (Diocese), Jamaica, Antilles
23	Aug	2020	Montelibano (Diocese), Colombia
05	Feb	2021	Montenegro (Diocese), Rio Grande do Sul, Brazil
12	Aug	2020	Monte Oliveto Maggiore (Territorial Abbey), Italy
20	Jan	2021	Montepulciano-Chiusi-Pienza (Diocese), Italy
08	Mar	2021	Monterey in California (Diocese), USA
26	Jul	2020	Montería (Diocese), Colombia
16	Jan	2021	Monterrey (Archdiocese), Nuevo León, México
01	Feb	2021	Montes Claros (Archdiocese), Minas Gerais, Brazil
01	Aug	2020	Montevergine (Territorial Abbey), Italy
21	Oct	2020	Montevideo (Archdiocese), Uruguay
15	Aug	2020	Mont-Laurier (Diocese), Québec, Canada
29	Apr	2021	Montpellier (-Lodève-Béziers-Agde-Saint-Pons-de-Thomières) (Archdiocese), France
19	Apr	2021	Montréal (Archdiocese), Québec, Canada
25	Feb	2021	Monze (Diocese), Zambia
20	Nov	2020	Mopti (Diocese), Mali
13	Aug	2020	Moramanga (Diocese), Madagascar
20	May	2021	Morelia (Archdiocese), Michoacán, México
18	Apr	2021	Morogoro (Diocese), Tanzania
25	Aug	2020	Morombe (Diocese), Madagascar
01	Jan	2021	Morón (Diocese), Argentina
26	Mar	2021	Morondava (Diocese), Madagascar

29	Sep	2020	Moroto (Diocese), Uganda
10	Mar	2021	Moshi (Diocese), Tanzania
17	Nov	2020	Mossoró (Diocese), Rio Grande do Norte, Brazil
15	Dec	2020	Mossul (Chaldean) (Archeparchy), Iraq
07	May	2021	Mossul (Syrian) (Archeparchy), Iraq
25	Oct	2020	Mostar-Duvno (-Trebinje e Mrkan) (Diocese), Bosnia and Herzegovina
02	Dec	2020	Motherwell (Diocese), Scotland, Great Britain
29	Oct	2020	Mouila (Diocese), Gabon
19	Oct	2020	Moulins (Diocese), France
04	Jun	2020	Moundou (Diocese), Chad
22	May	2021	Mount Hagen (Archdiocese), Papua New Guinea
20	Feb	2021	Moyobamba (Territorial Prelature), Peru
26	Feb	2021	Mpanda (Diocese), Tanzania
10	Apr	2021	Mpika (Diocese), Zambia
04	Jul	2020	Mtwara (Diocese), Tanzania
27	Oct	2020	Mukachevo (Munkács) (Ruthenian) (Eparchy), Ukraine
15	Sep	2020	Mukachevo (Munkács) (Diocese), Ukraine
13	Mar	2021	Multan (Diocese), Pakistan
08	Apr	2021	München und Freising {Munich} (Archdiocese), Germany
09	Jun	2020	Münster (Diocese), Germany
17	Jul	2020	Muranga (Diocese), Kenya
03	Oct	2020	Murska Sobota (Diocese), Slovenia
05	Sep	2020	Musoma (Diocese), Tanzania
03	Dec	2020	Mutare (Diocese), Zimbabwe
29	Jul	2020	Muvattupuzha (Syro-Malankara) (Eparchy), India
06	Aug	2020	Muyinga (Diocese), Burundi
25	Nov	2020	Muzaffarpur (Diocese), India
08	Apr	2021	Mwanza (Archdiocese), Tanzania
24	Jul	2020	Mweka (Diocese), Congo (Dem. Rep.)
06	Nov	2020	Myitkyina (Diocese), Myanmar
29	Jan	2021	Mymensingh (Diocese), Bangladesh
23	Jan	2021	Mysore (Diocese), India
16	Feb	2021	Mỹ Tho (Diocese), Viet Nam
02	Aug	2020	Mzuzu (Diocese), Malawi
23	Apr	2021	Nacala (Diocese), Mozambique
05	Nov	2020	Nagasaki (Archdiocese), Japan
18	Mar	2021	Nagoya (Diocese), Japan
23	Aug	2020	Nagpur (Archdiocese), India
03	Jun	2020	Naha (Diocese), Japan
17	Jan	2021	Nairobi (Archdiocese), Kenya
01	Sep	2020	Nakhon Ratchasima (Diocese), Thailand
04	Mar	2021	Nakhon Sawan (Diocese), Thailand
30	Jun	2020	Nakuru (Diocese), Kenya
12	Nov	2020	Nalgonda (Diocese), India

22	Jul	2020	Namibe (Diocese), Angola
11	Jul	2020	Nampula (Archdiocese), Mozambique
29	Nov	2020	Namur {Namen} (Diocese), Belgium
11	Apr	2021	Nanchang [Nanchang] (Archdiocese), China
20	Feb	2021	Nancheng [Nancheng] (Diocese), China
01	Aug	2020	Nanchong [Shunking] (Diocese), China
03	Aug	2020	Nancy (-Toul) (Diocese), France
03	Jun	2020	Nanjing [Nanking] (Archdiocese), China
10	Aug	2020	Nanning [Nanning] (Archdiocese), China
06	Jul	2020	Nanterre (Diocese), France
28	Dec	2020	Nantes (Diocese), France
11	Sep	2020	Nanyang [Nanyang] (Diocese), China
16	Sep	2020	Napo (Vicariate Apostolic), Ecuador
10	Jun	2020	Napoli {Naples} (Archdiocese), Italy
08	Feb	2021	Nardò-Gallipoli (Diocese), Italy
22	Jul	2020	Nashik (Diocese), India
17	Sep	2020	Nashville (Diocese), Tennessee, USA
21	Mar	2021	Nassau (Archdiocese), Bahamas, Antilles
05	Jul	2020	Natal (Archdiocese), Rio Grande do Norte, Brazil
17	Jan	2021	Natitingou (Diocese), Benin
03	Jun	2020	Naval (Diocese), Philippines
14	Nov	2020	Naviraí (Diocese), Mato Grosso do Sul, Brazil
10	Nov	2020	Navrongo-Bolgatanga (Diocese), Ghana
01	Jul	2020	Naxos, Andros, Tinos e Mykonos (Archdiocese), Greece
05	Feb	2021	Nazaré (Diocese), Pernambuco, Brazil
18	Jun	2020	Ndalatando (Diocese), Angola
21	Feb	2021	N'Dali (Diocese), Benin
04	Sep	2020	N'Djaména (Archdiocese), Chad
30	Jul	2020	Ndola (Diocese), Zambia
30	Apr	2021	Nebbi (Diocese), Uganda
14	Sep	2020	Neiva (Diocese), Colombia
21	Sep	2020	Nekemte (Vicariate Apostolic), Ethiopia
16	Dec	2020	Nellore (Diocese), India
16	Jul	2020	Nelson (Diocese), British Columbia, Canada
26	Mar	2021	Nepal (Vicariate Apostolic)
12	May	2021	Netherlands, Military (Military Ordinariate)
17	Apr	2021	Netzahualcóyotl (Diocese), México, México
21	Jul	2020	Neuquén (Diocese), Argentina
13	Apr	2021	Nevers (Diocese), France
19	Dec	2020	Newark (Archdiocese), New Jersey, USA
13	Sep	2020	New Orleans (Archdiocese), Louisiana, USA
20	Jan	2021	Newton (Our Lady of the Annunciation in Boston) (Melkite Greek) (Eparchy), USA
23	Nov	2020	New Ulm (Diocese), Minnesota, USA
21	Feb	2021	New Westminster (Ukrainian) (Eparchy), Canada

27	Feb	2021	New York (Archdiocese), New York, USA
23	Oct	2020	New Zealand, Military (Military Ordinariate)
15	Dec	2020	Neyyattinkara (Diocese), India
09	May	2021	Ngaoundéré (Diocese), Cameroon
05	Mar	2021	Ngong (Diocese), Kenya
29	Jul	2020	Ngozi (Diocese), Burundi
02	Jun	2020	Nha Trang (Diocese), Viet Nam
21	Nov	2020	Niamey (Archdiocese), Niger
09	Jun	2020	Nice (Diocese), France
26	Jun	2020	Nicolet (Diocese), Québec, Canada
02	Mar	2021	Nicopoli (Diocese), Bulgaria
03	Sep	2020	Nicosia (Diocese), Italy
06	Apr	2021	Niigata (Diocese), Japan
18	Jul	2020	Nîmes (-Uzès e Alès) (Diocese), France
07	Feb	2021	Ningbo [Ningpo] (Diocese), China
09	May	2021	Niterói (Archdiocese), Rio de Janeiro, Brazil
30	Nov	2020	Nitra (Diocese), Slovakia
04	Mar	2021	Njombe (Diocese), Tanzania
29	Apr	2021	Nkayi (Diocese), Congo
26	Dec	2020	Nkongsamba (Diocese), Cameroon
15	May	2021	Nnewi (Diocese), Nigeria
15	Feb	2021	Nocera Inferiore-Sarno (Diocese), Italy
12	Aug	2020	Nogales (Diocese), Sonora, México
05	Nov	2020	Nola (Diocese), Italy
08	Nov	2020	Nongstoin (Diocese), India
10	Nov	2020	Northampton (Diocese), England, Great Britain
20	Jul	2020	Northern Arabia (Vicariate Apostolic), Kuwait
23	Apr	2021	Norwich (Diocese), Connecticut, USA
14	May	2021	Nossa Senhora do Líbano em São Paulo (Maronite) (Eparchy), Sao Paulo, Brazil
14	Aug	2020	Nossa Senhora do Paraíso em São Paulo (Melkite Greek) (Eparchy), Sao Paulo, Brazil
31	Aug	2020	Noto (Diocese), Italy
03	Dec	2020	Notre-Dame du Liban de Paris (Maronite) (Eparchy), France
17	Jan	2021	Nottingham (Diocese), England, Great Britain
19	Mar	2021	Nouakchott (Diocese), Mauritania
23	Jan	2021	Nouméa (Archdiocese), New Caledonia, Pacific (Oceania)
26	Nov	2020	Nouna (Diocese), Burkina Faso
13	Nov	2020	Nova Friburgo (Diocese), Rio de Janeiro, Brazil
20	Oct	2020	Nova Iguaçu (Diocese), Rio de Janeiro, Brazil
27	Mar	2021	Novaliches (Diocese), Philippines
13	Mar	2021	Novara (Diocese), Italy
15	Apr	2021	Novo Hamburgo (Diocese), Rio Grande do Sul, Brazil
13	Dec	2020	Novo Mesto (Diocese), Slovenia
09	Jun	2020	Nsukka (Diocese), Nigeria
09	Jul	2020	Nuestra Señora de la Altagracia en Higüey (Diocese), Dominican Republic

25	Apr	2021	Nuestra Señora de los Mártires del Libano en México (Maronite) (Eparchy)
03	Jan	2021	Nuestra Señora del Paraíso en México (Melkite Greek) (Eparchy)
24	Jan	2021	Nueva Pamplona (Archdiocese), Colombia
30	Aug	2020	Nueva Segovia (Archdiocese), Philippines
23	Oct	2020	Nueve de Julio (Diocese), Argentina
21	Jun	2020	Nuevo Casas Grandes (Diocese), Chihuahua, México
10	Aug	2020	Nuevo Laredo (Diocese), Tamaulipas, México
01	Jul	2020	Ñuflo de Chávez (Vicariate Apostolic), Bolivia
30	Dec	2020	Nuoro (Diocese), Italy
15	May	2021	Nyahururu (Diocese), Kenya
08	Feb	2021	Nyeri (Archdiocese), Kenya
14	Feb	2021	Nyíregyháza (Hungarian) (Eparchy), Hungary
25	Jun	2020	Nyundo (Diocese), Rwanda
27	Mar	2021	N'Zérékoré (Diocese), Guinea
19	Oct	2020	Oakland (Diocese), California, USA
20	Apr	2021	Obala (Diocese), Cameroon
01	Oct	2020	Oberá (Diocese), Argentina
21	Aug	2020	Óbidos (Diocese), Para, Brazil
18	Jun	2020	Obuasi (Diocese), Ghana
11	Oct	2020	Ocaña (Diocese), Colombia
03	Dec	2020	Odessa (Ukrainian) (Archiepiscopal Exarchate), Ukraine
06	Oct	2020	Odessa-Simferopol (Diocese), Ukraine
09	Dec	2020	Odienné (Diocese), Côte d'Ivoire
16	Aug	2020	Oeiras (Diocese), Piaui, Brazil
28	Aug	2020	Ogdensburg (Diocese), New York, USA
12	Apr	2021	Ogoja (Diocese), Nigeria
22	Apr	2021	Oita (Diocese), Japan
02	Mar	2021	Okigwe (Diocese), Nigeria
16	Jun	2020	Oklahoma City (Archdiocese), Oklahoma, USA
17	Jun	2020	Olinda e Recife (Archdiocese), Pernambuco, Brazil
26	Jul	2020	Oliveira (Diocese), Minas Gerais, Brazil
26	Apr	2021	Olomouc (Archdiocese), Czech Republic
19	Dec	2020	Omaha (Archdiocese), Nebraska, USA
17	Jul	2020	Ondjiva (Diocese), Angola
24	Oct	2020	Ondo (Diocese), Nigeria
31	Dec	2020	Onitsha (Archdiocese), Nigeria
17	Feb	2021	Ootacamund (Diocese), India
05	Jun	2020	Opole (Diocese), Poland
20	Dec	2020	Oppido Mamertina-Palmi (Diocese), Italy
29	Jun	2020	Opus Dei (Personal Prelature), N/A
02	Jul	2020	Oradea Mare {Gran Varadino, Nagyvárad} (Diocese), Romania
20	Apr	2021	Oradea Mare {Gran Varadino} (Romanian) (Diocese), Romania
29	Aug	2020	Orán (Diocese), Argentina
14	Mar	2021	Oran (Diocese), Algeria

15	Jan	2021	Orange in California (Diocese), USA
27	Jul	2020	Orense (Diocese), Spain
02	May	2021	Oria (Diocese), Italy
23	Oct	2020	Orihuela-Alicante (Diocese), Spain
16	Aug	2020	Oristano (Archdiocese), Italy
31	Oct	2020	Orizaba (Diocese), Veracruz, México
15	Mar	2021	Orlando (Diocese), Florida, USA
08	Apr	2021	Orléans (Diocese), France
16	Jun	2020	Orlu (Diocese), Nigeria
05	Nov	2020	Oruro (Diocese), Bolivia
27	Sep	2020	Orvieto-Todi (Diocese), Italy
13	Apr	2021	Osaka (Archdiocese), Japan
15	Jan	2021	Osasco (Diocese), Sao Paulo, Brazil
02	Apr	2021	Oslo (Diocese), Norway
10	Sep	2020	Osma-Soria (Diocese), Spain
07	Dec	2020	Osnabrück (Diocese), Germany
10	Jul	2020	Osogbo (Diocese), Nigeria
03	Jul	2020	Osório (Diocese), Rio Grande do Sul, Brazil
08	Dec	2020	Osorno (Diocese), Chile
01	Nov	2020	Ossory (Diocese), Ireland
04	Apr	2021	Ostia (Suburbicarian See), Italy
28	Nov	2020	Ostrava-Opava (Diocese), Czech Republic
13	Jan	2021	Otranto (Archdiocese), Italy
26	Aug	2020	Ottawa-Cornwall (Archdiocese), Ontario, Canada
22	Jan	2021	Otukpo (Diocese), Nigeria
10	May	2021	Ouagadougou (Archdiocese), Burkina Faso
28	Jun	2020	Ouahigouya (Diocese), Burkina Faso
18	Oct	2020	Oudtshoorn (Diocese), South Africa
23	Jun	2020	Ouesso (Diocese), Congo
15	Nov	2020	Ourinhos (Diocese), Sao Paulo, Brazil
05	Feb	2021	Our Lady of Deliverance of Newark (Syrian) (Eparchy), USA
08	May	2021	Our Lady of Lebanon of Los Angeles (Maronite) (Eparchy), California, USA
30	Jan	2021	Our Lady of Nareg in Glendale (Armenian) (Eparchy), California, USA
13	Aug	2020	Our Lady of the Annunciation at Ibadan (Annunciazione) (Maronite) (Eparchy),
17	Jul	2020	Our Lady of the Southern Cross (Personal Ordinariate), Australia
01	Jul	2020	Our Lady of Walsingham (Personal Ordinariate), England, Great Britain
26	Nov	2020	Oviedo (Archdiocese), Spain
01	Jun	2020	Owando (Diocese), Congo
27	Feb	2021	Owensboro (Diocese), Kentucky, USA
14	Oct	2020	Owerri (Archdiocese), Nigeria
24	Apr	2021	Oyem (Diocese), Gabon
12	Jan	2021	Oyo (Diocese), Nigeria
17	Jan	2021	Ozamiz (Archdiocese), Philippines
19	Feb	2021	Ozieri (Diocese), Italy

29	Aug	2020	Padang (Diocese), Indonesia
04	Apr	2021	Paderborn (Archdiocese), Germany
25	Jun	2020	Padova {Padua} (Diocese), Italy
15	Apr	2021	Pagadian (Diocese), Philippines
28	Jul	2020	Paisley (Diocese), Scotland, Great Britain
12	Sep	2020	Paksé (Vicariate Apostolic), Laos
14	Nov	2020	Pala (Diocese), Chad
18	Nov	2020	Palai (Syro-Malabar) (Diocese), India
27	Aug	2020	Palangkaraya (Diocese), Indonesia
27	Feb	2021	Palayamkottai (Diocese), India
12	Apr	2021	Palembang (Archdiocese), Indonesia
04	Mar	2021	Palencia (Diocese), Spain
29	Jun	2020	Palermo (Archdiocese), Italy
22	Oct	2020	Palestrina (Suburbicarian See), Italy
01	Feb	2021	Palghat (Syro-Malabar) (Diocese), India
17	Dec	2020	Palmares (Diocese), Pernambuco, Brazil
20	Mar	2021	Palmas (Archdiocese), Tocatins, Brazil
19	Jan	2021	Palmas-Francisco Beltrão (Diocese), Parana, Brazil
08	Jun	2020	Palm Beach (Diocese), Florida, USA
30	Jul	2020	Palmeira dos Índios (Diocese), Alagoas, Brazil
02	May	2021	Palmerston North (Diocese), New Zealand
27	Dec	2020	Palmira (Diocese), Colombia
18	Nov	2020	Palo (Archdiocese), Philippines
22	Jul	2020	Pamiers (-Couserans-Mirepoix) (Diocese), France
22	Dec	2020	Pamplona y Tudela (Archdiocese), Spain
14	Mar	2021	Panamá (Archdiocese)
01	May	2021	Pando (Vicariate Apostolic), Bolivia
05	Feb	2021	Panevėžys (Diocese), Lithuania
12	Jan	2021	Pangkalpinang (Diocese), Indonesia
17	Aug	2020	Pankshin (Diocese), Nigeria
23	Jul	2020	Pannonhalma (Territorial Abbey), Hungary
26	Oct	2020	Papantla (Diocese), Puebla, México
21	May	2021	Papeete (Archdiocese), French Polynesia, Pacific (Oceania)
27	Jan	2021	Paracatu (Diocese), Minas Gerais, Brazil
19	Jul	2020	Paraguay, Military (Military Ordinariate)
22	May	2021	Paraíba (Archdiocese), Brazil
24	Jun	2020	Parakou (Archdiocese), Benin
13	Feb	2021	Paramaribo (Diocese), Suriname, Antilles
03	May	2021	Paraná (Archdiocese), Argentina
03	Jun	2020	Paranaguá (Diocese), Parana, Brazil
18	Jun	2020	Parañaque (Diocese), Philippines
01	Jun	2020	Paranavaí (Diocese), Parana, Brazil
21	May	2021	Parassala (Syro-Malankara) (Eparchy), India
18	Jan	2021	Parintins (Diocese), Amazonas, Brazil

28	Apr	2021	Paris (Archdiocese), France
05	Jan	2021	Parma (Ruthenian) (Eparchy), Ohio, USA
22	Jan	2021	Parma (-Fontevivo) (Diocese), Italy
28	Jan	2021	Parnaíba (Diocese), Piaui, Brazil
06	Mar	2021	Parral (Diocese), Chihuahua, México
20	Jun	2020	Parramatta (Diocese), Australia
21	Jun	2020	Pasig (Diocese), Philippines
15	Oct	2020	Passaic (Ruthenian) (Eparchy), New Jersey, USA
21	Jan	2021	Passau (Diocese), Germany
03	Jul	2020	Passo Fundo (Archdiocese), Rio Grande do Sul, Brazil
24	Sep	2020	Pasto (Diocese), Colombia
25	Oct	2020	Paterson (Diocese), New Jersey, USA
23	Dec	2020	Pathanamthitta (Syro-Malankara) (Eparchy), India
21	Oct	2020	Pathein (Diocese), Myanmar
03	Aug	2020	Patna (Archdiocese), India
24	Feb	2021	Patos (Diocese), Paraiba, Brazil
15	May	2021	Patos de Minas (Diocese), Minas Gerais, Brazil
07	Sep	2020	Patti (Diocese), Italy
22	Sep	2020	Paulo Afonso (Diocese), Bahia, Brazil
06	Sep	2020	Pavia (Diocese), Italy
20	Jul	2020	Pécs (Diocese), Hungary
24	Jul	2020	Pekhon (Diocese), Myanmar
08	Dec	2020	Pelotas (Archdiocese), Rio Grande do Sul, Brazil
27	Sep	2020	Pelplin (Diocese), Poland
25	Jun	2020	Pemba (Diocese), Mozambique
22	Feb	2021	Pembroke (Diocese), Ontario, Canada
25	Nov	2020	Penang (Diocese), Malaysia
28	Jun	2020	Penedo (Diocese), Alagoas, Brazil
17	Jan	2021	Penonomé (Diocese), Panama
28	Jul	2020	Pensacola-Tallahassee (Diocese), Florida, USA
02	Jan	2021	Peoria (Diocese), Illinois, USA
30	Aug	2020	Pereira (Diocese), Colombia
22	Nov	2020	Périgueux (-Sarlat) (Diocese), France
14	Dec	2020	Perpignan-Elne (Diocese), France
21	Dec	2020	Perth (Archdiocese), Australia
21	Feb	2021	Peru, Military (Military Ordinariate)
16	May	2021	Perugia-Città della Pieve (Archdiocese), Italy
14	Mar	2021	Pesaro (Archdiocese), Italy
20	Dec	2020	Pescara-Penne (Archdiocese), Italy
17	Apr	2021	Pescia (Diocese), Italy
01	Jun	2020	Pesqueira (Diocese), Pernambuco, Brazil
01	Jan	2021	Peterborough (Diocese), Ontario, Canada
18	Jun	2020	Petra e Filadelfia (Melkite Greek) (Archeparchy), Jordan
23	Sep	2020	Petrolina (Diocese), Pernambuco, Brazil

17	Nov	2020	Petrópolis (Diocese), Rio de Janeiro, Brazil
14	Jun	2020	Phan Thiết (Diocese), Viet Nam
31	May	2020	Phát Diệm (Diocese), Viet Nam
08	Apr	2021	Philadelphia (Archdiocese), Pennsylvania, USA
17	Oct	2020	Philadelphia (Ukrainian) (Archeparchy), Pennsylvania, USA
11	Dec	2020	Philippines, Military (Military Ordinariate)
13	Jun	2020	Phnom-Penh (Vicariate Apostolic), Cambodia
04	Oct	2020	Phoenix (Diocese), Arizona, USA
13	Mar	2021	Phú Cường (Diocese), Viet Nam
05	Dec	2020	Piacenza-Bobbio (Diocese), Italy
10	Feb	2021	Piana degli Albanesi (Italo-Albanese) (Eparchy), Italy
03	Nov	2020	Piazza Armerina (Diocese), Italy
20	Apr	2021	Picos (Diocese), Piaui, Brazil
31	Aug	2020	Piedras Negras (Diocese), Coahuila, México
12	Nov	2020	Pilcomayo (Vicariate Apostolic), Paraguay
05	Jul	2020	Pinar del Rio (Diocese), Cuba
20	Jan	2021	Pinerolo (Diocese), Italy
09	Apr	2021	Pingliang [Pingliang] (Diocese), China
16	Aug	2020	Pinheiro (Diocese), Maranhão, Brazil
03	Mar	2021	Pinsk (Diocese), Belarus
05	Feb	2021	Piracicaba (Diocese), Sao Paulo, Brazil
03	Sep	2020	Pisa (Archdiocese), Italy
02	Feb	2021	Pistoia (Diocese), Italy
14	Jul	2020	Pitigliano-Sovana-Orbetello (Diocese), Italy
29	Mar	2021	Pittsburgh (Ruthenian) (Archeparchy), Pennsylvania, USA
22	Apr	2021	Pittsburgh (Diocese), Pennsylvania, USA
12	Feb	2021	Piura (Archdiocese), Peru
19	Jul	2020	Plasencia (Diocese), Spain
16	Dec	2020	Płock (Diocese), Poland
30	Jul	2020	Plymouth (Diocese), England, Great Britain
12	Nov	2020	Plzeň (Diocese), Czech Republic
24	Sep	2020	Pointe-Noire (Diocese), Congo
20	Mar	2021	Poitiers (Archdiocese), France
29	Apr	2021	Poland, Military (Military Ordinariate)
08	Dec	2020	Poland, Faithful of Eastern Rites (Ordinariate)
14	May	2021	Polokwane (Diocese), South Africa
27	Jan	2021	Pompei o Beatissima Vergine Maria del Santissimo Rosario (Territorial Prelature), Italy
10	Nov	2020	Ponce (Diocese), Puerto Rico
20	May	2021	Pondicherry and Cuddalore (Archdiocese), India
29	Jan	2021	Ponta de Pedras (Diocese), Para, Brazil
21	Mar	2021	Ponta Grossa (Diocese), Parana, Brazil
02	Aug	2020	Pontianak (Archdiocese), Indonesia
19	Mar	2021	Pontoise (Diocese), France
02	Nov	2020	Poona (Diocese), India

28	Oct	2020	Popayán (Archdiocese), Colombia
01	Jul	2020	Popokabaka (Diocese), Congo (Dem. Rep.)
08	Nov	2020	Poreč i Pula (Diocese), Croatia
23	Jan	2021	Portalegre-Castelo Branco (Diocese), Portugal
15	Oct	2020	Port-au-Prince (Archdiocese), Haïti
29	Nov	2020	Port-Bergé (Diocese), Madagascar
24	Mar	2021	Port Blair (Diocese), India
13	Dec	2020	Port-de-Paix (Diocese), Haïti
07	Apr	2021	Port Elizabeth (Diocese), South Africa
22	Sep	2020	Port-Gentil (Diocese), Gabon
06	Mar	2021	Port Harcourt (Diocese), Nigeria
25	Jan	2021	Portland (Diocese), Maine, USA
18	Aug	2020	Portland in Oregon (Archdiocese), USA
11	Feb	2021	Port-Louis (Diocese), Mauritius
13	Feb	2021	Port Moresby (Archdiocese), Papua New Guinea
12	Aug	2020	Porto (Diocese), Portugal
12	Jun	2020	Porto Alegre (Archdiocese), Rio Grande do Sul, Brazil
04	Jun	2020	Port of Spain (Archdiocese), Trinidad and Tobago, Antilles
24	Jan	2021	Porto Nacional (Diocese), Tocatins, Brazil
25	Jan	2021	Porto Novo (Diocese), Benin
09	Sep	2020	Porto-Santa Rufina (Suburbicarian See), Italy
15	Sep	2020	Porto Velho (Archdiocese), Rondonia, Brazil
29	Apr	2021	Portoviejo (Archdiocese), Ecuador
10	May	2021	Port Pirie (Diocese), Australia
25	Nov	2020	Portsmouth (Diocese), England, Great Britain
19	Apr	2021	Portugal, Military (Military Ordinariate)
27	Nov	2020	Port Victoria o Seychelles (Diocese)
20	Oct	2020	Port-Vila (Diocese), Vanuatu, Pacific (Oceania)
10	Dec	2020	Posadas (Diocese), Argentina
12	Mar	2021	Potenza-Muro Lucano-Marsico Nuovo (Archdiocese), Italy
01	Apr	2021	Potosí (Diocese), Bolivia
14	Apr	2021	Pouso Alegre (Archdiocese), Minas Gerais, Brazil
28	Sep	2020	Požega (Diocese), Croatia
05	Sep	2020	Poznań (Archdiocese), Poland
10	Feb	2021	Pozzuoli (Diocese), Italy
09	May	2021	Praha {Prague} (Archdiocese), Czech Republic
06	Sep	2020	Prato (Diocese), Italy
05	Jun	2020	Presidente Prudente (Diocese), Sao Paulo, Brazil
17	Jul	2020	Prešov (Prjašev) (Slovakian) (Archdiocese), Slovakia
18	Sep	2020	Pretoria (Archdiocese), South Africa
18	Jul	2020	Primavera do Leste - Paranatinga (Diocese), Mato Grosso, Brazil
05	Oct	2020	Prince-Albert (Diocese), Saskatchewan, Canada
22	Oct	2020	Prince George (Diocese), British Columbia, Canada
29	Dec	2020	Prizren-Prishtina (Diocese), Serbia

04	Mar	2021	Propriá (Diocese), Sergipe, Brazil
16	Jan	2021	Providence (Diocese), Rhode Island, USA
04	Oct	2020	Przemyśl (Archdiocese), Poland
15	Mar	2021	Przemyśl-Warszawa {-Warsaw} (Ukrainian) (Archdiocese), Poland
01	Nov	2020	Pucallpa (Vicariate Apostolic), Peru
29	Oct	2020	Puebla de los Ángeles, Puebla (Archdiocese), México
12	Apr	2021	Pueblo (Diocese), Colorado, USA
28	Oct	2020	Puerto Ayacucho (Vicariate Apostolic), Venezuela
18	Jan	2021	Puerto Cabello (Diocese), Venezuela
16	Mar	2021	Puerto Carreño (Vicariate Apostolic), Colombia
06	Jun	2020	Puerto Escondido (Diocese), Oaxaca, México
17	Oct	2020	Puerto Gaitán (Vicariate Apostolic), Colombia
31	May	2020	Puerto Iguazú (Diocese), Argentina
06	Apr	2021	Puerto Leguízamo-Solano (Vicariate Apostolic), Colombia
26	Nov	2020	Puerto Maldonado (Vicariate Apostolic), Peru
31	Oct	2020	Puerto Montt (Archdiocese), Chile
12	Sep	2020	Puerto Plata (Diocese), Dominican Republic
25	Mar	2021	Puerto Princesa (Vicariate Apostolic), Philippines
22	Jan	2021	Punalur (Diocese), India
05	Mar	2021	Puno (Diocese), Peru
06	Nov	2020	Punta Arenas (Diocese), Chile
17	Feb	2021	Puntarenas (Diocese), Costa Rica
11	Jan	2021	Punto Fijo (Diocese), Venezuela
12	Mar	2021	Puqi [Puchi] (Diocese), China
27	Jun	2020	Purnea (Diocese), India
03	Apr	2021	Purwokerto (Diocese), Indonesia
01	Dec	2020	Puthur (Syro-Malankara) (Eparchy), India
16	May	2021	Puyo (Vicariate Apostolic), Ecuador
13	Jul	2020	Pyay (Diocese), Myanmar
29	Mar	2021	P'yŏng-yang (Diocese), Korea (North)
11	Jan	2021	Qacha's Nek (Diocese), Lesotho
21	Jan	2021	Qichun [Kichow] (Diocese), China
10	Apr	2021	Qingdao [Tsingtao] (Diocese), China
13	Jun	2020	Qiqihar [Tsitsihar] (Prefecture Apostolic), China
30	Jan	2021	Québec (Archdiocese), Canada
01	Jun	2020	Queenstown (Diocese), South Africa
02	Jul	2020	Quelimane (Diocese), Mozambique
19	Nov	2020	Querétaro (Diocese), México
12	Oct	2020	Quetta (Vicariate Apostolic), Pakistan
08	Nov	2020	Quibdó (Diocese), Colombia
15	Sep	2020	Quiché (Diocese), Guatemala
11	Apr	2021	Quilmes (Diocese), Argentina
08	Mar	2021	Quilon (Diocese), India
08	Dec	2020	Quimper [Cornouailles] (-Léon) (Diocese), France

17	May	2021	Quito (Archdiocese), Ecuador
30	Sep	2020	Quixadá (Diocese), Ceara, Brazil
23	Aug	2020	Quy Nhơn (Qui Nhơn) (Diocese), Viet Nam
20	Oct	2020	Rabat (Archdiocese), Morocco
02	Jun	2020	Rabaul (Archdiocese), Papua New Guinea
02	Aug	2020	Radom (Diocese), Poland
06	May	2021	Rafaela (Diocese), Argentina
09	Nov	2020	Ragusa (Diocese), Italy
11	Sep	2020	Raiganj (Diocese), India
02	Oct	2020	Raigarh (Diocese), India
11	Dec	2020	Raipur (Archdiocese), India
23	Aug	2020	Rajkot (Syro-Malabar) (Diocese), India
13	Jul	2020	Rajshahi (Diocese), Bangladesh
13	May	2021	Raleigh (Diocese), North Carolina, USA
21	Apr	2021	Ramanathapuram (Syro-Malabar) (Eparchy), India
06	Feb	2021	Rancagua (Diocese), Chile
01	Mar	2021	Ranchi (Archdiocese), India
11	Jul	2020	Raphoe (Diocese), Ireland
18	Mar	2021	Rapid City (Diocese), South Dakota, USA
14	Feb	2021	Rarotonga (Diocese), Cook Islands, Pacific (Oceania)
06	Jan	2021	Ratchaburi (Diocese), Thailand
10	Aug	2020	Ratnapura (Diocese), Sri Lanka
31	Dec	2020	Ravenna-Cervia (Archdiocese), Italy
09	Mar	2021	Rayagada (Diocese), India
22	May	2021	Reconquista (Diocese), Argentina
10	Dec	2020	Regensburg (Diocese), Germany
22	Mar	2021	Reggio Calabria-Bova (Archdiocese), Italy
28	Aug	2020	Reggio Emilia-Guastalla (Diocese), Italy
18	Aug	2020	Regina (Archdiocese), Saskatchewan, Canada
05	Oct	2020	Registro (Diocese), Sao Paulo, Brazil
26	Jan	2021	Reims (Archdiocese), France
04	Jan	2021	Rennes (-Dol-Saint-Malo) (Archdiocese), France
03	Oct	2020	Reno (Diocese), Nevada, USA
30	Jan	2021	Requena (Vicariate Apostolic), Peru
13	Oct	2020	Resistencia (Archdiocese), Argentina
08	Sep	2020	Reyes (Vicariate Apostolic), Bolivia
10	Jan	2021	Reykjavik (Diocese), Iceland
23	Aug	2020	Rēzekne-Aglona (Diocese), Latvia
31	May	2020	Rhodos {Rhodes} (Archdiocese), Greece
13	Dec	2020	Ribeirão Preto (Archdiocese), Sao Paulo, Brazil
01	Apr	2021	Richmond (Diocese), Virginia, USA
08	May	2021	Rieti (-S. Salvatore Maggiore) (Diocese), Italy
19	Oct	2020	Riga (Archdiocese), Latvia
14	Jun	2020	Rijeka (Archdiocese), Croatia

15	Jul	2020	Rimini (Diocese), Italy
08	Nov	2020	Rimouski (Archdiocese), Québec, Canada
22	Jul	2020	Riobamba (Diocese), Ecuador
10	Dec	2020	Rio Branco (Diocese), Acre, Brazil
13	Dec	2020	Rio do Sul (Diocese), Santa Catarina, Brazil
15	Aug	2020	Río Gallegos (Diocese), Argentina
12	Jan	2021	Rio Grande (Diocese), Rio Grande do Sul, Brazil
18	Aug	2020	Riohacha (Diocese), Colombia
16	Sep	2020	Robe (Prefecture Apostolic), Ethiopia
24	Feb	2021	Rochester (Diocese), New York, USA
17	Aug	2020	Rockford (Diocese), Illinois, USA
22	Sep	2020	Rockhampton (Diocese), Australia
31	Aug	2020	Rockville Centre (Diocese), New York, USA
04	Aug	2020	Rodez (-Vabres) (Diocese), France
24	Nov	2020	Rodrigues (Vicariate Apostolic), Mauritius
12	Oct	2020	Roermond (Diocese), Netherlands
31	Mar	2021	Roma {Rome} (Diocese), Italy
22	Sep	2020	Romania (Armenian) (Ordinariate)
02	Mar	2021	Romblon (Diocese), Philippines
04	Jun	2020	Rondonópolis - Guiratinga (Diocese), Mato Grosso, Brazil
11	Jun	2020	Roraima (Diocese), Roraima, Brazil
04	Apr	2021	Rosario (Archdiocese), Argentina
13	Mar	2021	Roseau (Diocese), Dominica, Antilles
02	Apr	2021	Rossano-Cariati (Archdiocese), Italy
04	Jun	2020	Rottenburg-Stuttgart (Diocese), Germany
19	Aug	2020	Rotterdam (Diocese), Netherlands
04	May	2021	Rouen (Archdiocese), France
08	Jul	2020	Rourkela (Diocese), India
29	Sep	2020	Rouyn-Noranda (Diocese), Québec, Canada
11	Jan	2021	Rožňava (Diocese), Slovakia
29	Sep	2020	Rrëshen (Diocese), Albania
07	Jan	2021	Rubiataba-Mozarlândia (Diocese), Goias, Brazil
27	Jul	2020	Ruhengeri (Diocese), Rwanda
09	Jul	2020	Rulenge-Ngara (Diocese), Tanzania
29	Nov	2020	Rumbek (Diocese), South Sudan
03	Sep	2020	Rundu (Vicariate Apostolic), Namibia
04	Jul	2020	Russia (Russian) (Apostolic Exarchate)
17	Oct	2020	Rustenburg (Diocese), South Africa
05	Sep	2020	Rutana (Diocese), Burundi
13	Nov	2020	Ruteng (Diocese), Indonesia
06	May	2021	Ruy Barbosa (Rui Barbosa) (Diocese), Bahia, Brazil
18	Nov	2020	Ruyigi (Diocese), Burundi
07	Sep	2020	Rzeszów (Diocese), Poland
22	Oct	2020	Sabina-Poggio Mirteto (Suburbicarian See), Italy

30	Oct	2020	Sacramento (Diocese), California, USA
02	Feb	2021	Sagar (Syro-Malabar) (Diocese), India
17	Mar	2021	Saginaw (Diocese), Michigan, USA
12	Jun	2020	Saïdā (Sidone) (Maronite) (Eparchy), Lebanon
05	Feb	2021	Saïdā (Sidone) (Melkite Greek) (Archeparchy), Lebanon
21	Jan	2021	Saint Andrews and Edinburgh (Archdiocese), Scotland, Great Britain
01	Nov	2020	Saint Augustine (Diocese), Florida, USA
15	Jun	2020	Saint-Boniface (Archdiocese), Manitoba, Canada
18	Feb	2021	Saint-Brieuc (-Tréguier) (Diocese), France
22	Nov	2020	Saint Catharines (Diocese), Ontario, Canada
01	Sep	2020	Saint-Claude (Diocese), France
26	Dec	2020	Saint Cloud (Diocese), Minnesota, USA
07	Nov	2020	Saint-Denis (Diocese), France
31	Jan	2021	Saint-Denis-de-La Réunion (Diocese)
03	Dec	2020	Saint-Dié (Diocese), France
20	Oct	2020	Sainte-Anne-de-la-Pocatière (Diocese), Québec, Canada
14	Oct	2020	Sainte-Croix-de-Paris (Armenian) (Eparchy), France
28	Oct	2020	Saint Ephrem of Khadki (Syro-Malankara) (Eparchy), India
22	Jul	2020	Saint-Etienne (Diocese), France
07	Apr	2021	Saint-Flour (Diocese), France
23	Jul	2020	Saint George's in Canton (Romanian) (Eparchy), USA
20	May	2021	Saint George's in Grenada (Diocese), Antilles
15	Apr	2021	Saint Helena, Ascension and Tristan da Cunha (Mission Sui Iuris)
28	Apr	2021	Saint-Hyacinthe (Diocese), Québec, Canada
01	Aug	2020	Saint-Jean-Longueuil (Diocese), Québec, Canada
20	Sep	2020	Saint-Jérôme (Diocese), Québec, Canada
09	Oct	2020	Saint John Chrysostom of Gurgaon (Syro-Malankara) (Eparchy), India
15	May	2021	Saint John, New Brunswick (Diocese), Canada
10	Oct	2020	Saint John's-Basseterre (Diocese), Virgin Islands (British), Antilles
06	Oct	2020	Saint John's, Newfoundland (Archdiocese), Canada
07	Jun	2020	Saint John XXIII of Sofia (Bulgarian) (Eparchy), Bulgaria
04	Jul	2020	Saint Josaphat in Parma (Ukrainian) (Eparchy), USA
28	Oct	2020	Saint Louis (Archdiocese), Missouri, USA
21	Sep	2020	Saint-Louis du Sénégal (Diocese)
20	Nov	2020	Saint-Maron de Montréal (Maronite) (Eparchy), Canada
20	Nov	2020	Saint Maron of Brooklyn (Maronite) (Eparchy), New York, USA
09	May	2021	Saint Maron of Sydney (Maronite) (Eparchy), Australia
28	Jul	2020	Saint Mary, Queen of Peace (Syro-Malankara) (Eparchy), USA
31	May	2020	Saint-Maurice (Territorial Abbey), Switzerland
29	Sep	2020	Saint Michael's of Sydney (Melkite Greek) (Eparchy), Australia
22	Mar	2021	Saint Nicholas of Chicago (Ukrainian) (Eparchy), Illinois, USA
04	Aug	2020	Saint Paul and Minneapolis (Archdiocese), Minnesota, USA
14	Oct	2020	Saint Paul in Alberta (Diocese), Canada
09	May	2021	Saint Petersburg (Diocese), Florida, USA

06	Sep	2020	Saint Peter the Apostle of San Diego (Chaldean) (Eparchy), USA
30	Jul	2020	Saint-Sauveur de Montréal (Melkite Greek) (Eparchy), Canada
03	Apr	2021	Saints Cyril and Methodius of Toronto (Slovakian) (Eparchy), Canada
31	Dec	2020	Saints Peter and Paul of Melbourne (Ukrainian) (Eparchy), Australia
29	Mar	2021	Saint Thomas (Diocese), American Virgin Islands, USA
18	Sep	2020	Saint Thomas the Apostle of Chicago (Syro-Malabar) (Eparchy), Illinois, USA
16	Mar	2021	Saint Thomas the Apostle of Detroit (Chaldean) (Eparchy), USA
15	May	2021	Saint Thomas the Apostle of Melbourne (Syro-Malabar) (Eparchy), Australia
17	Feb	2021	Saint Thomas the Apostle of Sydney (Chaldean) (Eparchy), Australia
27	Jun	2020	Saint Vladimir-Le-Grand de Paris (Ukrainian) (Eparchy)
13	Apr	2021	Saitama (Diocese), Japan
04	Oct	2020	Sakania-Kipushi (Diocese), Congo (Dem. Rep.)
16	Nov	2020	Salamanca (Diocese), Spain
11	Mar	2021	Sale (Diocese), Australia
08	Aug	2020	Salem (Diocese), India
09	Sep	2020	Salerno-Campagna-Acerno (Archdiocese), Italy
20	Jan	2021	Salford (Diocese), England, Great Britain
19	Jul	2020	Salgueiro (Diocese), Pernambuco, Brazil
27	Apr	2021	Salina (Diocese), Kansas, USA
17	Jun	2020	Salmas {Shahpour} (Chaldean) (Diocese), Iran
28	Jan	2021	Salta (Archdiocese), Argentina
28	Jan	2021	Saltillo (Diocese), Coahuila, México
01	Apr	2021	Salt Lake City (Diocese), Utah, USA
27	Jan	2021	Salto (Diocese), Uruguay
24	Feb	2021	Saluzzo (Diocese), Italy
09	May	2021	Salzburg (Archdiocese), Austria
09	Sep	2020	Samarinda (Archdiocese), Indonesia
09	Dec	2020	Sambalpur (Diocese), India
28	Mar	2021	Sambir-Drohobych (Ukrainian) (Eparchy), Ukraine
02	Sep	2020	Same (Diocese), Tanzania
08	Oct	2020	Samoa-Apia (Archdiocese), Samoa, Pacific (Oceania)
18	Feb	2021	Samoa-Pago Pago (Diocese), American Samoa, Pacific (Oceania)
08	Aug	2020	San (Diocese), Mali
02	Nov	2020	San Andrés Tuxtla (Diocese), Veracruz, México
24	Aug	2020	San Andrés y Providencia (Vicariate Apostolic), Colombia
17	Jun	2020	San Angelo (Diocese), Texas, USA
26	Jan	2021	San Antonio (Archdiocese), Texas, USA
11	Aug	2020	San Bartolomé de Chillán (Diocese), Chile
05	Sep	2020	San Benedetto del Tronto-Ripatransone-Montalto (Diocese), Italy
23	Aug	2020	San Bernardino (Diocese), California, USA
01	Jun	2020	San Bernardo (Diocese), Chile
02	Nov	2020	San Carlos (Diocese), Philippines
03	Aug	2020	San Carlos de Ancud (Diocese), Chile
10	Sep	2020	San Carlos de Bariloche (Diocese), Argentina

12	Nov	2020	San Carlos de Venezuela (Diocese)
14	Feb	2021	San Charbel en Buenos Aires (Maronite) (Eparchy), Argentina
18	Feb	2021	San Clemente a Saratov (Diocese), Russian Federation
31	Jan	2021	San Cristobal de la Habana (Archdiocese), Cuba
26	Feb	2021	San Cristóbal de La Laguna o Tenerife (Diocese), Spain
18	Jun	2020	San Cristóbal de Las Casas (Diocese), Chiapas, México
07	Jun	2020	San Cristóbal de Venezuela (Diocese)
20	Jan	2021	Sandakan (Diocese), Malaysia
05	Jan	2021	Sandhurst (Diocese), Australia
18	Apr	2021	San Diego (Diocese), California, USA
16	Oct	2020	Sandomierz (Diocese), Poland
18	Dec	2020	San Felipe (Diocese), Chile
14	Mar	2021	San Felipe (Diocese), Venezuela
29	Oct	2020	San Fernando (Archdiocese), Philippines
18	Dec	2020	San Fernando de Apure (Diocese), Venezuela
13	Dec	2020	San Fernando de La Union (Diocese), Philippines
24	Sep	2020	San Francisco (Diocese), Argentina
12	Dec	2020	San Francisco (Archdiocese), California, USA
28	Nov	2020	San Francisco de Asís de Jutiapa (Diocese), Guatemala
18	Jan	2021	San Francisco de Macorís (Diocese), Dominican Republic
29	Jan	2021	Sanggau (Diocese), Indonesia
17	May	2021	San Giuseppe a Irkutsk (Diocese), Russian Federation
18	May	2021	Sangmélima (Diocese), Cameroon
15	Aug	2020	San Gregorio de Narek en Buenos Aires (Armenian) (Eparchy), Argentina
09	Mar	2021	San Ignacio de Velasco (Diocese), Bolivia
21	Mar	2021	San Isidro (Diocese), Argentina
20	Oct	2020	San Isidro de El General (Diocese), Costa Rica
25	Sep	2020	San Jacinto (Diocese), Ecuador
15	Apr	2021	San Jose (Diocese), Philippines
23	Nov	2020	San Jose de Antique (Diocese), Philippines
12	Mar	2021	San José de Costa Rica (Archdiocese)
30	Sep	2020	San José del Amazonas (Vicariate Apostolic), Peru
17	Apr	2021	San José del Guaviare (Diocese), Colombia
14	Sep	2020	San José de Mayo (Diocese), Uruguay
15	Jun	2020	San Jose in California (Diocese), USA
19	Nov	2020	San Jose in Mindoro (Vicariate Apostolic), Philippines
27	Apr	2021	San Juan Bautista de Calama (Diocese), Chile
01	Nov	2020	San Juan Bautista de las Misiones (Diocese), Paraguay
09	Apr	2021	San Juan de Cuyo (Archdiocese), Argentina
20	Jun	2020	San Juan de la Maguana (Diocese), Dominican Republic
11	Apr	2021	San Juan de los Lagos (Diocese), Jalisco, México
12	Mar	2021	San Juan de Puerto Rico (Archdiocese)
30	Sep	2020	San Justo (Diocese), Argentina
29	Aug	2020	Sankt Gallen (Diocese), Switzerland

23	Mar	2021	Sankt Pölten (Diocese), Austria
09	Oct	2020	San Lorenzo (Diocese), Paraguay
15	Sep	2020	San Luis (Diocese), Argentina
22	Oct	2020	San Luis Potosí (Archdiocese), México
05	Aug	2020	San Marco Argentano-Scalea (Diocese), Italy
21	Jul	2020	San Marcos (Diocese), Guatemala
01	Jun	2020	San Marcos de Arica (Diocese), Chile
07	Oct	2020	San Marino-Montefeltro (Diocese), Italy
22	Aug	2020	San Martín (Diocese), Argentina
13	Aug	2020	San Miguel (Diocese), Argentina
26	Jul	2020	San Miguel (Diocese), El Salvador
06	Nov	2020	San Miguel de Sucumbíos (Vicariate Apostolic), Ecuador
20	May	2021	San Miniato (Diocese), Italy
13	Aug	2020	San Nicola di Ruski Krstur (Križevci) (Eparchy)
09	Feb	2021	San Nicolás de los Arroyos (Diocese), Argentina
16	Apr	2021	San Pablo (Diocese), Philippines
24	Nov	2020	San Pedro (Diocese), Paraguay
06	Aug	2020	San Pedro de Macorís (Diocese), Dominican Republic
13	Nov	2020	San Pedro-en-Côte d'Ivoire (Diocese)
12	Aug	2020	San Pedro Sula (Diocese), Honduras
07	Sep	2020	San Rafael (Diocese), Argentina
21	Apr	2021	San Ramón (Vicariate Apostolic), Peru
18	Feb	2021	San Roque de Presidencia Roque Sáenz Peña (Diocese), Argentina
26	Jul	2020	San Salvador (Archdiocese), El Salvador
21	Sep	2020	San Sebastián (Diocese), Spain
09	Apr	2021	San Severo (Diocese), Italy
24	Apr	2021	Santa Ana (Diocese), El Salvador
30	Sep	2020	Santa Clara (Diocese), Cuba
25	Jan	2021	Santa Cruz de la Sierra (Archdiocese), Bolivia
01	Aug	2020	Santa Cruz do Sul (Diocese), Rio Grande do Sul, Brazil
30	Nov	2020	Santa Fe (Archdiocese), New Mexico, USA
11	Apr	2021	Santa Fe de Antioquia (Archdiocese), Colombia
22	Aug	2020	Santa Fe de la Vera Cruz (Archdiocese), Argentina
23	Nov	2020	Santa Maria (Archdiocese), Rio Grande do Sul, Brazil
30	Apr	2021	Santa Maria de Los Ángeles (Diocese), Chile
24	Mar	2021	Santa María del Patrocinio en Buenos Aires (Ukrainian) (Eparchy), Argentina
16	Apr	2021	Santa Maria di Grottaferrata (Italo-Albanese) (Territorial Abbey), Italy
07	Jan	2021	Santa Marta (Diocese), Colombia
28	Jun	2020	Santander (Diocese), Spain
13	Sep	2020	Sant'Angelo dei Lombardi-Conza-Nusco-Bisaccia (Archdiocese), Italy
30	Apr	2021	Santarém (Archdiocese), Para, Brazil
25	Feb	2021	Santarém (Diocese), Portugal
20	Aug	2020	Santa Rosa (in California) (Diocese), USA
05	Aug	2020	Santa Rosa (Diocese), Argentina

17	Apr	2021	Santa Rosa de Copán (Diocese), Honduras
08	May	2021	Santa Rosa de Lima (Diocese), Guatemala
25	Nov	2020	Santa Rosa de Osos (Diocese), Colombia
08	Dec	2020	Sant Feliu de Llobregat (Diocese), Spain
10	Oct	2020	Santiago Apóstol de Huancané (Territorial Prelature), Peru
24	Mar	2021	Santiago de Cabo Verde (Diocese)
20	May	2021	Santiago de Chile (Archdiocese)
10	Dec	2020	Santiago de Compostela (Archdiocese), Spain
14	Apr	2021	Santiago de Cuba (Archdiocese)
03	Mar	2021	Santiago de Guatemala (Archdiocese), Guatemala
29	Jun	2020	Santiago del Estero (Diocese), Argentina
17	Oct	2020	Santiago de los Caballeros (Archdiocese), Dominican Republic
21	Sep	2020	Santiago de María (Diocese), El Salvador
23	Jul	2020	Santiago de Veraguas (Diocese), Panama
20	Jul	2020	Santisimo Salvador de Bayamo y Manzanillo (Diocese), Cuba
09	Sep	2020	Santíssima Conceição do Araguaia (Diocese), Brazil
22	Apr	2021	Santissima Trinità di Cava de' Tirreni (Territorial Abbey), Italy
25	Sep	2020	Santissima Trinità in Almaty (Diocese), Kazakhstan
01	May	2021	Santo Amaro (Diocese), Sao Paulo, Brazil
01	Aug	2020	Santo André (Diocese), Sao Paulo, Brazil
19	Apr	2021	Santo Ângelo (Diocese), Rio Grande do Sul, Brazil
08	Feb	2021	Santo Domingo (Archdiocese), Dominican Republic
18	Jan	2021	Santo Domingo en Ecuador (Diocese)
04	Sep	2020	Santorini {Thira} (Diocese), Greece
07	Mar	2021	Santos (Diocese), Sao Paulo, Brazil
25	Nov	2020	Santo Tomé (Diocese), Argentina
08	Sep	2020	San Vicente (Diocese), El Salvador
09	Aug	2020	San Vicente del Caguán (Diocese), Colombia
31	May	2020	Sanyuan [Sanyüan] (Diocese), China
05	Aug	2020	São Carlos (Diocese), Sao Paulo, Brazil
22	Jul	2020	São Félix (Territorial Prelature), Mato Grosso, Brazil
01	Jul	2020	São Gabriel da Cachoeira (Diocese), Amazonas, Brazil
22	Jul	2020	São João Batista em Curitiba (Ukrainian) (Archeparchy), Brazil
20	Apr	2021	São João da Boa Vista (Diocese), Sao Paulo, Brazil
14	Jun	2020	São João del Rei (Diocese), Minas Gerais, Brazil
22	Jun	2020	São João Maria Vianney (Apostolic Administration), Rio de Janeiro, Brazil
30	Dec	2020	São José do Rio Preto (Diocese), Sao Paulo, Brazil
08	Dec	2020	São José dos Campos (Diocese), Sao Paulo, Brazil
24	Jun	2020	São José dos Pinhais (Diocese), Parana, Brazil
30	Jun	2020	São Luís de Montes Belos (Diocese), Goias, Brazil
10	Feb	2021	São Luís do Maranhão (Archdiocese), Brazil
09	Apr	2021	São Luíz de Cáceres (Diocese), Mato Grosso, Brazil
12	Feb	2021	São Mateus (Diocese), Espirito Santo, Brazil
09	Jul	2020	São Miguel Paulista (Diocese), Sao Paulo, Brazil

29	Apr	2021	São Paulo (Archdiocese), Brazil
13	Jun	2020	São Raimundo Nonato (Diocese), Piaui, Brazil
05	Dec	2020	São Salvador da Bahia (Archdiocese), Brazil
29	Jan	2021	São Sebastião do Rio de Janeiro (Archdiocese), Brazil
21	Dec	2020	São Tomé e Príncipe (Diocese)
11	Nov	2020	Sapë (Diocese), Albania
14	Sep	2020	Sapporo (Diocese), Japan
20	Feb	2021	Sarh (Diocese), Chad
22	Jun	2020	Saskatoon (Diocese), Saskatchewan, Canada
10	Apr	2021	Saskatoon (Ukrainian) (Eparchy), Canada
29	Mar	2021	Sassari (Archdiocese), Italy
17	May	2021	Satna (Syro-Malabar) (Diocese), India
21	Dec	2020	Satu Mare {Szatmár} (Diocese), Romania
16	Sep	2020	Sault Sainte Marie (Diocese), Ontario, Canada
01	Apr	2021	Saurimo (Archdiocese), Angola
11	Oct	2020	Savannah (Diocese), Georgia, USA
04	Jan	2021	Savannakhet (Vicariate Apostolic), Laos
25	Dec	2020	Savona-Noli (Diocese), Italy
07	Feb	2021	Scranton (Diocese), Pennsylvania, USA
22	Oct	2020	Seattle (Archdiocese), Washington, USA
09	Nov	2020	Sées {Séez} (Diocese), France
15	Feb	2021	Segheneity (Eritrean) (Eparchy), Eritrea
23	Sep	2020	Segorbe-Castellón de la Plana (Diocese), Spain
04	Mar	2021	Ségou (Diocese), Mali
09	Dec	2020	Segovia (Diocese), Spain
20	Jan	2021	Sekondi-Takoradi (Diocese), Ghana
28	Sep	2020	Semarang (Archdiocese), Indonesia
26	Mar	2021	Sendai (Diocese), Japan
28	Sep	2020	Senigallia (Diocese), Italy
05	Jun	2020	Sens (-Auxerre) (Archdiocese), France
05	Apr	2021	Seoul (Archdiocese), Korea (South)
19	May	2021	Serrinha (Diocese), Bahia, Brazil
01	Nov	2020	Sessa Aurunca (Diocese), Italy
01	Apr	2021	Sete Lagoas (Diocese), Minas Gerais, Brazil
10	Jul	2020	Setúbal (Diocese), Portugal
13	May	2021	Sevilla {Seville} (Archdiocese), Spain
27	Mar	2021	Sfântul Vasile cel Mare de Bucureşti (Romanian) (Eparchy), Romania
14	Apr	2021	Shamshabad (Syro-Malabar) (Eparchy), India
14	Jan	2021	Shanba (Patriotic) (Diocese), China
09	Mar	2021	Shanghai [Shanghai] (Diocese), China
28	Sep	2020	Shangqiu [Kweiteh] (Diocese), China
16	Jul	2020	Shantou [Swatow] (Diocese), China
20	Jun	2020	Shaoguan [Shiuchow] (Diocese), China
29	Aug	2020	Shaowu [Shaowu] (Prefecture Apostolic), China

19	Nov	2020	Shashi [Shasi] (Prefecture Apostolic), China
26	Sep	2020	Shendam (Diocese), Nigeria
08	Oct	2020	Shenyang [Mukden, Fengtien] (Archdiocese), China
28	Jan	2021	Sherbrooke (Archdiocese), Québec, Canada
19	Aug	2020	's Hertogenbosch (Bois-le-Duc) (Diocese), Netherlands
25	Sep	2020	Shillong (Archdiocese), India
16	Apr	2021	Shimoga (Diocese), India
20	Aug	2020	Shinyanga (Diocese), Tanzania
18	Dec	2020	Shiqian [Shihtsien] (Prefecture Apostolic), China
11	Jan	2021	Shkodrë-Pult (Archdiocese), Albania
21	Mar	2021	Shreveport (Diocese), Louisiana, USA
28	Sep	2020	Shrewsbury (Diocese), England, Great Britain
30	Aug	2020	Shuoxian [Shohchow] (Diocese), China
07	Nov	2020	Šiauliai (Diocese), Lithuania
20	Aug	2020	Šibenik (Knin) (Diocese), Croatia
01	Sep	2020	Sibolga (Diocese), Indonesia
16	Mar	2021	Sibu (Diocese), Malaysia
18	Aug	2020	Sicuani (Territorial Prelature), Peru
22	Apr	2021	Siedlce (Diocese), Poland
08	Aug	2020	Siena-Colle di Val d'Elsa-Montalcino (Archdiocese), Italy
23	Feb	2021	Sigüenza-Guadalajara (Diocese), Spain
02	Sep	2020	Sikasso (Diocese), Mali
11	Jan	2021	Simdega (Diocese), India
10	Jun	2020	Simla and Chandigarh (Diocese), India
16	Aug	2020	Sincelejo (Diocese), Colombia
01	May	2021	Sindhudurg (Diocese), India
08	Jan	2021	Singapore (Archdiocese)
10	Sep	2020	Singida (Diocese), Tanzania
15	Jan	2021	Sinop (Diocese), Mato Grosso, Brazil
11	Aug	2020	Sintang (Diocese), Indonesia
07	Mar	2021	Sion {Sitten} (Diocese), Switzerland
31	Oct	2020	Sioux City (Diocese), Iowa, USA
04	Nov	2020	Sioux Falls (Diocese), South Dakota, USA
20	Nov	2020	Siping [Szepingkai] (Diocese), China
05	Jun	2020	Siracusa (Archdiocese), Italy
30	Nov	2020	Sisak (Diocese), Croatia
16	Sep	2020	Siuna (Diocese), Nicaragua
04	Dec	2020	Sivagangai (Diocese), India
24	Aug	2020	Skopje (Diocese), North Macedonia
05	Jan	2021	Slovakia, Military (Military Ordinariate)
16	Jun	2020	Soacha (Diocese), Colombia
30	Sep	2020	Sobral (Diocese), Ceara, Brazil
12	Dec	2020	Socorro y San Gil (Diocese), Colombia
07	Oct	2020	Soddo (Vicariate Apostolic), Ethiopia

08	Aug	2020	Sofia e Plovdiv (Diocese), Bulgaria
13	Jul	2020	Sohag (Coptic) (Eparchy), Egypt
24	Jul	2020	Soissons (-Laon-Saint-Quentin) (Diocese), France
19	Jul	2020	Sokal-Zhovkva (Ukrainian) (Eparchy), Ukraine
01	May	2021	Sokodé (Diocese), Togo
07	Jun	2020	Sokoto (Diocese), Nigeria
24	Apr	2021	Sololá-Chimaltenango (Diocese), Guatemala
17	Mar	2021	Solsona (Diocese), Spain
30	Mar	2021	Solwezi (Diocese), Zambia
20	Jun	2020	Songea (Archdiocese), Tanzania
01	Jan	2021	Sonsonate (Diocese), El Salvador
22	Jul	2020	Sonsón-Rionegro (Diocese), Colombia
17	May	2021	Sora-Cassino-Aquino-Pontecorvo (Diocese), Italy
23	Oct	2020	Sorocaba (Archdiocese), Sao Paulo, Brazil
22	May	2021	Soroti (Diocese), Uganda
21	Aug	2020	Sorrento-Castellammare di Stabia (Archdiocese), Italy
15	Jul	2020	Sorsogon (Diocese), Philippines
21	Aug	2020	Sosnowiec (Diocese), Poland
28	Jul	2020	South Africa, Military (Military Ordinariate)
06	Feb	2021	Southern Albania {Albania Meridionale} (Albanian) (Apostolic Administration)
12	Sep	2020	Southern Arabia (Vicariate Apostolic), Yemen
07	Aug	2020	Southwark (Archdiocese), England, Great Britain
28	Jul	2020	Spain, Military (Military Ordinariate)
09	Jul	2020	Spain, Faithful of Eastern Rites (Ordinariate)
08	Jul	2020	Speyer (Diocese), Germany
20	Jun	2020	Spiš (Diocese), Slovakia
15	Nov	2020	Split-Makarska (Archdiocese), Croatia
08	Jul	2020	Spokane (Diocese), Washington, USA
21	Dec	2020	Spoleto-Norcia (Archdiocese), Italy
11	Sep	2020	Springfield-Cape Girardeau (Diocese), Missouri, USA
29	Oct	2020	Springfield in Illinois (Diocese), USA
27	Jun	2020	Springfield in Massachusetts (Diocese), USA
24	Oct	2020	Srijem (Diocese), Serbia
09	Feb	2021	Srikakulam (Diocese), India
06	May	2021	Stamford (Ukrainian) (Eparchy), USA
06	May	2021	Steubenville (Diocese), Ohio, USA
10	Oct	2020	Stockholm (Diocese), Sweden
23	Feb	2021	Stockton (Diocese), California, USA
07	May	2021	Strasbourg (Archdiocese), France
06	Sep	2020	Stryj (Ukrainian) (Eparchy), Ukraine
08	Mar	2021	Subiaco (Territorial Abbey), Italy
24	Apr	2021	Subotica (Diocese), Serbia
01	Apr	2021	Suchitepéquez-Retalhuleu (Diocese), Guatemala
12	May	2021	Sucre (Archdiocese), Bolivia

08	Jul	2020	Sudan and South Sudan (Syrian) (Patriarchal Dependent Territory)
22	Mar	2021	Suixian [Suihsien] (Prefecture Apostolic), China
21	Dec	2020	Sulmona-Valva (Diocese), Italy
25	Feb	2021	Sultanpet (Diocese), India
07	Oct	2020	Sumbawanga (Diocese), Tanzania
04	Apr	2021	Sumbe (Diocese), Angola
02	Oct	2020	Sunyani (Diocese), Ghana
11	Dec	2020	Superior (Diocese), Wisconsin, USA
10	Apr	2021	Surabaya (Diocese), Indonesia
03	Mar	2021	Surat Thani (Diocese), Thailand
27	Aug	2020	Surigao (Diocese), Philippines
01	Jan	2021	Susa (Diocese), Italy
12	Dec	2020	Suva (Archdiocese), Fiji, Pacific (Oceania)
20	Oct	2020	Suwon (Diocese), Korea (South)
04	Jul	2020	Suzhou [Soochow] (Diocese), China
14	Dec	2020	Świdnica (Diocese), Poland
14	Oct	2020	Sydney (Archdiocese), Australia
28	Oct	2020	Sylhet (Diocese), Bangladesh
05	Aug	2020	Syracuse (Diocese), New York, USA
03	Aug	2020	Syros (e Milos) (Diocese), Greece
26	Sep	2020	Szczecin-Kamień (Archdiocese), Poland
10	Jan	2021	Szeged-Csanád (Diocese), Hungary
26	Feb	2021	Székesfehérvár (Albareale) (Diocese), Hungary
11	May	2021	Szombathely (Diocese), Hungary
25	Dec	2020	Tabasco (Diocese), México
14	Oct	2020	Tabora (Archdiocese), Tanzania
09	Sep	2020	Tabuk (Vicariate Apostolic), Philippines
17	Sep	2020	Tacámbaro (Diocese), Michoacán, México
16	Nov	2020	Tacna y Moquegua (Diocese), Peru
06	Jul	2020	Tacuarembó (Diocese), Uruguay
26	Dec	2020	Tadjikistan (Mission Sui Iuris)
02	May	2021	Tagbilaran (Diocese), Philippines
11	Aug	2020	Tagum (Diocese), Philippines
20	Oct	2020	Taichung (Diocese), Taiwan
13	Jun	2020	Tainan (Diocese), Taiwan
20	Mar	2021	Taiohae o Tefenuaenata (Diocese), French Polynesia, Pacific (Oceania)
01	Dec	2020	Taipei (Archdiocese), Taiwan
26	Mar	2021	Taiyuan [Taiyüan] (Archdiocese), China
19	May	2021	Takamatsu (Diocese), Japan
16	Jul	2020	Talca (Diocese), Chile
03	Aug	2020	Talibon (Diocese), Philippines
21	Mar	2021	Tamale (Archdiocese), Ghana
27	Dec	2020	Tambacounda (Diocese), Senegal
04	Oct	2020	Tampico (Diocese), Tamaulipas, México

13	Jul	2020	Tandag (Diocese), Philippines
07	Jul	2020	Tanga (Diocese), Tanzania
18	Dec	2020	Tanger (Archdiocese), Morocco
03	Jul	2020	Tanjore (Diocese), India
07	Nov	2020	Tanjungkarang (Diocese), Indonesia
07	Feb	2021	Tanjung Selor (Diocese), Indonesia
15	Jun	2020	Tapachula (Diocese), Chiapas, México
22	Jun	2020	Tarahumara (Diocese), Chihuahua, México
01	Jan	2021	Taranto (Archdiocese), Italy
21	Oct	2020	Tarawa and Nauru (Diocese), Kiribati, Pacific (Oceania)
06	Dec	2020	Tarazona (Diocese), Spain
24	Jan	2021	Tarbes et Lourdes (Diocese), France
20	Dec	2020	Tarija (Diocese), Bolivia
08	Feb	2021	Tarlac (Diocese), Philippines
24	Jun	2020	Tarma (Diocese), Peru
03	Mar	2021	Tarnów (Diocese), Poland
28	Apr	2021	Tarragona (Archdiocese), Spain
05	Jul	2020	Taubaté (Diocese), Sao Paulo, Brazil
08	Apr	2021	Taunggyi (Archdiocese), Myanmar
26	Dec	2020	Taungngu (Diocese), Myanmar
24	Aug	2020	Taytay (Vicariate Apostolic), Philippines
13	Nov	2020	Teano-Calvi (Diocese), Italy
28	Aug	2020	Techiman (Diocese), Ghana
21	Aug	2020	Tefé (Territorial Prelature), Amazonas, Brazil
23	Nov	2020	Teggiano-Policastro (Diocese), Italy
10	Jun	2020	Tegucigalpa (Archdiocese), Honduras
12	Apr	2021	Teheran (Chaldean) (Archdiocese), Iran
19	Dec	2020	Tehuacán (Diocese), Puebla, México
15	Apr	2021	Tehuantepec (Diocese), Oaxaca, México
04	May	2021	Teixeira de Freitas-Caravelas (Diocese), Bahia, Brazil
14	Dec	2020	Tellicherry (Syro-Malabar) (Archeparchy), India
30	Sep	2020	Telšiai (-Klaipeda) (Diocese), Lithuania
18	May	2021	Tempio-Ampurias (Diocese), Italy
16	Sep	2020	Temuco (Diocese), Chile
13	Apr	2021	Tenancingo (Diocese), México, México
16	Sep	2020	Tenkodogo (Diocese), Burkina Faso
05	Sep	2020	Teófilo Otoni (Diocese), Minas Gerais, Brazil
23	Nov	2020	Teotihuacán (Diocese), México, México
01	Dec	2020	Tepic (Diocese), Nayarit, México
22	Aug	2020	Teramo-Atri (Diocese), Italy
25	Jul	2020	Teresina (Archdiocese), Piaui, Brazil
25	Mar	2021	Termoli-Larino (Diocese), Italy
20	Aug	2020	Terni-Narni-Amelia (Diocese), Italy
05	Jan	2021	Ternopil-Zboriv (Ukrainian) (Archeparchy), Ukraine

03	May	2021	Terrassa (Diocese), Spain
07	Sep	2020	Teruel y Albarracín (Diocese), Spain
09	Mar	2021	Tete (Diocese), Mozambique
04	Aug	2020	Texcoco (Diocese), México, México
23	Mar	2021	Tezpur (Diocese), India
25	Jul	2020	Thái Bình (Diocese), Viet Nam
29	Oct	2020	Thamarasserry (Syro-Malabar) (Diocese), India
05	Jan	2021	Thanh Hoá (Diocese), Viet Nam
23	Jun	2020	Thành-Phô Hồ Chí Minh (Hôchiminh Ville) (Archdiocese), Viet Nam
22	Jan	2021	Thare and Nonseng (Archdiocese), Thailand
24	Jul	2020	Thessaloniki (Vicariate Apostolic), Greece
30	Mar	2021	Thiès (Diocese), Senegal
29	Jul	2020	Thuckalay (Syro-Malabar) (Diocese), India
29	Aug	2020	Thunder Bay (Diocese), Ontario, Canada
27	Mar	2021	Tianguá (Diocese), Ceara, Brazil
17	Jun	2020	Tianjin [Tientsin] (Diocese), China
26	Oct	2020	Tianshui [Tsinchow] (Diocese), China
17	Oct	2020	Tibú (Diocese), Colombia
26	Jan	2021	Tierradentro (Vicariate Apostolic), Colombia
06	Jun	2020	Tijuana (Archdiocese), Baja California Norte, México
06	Jul	2020	Tilarán-Liberia (Diocese), Costa Rica
13	Feb	2021	Timika (Diocese), Indonesia
31	Mar	2021	Timişoara (Diocese), Romania
21	Jan	2021	Timmins (Diocese), Ontario, Canada
30	Nov	2020	Tiranë-Durrës (Archdiocese), Albania
13	Jun	2020	Tiruchirapalli (Diocese), India
23	Oct	2020	Tiruvalla (Syro-Malankara) (Archeparchy), India
10	Feb	2021	Tivoli (Diocese), Italy
22	Feb	2021	Tlalnepantla (Archdiocese), México, México
11	Sep	2020	Tlapa (Diocese), Guerrero, México
31	Jan	2021	Tlaxcala (Diocese), México
19	Sep	2020	Toamasina (Archdiocese), Madagascar
14	Dec	2020	Tocantinópolis (Diocese), Tocatins, Brazil
07	Mar	2021	Tokelau (Mission Sui Iuris), Pacific (Oceania)
03	Feb	2021	Tŏkwon {Tokugen} (Territorial Abbey), Korea (North)
18	Oct	2020	Tōkyō (Archdiocese), Japan
15	Jul	2020	Tôlagnaro (Diocese), Madagascar
12	Aug	2020	Toledo (in America) (Diocese), Ohio, USA
20	Feb	2021	Toledo (Diocese), Parana, Brazil
16	Jun	2020	Toledo (Archdiocese), Spain
24	Oct	2020	Toliara (Archdiocese), Madagascar
18	Dec	2020	Toluca (Archdiocese), México, México
26	Aug	2020	Tombura-Yambio (Diocese), South Sudan
08	May	2021	Tonga (Diocese), Pacific (Oceania)

17	Aug	2020	Tongzhou [Tungchow] (Prefecture Apostolic), China
22	Nov	2020	Toowoomba (Diocese), Australia
09	Jun	2020	Torino {Turin} (Archdiocese), Italy
19	Oct	2020	Torit (Diocese), South Sudan
15	Feb	2021	Toronto (Archdiocese), Ontario, Canada
04	May	2021	Toronto (Ukrainian) (Eparchy), Canada
11	Sep	2020	Tororo (Archdiocese), Uganda
07	May	2021	Torreón (Diocese), Coahuila, México
26	Dec	2020	Tortona (Diocese), Italy
23	Sep	2020	Tortosa (Diocese), Spain
07	Jan	2021	Toruń (Diocese), Poland
12	Oct	2020	Toulouse (-Saint Bertrand de Comminges-Rieux) (Archdiocese), France
02	Jun	2020	Tournai {Doornik} (Diocese), Belgium
05	Nov	2020	Tours (Archdiocese), France
07	May	2021	Townsville (Diocese), Australia
17	Oct	2020	Trani-Barletta-Bisceglie (-Nazareth) (Archdiocese), Italy
11	May	2021	Trapani (Diocese), Italy
03	Apr	2021	Trasfigurazione a Novosibirsk (Diocese), Russian Federation
27	Aug	2020	Trento (Archdiocese), Italy
13	Jan	2021	Trenton (Diocese), New Jersey, USA
02	Nov	2020	Três Lagoas (Diocese), Mato Grosso do Sul, Brazil
03	Oct	2020	Treviso (Diocese), Italy
14	Feb	2021	Tricarico (Diocese), Italy
22	Dec	2020	Trichur (Syro-Malabar) (Archdiocese), India
18	Sep	2020	Trier (Diocese), Germany
09	Jul	2020	Trieste (Diocese), Italy
17	Dec	2020	Trincomalee (Diocese), Sri Lanka
28	Aug	2020	Trinidad (Vicariate Apostolic), Colombia
19	Feb	2021	Tripoli (Vicariate Apostolic), Libya
14	Jan	2021	Tripoli del Libano {Tarabulus} (Maronite) (Archeparchy)
28	Aug	2020	Tripoli del Libano {Tarabulus} (Melkite Greek) (Archeparchy)
01	May	2021	Trivandrum (Syro-Malankara) (Archeparchy), India
15	Oct	2020	Trivandrum (Archdiocese), India
22	Apr	2021	Trivento (Diocese), Italy
04	Mar	2021	Trnava (Archdiocese), Slovakia
16	Feb	2021	Trois-Rivières (Diocese), Québec, Canada
23	Dec	2020	Tromsø (Territorial Prelature), Norway
07	Dec	2020	Trondheim (Territorial Prelature), Norway
01	Sep	2020	Troyes (Diocese), France
29	Jan	2021	Trujillo (Diocese), Honduras
06	Mar	2021	Trujillo (Archdiocese), Peru
24	Feb	2021	Trujillo (Diocese), Venezuela
02	Aug	2020	Tshumbe (Diocese), Congo (Dem. Rep.)
02	Sep	2020	Tsiroanomandidy (Diocese), Madagascar

25	Feb	2021	Tuam (Archdiocese), Ireland
09	Jul	2020	Tubarão (Diocese), Santa Catarina, Brazil
25	Oct	2020	Tucson (Diocese), Arizona, USA
15	Jun	2020	Tucumán (Archdiocese), Argentina
10	Sep	2020	Tucupita (Vicariate Apostolic), Venezuela
02	Feb	2021	Tuguegarao (Archdiocese), Philippines
12	Jun	2020	Tui-Vigo (Diocese), Spain
27	Mar	2021	Tula (Diocese), Hidalgo, México
22	Nov	2020	Tulancingo (Archdiocese), Hidalgo, México
09	Dec	2020	Tulcán (Diocese), Ecuador
16	Jun	2020	Tulle (Diocese), France
21	Nov	2020	Tulsa (Diocese), Oklahoma, USA
23	Apr	2021	Tumaco (Diocese), Colombia
15	Aug	2020	Tunduru-Masasi (Diocese), Tanzania
18	Jul	2020	Tunis (Archdiocese), Tunisia
30	Mar	2021	Tunja (Archdiocese), Colombia
18	Mar	2021	Tunxi [Tunki] (Prefecture Apostolic), China
07	Dec	2020	Tura (Diocese), India
15	May	2021	Turkey (Syrian) (Patriarchal Exarchate)
26	Aug	2020	Turkmenistan (Mission Sui Iuris)
11	Mar	2021	Turks and Caicos (Mission Sui Iuris), Antilles
13	Jan	2021	Tursi-Lagonegro (Diocese), Italy
07	Jul	2020	Tuticorin (Diocese), India
03	Jul	2020	Tuxpan (Diocese), Veracruz, México
28	Apr	2021	Tuxtepec (Diocese), Oaxaca, México
11	Jul	2020	Tuxtla Gutiérrez (Archdiocese), Chiapas, México
03	Nov	2020	Tyler (Diocese), Texas, USA
10	Aug	2020	Tyr (Maronite) (Archeparchy), Lebanon
29	Dec	2020	Tyr (Melkite Greek) (Archdiocese), Lebanon
08	Jun	2020	Tzaneen (Diocese), South Africa
14	Feb	2021	Uberaba (Archdiocese), Minas Gerais, Brazil
10	Oct	2020	Uberlândia (Diocese), Minas Gerais, Brazil
27	Mar	2021	Ubon Ratchathani (Diocese), Thailand
14	May	2021	Udaipur (Diocese), India
21	Apr	2021	Udine (Archdiocese), Italy
28	Feb	2021	Udon Thani (Diocese), Thailand
14	Sep	2020	Udupi (Diocese), India
23	Feb	2021	Uganda, Military (Military Ordinariate)
17	Sep	2020	Ugento-Santa Maria di Leuca (Diocese), Italy
17	Jul	2020	Uije (Diocese), Angola
01	Feb	2021	Uijeongbu (Diocese), Korea (South)
31	Oct	2020	Ujjain (Syro-Malabar) (Diocese), India
24	Jul	2020	Ulaanbaatar (Prefecture Apostolic), Mongolia
14	Feb	2021	Umtata (Diocese), South Africa

21	Apr	2021	Umuahia (Diocese), Nigeria
05	Sep	2020	Umuarama (Diocese), Parana, Brazil
18	Dec	2020	Umzimkulu (Diocese), South Africa
25	Oct	2020	União da Vitória (Diocese), Parana, Brazil
31	Jul	2020	United States of America, Military (Military Ordinariate)
03	Oct	2020	Urbino-Urbania-Sant'Angelo in Vado (Archdiocese), Italy
19	Jun	2020	Urdaneta (Diocese), Philippines
09	Jan	2021	Urgell (Diocese), Spain
22	Mar	2021	Urmyā {Rezayeh} (Chaldean) (Archdiocese), Iran
04	Sep	2020	Uromi (Diocese), Nigeria
25	Aug	2020	Uruaçu (Uruassu) (Diocese), Goias, Brazil
02	Feb	2021	Uruguaiana (Diocese), Rio Grande do Sul, Brazil
22	Jan	2021	Utrecht (Archdiocese), Netherlands
15	Aug	2020	Uvira (Diocese), Congo (Dem. Rep.)
10	Mar	2021	Uyo (Diocese), Nigeria
28	Feb	2021	Uzbekistan (Apostolic Administration)
05	Dec	2020	Vác (Diocese), Hungary
13	Sep	2020	Vacaria (Diocese), Rio Grande do Sul, Brazil
14	Apr	2021	Vaduz (Archdiocese), Liechtenstein
18	Feb	2021	Valdivia (Diocese), Chile
03	Oct	2020	Valença (Diocese), Rio de Janeiro, Brazil
15	Dec	2020	Valence (-Die-Saint-Paul-Trois-Châteaux) (Diocese), France
03	Jan	2021	Valencia (Archdiocese), Spain
30	Apr	2021	Valencia en Venezuela (Archdiocese)
17	Dec	2020	Valladolid (Archdiocese), Spain
16	Apr	2021	Valle de Chalco (Diocese), México, México
26	Apr	2021	Valle de la Pascua (Diocese), Venezuela
01	Oct	2020	Valledupar (Diocese), Colombia
05	Jun	2020	Valleyfield (Diocese), Québec, Canada
01	Dec	2020	Vallo della Lucania (Diocese), Italy
02	Nov	2020	Valparaíso (Diocese), Chile
11	Jul	2020	Vancouver (Archdiocese), British Columbia, Canada
03	Aug	2020	Vanimo (Diocese), Papua New Guinea
22	Sep	2020	Vannes (Diocese), France
01	Apr	2021	Varanasi (Diocese), India
10	Mar	2021	Varaždin (Diocese), Croatia
20	Sep	2020	Vasai (Diocese), India
14	Jan	2021	Vélez (Diocese), Colombia
26	Feb	2021	Velletri-Segni (Suburbicarian See), Italy
10	May	2021	Vellore (Diocese), India
19	Feb	2021	Venado Tuerto (Diocese), Argentina
28	Apr	2021	Venezia {Venice} (Patriarchate), Italy
30	Oct	2020	Venezuela, Military (Military Ordinariate)
04	Feb	2021	Venezuela (Melkite Greek) (Apostolic Exarchate)

18	Mar	2021	Venezuela (Syrian) (Apostolic Exarchate)
30	Dec	2020	Venice (Diocese), Florida, USA
25	Apr	2021	Ventimiglia-San Remo (Diocese), Italy
08	Oct	2020	Veracruz (Diocese), México
30	Mar	2021	Verapaz, Cobán (Diocese), Guatemala
12	Jan	2021	Verapoly (Archdiocese), India
13	May	2021	Vercelli (Archdiocese), Italy
03	May	2021	Verdun (Diocese), France
30	Aug	2020	Verona (Diocese), Italy
03	Sep	2020	Versailles (Diocese), France
14	Jul	2020	Veszprém (Archdiocese), Hungary
21	Sep	2020	Viana (Diocese), Angola
09	Aug	2020	Viana (Diocese), Maranhão, Brazil
09	Feb	2021	Viana do Castelo (Diocese), Portugal
27	Oct	2020	Vic (Diocese), Spain
06	Jul	2020	Vicenza (Diocese), Italy
23	Feb	2021	Victoria (Diocese), British Columbia, Canada
15	Dec	2020	Victoria in Texas (Diocese), USA
14	Jan	2021	Viedma (Diocese), Argentina
16	Nov	2020	Vientiane (Vicariate Apostolic), Laos
31	Mar	2021	Vigevano (Diocese), Italy
18	Feb	2021	Vijayapuram (Diocese), India
17	Apr	2021	Vijayawada (Diocese), India
03	May	2021	Vila Real (Diocese), Portugal
15	Aug	2020	Vilkaviškis (Diocese), Lithuania
12	Jan	2021	Villa de la Concepción del Río Cuarto (Diocese), Argentina
01	Nov	2020	Villa María (Diocese), Argentina
24	Oct	2020	Villarrica (Diocese), Chile
23	Jun	2020	Villarrica del Espíritu Santo (Diocese), Paraguay
25	Aug	2020	Villavicencio (Archdiocese), Colombia
11	Dec	2020	Vilnius (Archdiocese), Lithuania
23	Jan	2021	Vinh (Diocese), Viet Nam
15	Jan	2021	Vĩnh Long (Diocese), Viet Nam
21	Nov	2020	Virac (Diocese), Philippines
16	Jan	2021	Visakhapatnam (Archdiocese), India
10	Nov	2020	Viseu (Diocese), Portugal
05	Jan	2021	Vitebsk (Diocese), Belarus
15	Feb	2021	Viterbo (Diocese), Italy
13	Jun	2020	Vitória (Archdiocese), Espirito Santo, Brazil
21	May	2021	Vitoria (Diocese), Spain
10	Apr	2021	Vitória da Conquista (Archdiocese), Bahia, Brazil
19	Jul	2020	Vittorio Veneto (Diocese), Italy
07	Nov	2020	Viviers (Diocese), France
10	Apr	2021	Volterra (Diocese), Italy

04	Oct	2020	Votuporanga (Diocese), Sao Paulo, Brazil
13	Jan	2021	Vrhbosna {Sarajevo} (Archdiocese), Bosnia and Herzegovina
13	Jan	2021	Wa (Diocese), Ghana
31	Jul	2020	Wabag (Diocese), Papua New Guinea
19	Dec	2020	Wagga Wagga (Diocese), Australia
06	Jun	2020	Wallis et Futuna (Diocese), Wallis and Futuna, Pacific (Oceania)
30	Dec	2020	Wamba (Diocese), Congo (Dem. Rep.)
26	Sep	2020	Wanxian [Wanhsien] (Diocese), China
14	Nov	2020	Warangal (Diocese), India
19	Sep	2020	Warmia (Archdiocese), Poland
02	Jan	2021	Warri (Diocese), Nigeria
16	Feb	2021	Warszawa {Warsaw} (Archdiocese), Poland
06	Dec	2020	Warszawa-Praga (Diocese), Poland
20	Mar	2021	Washington (Archdiocese), District of Columbia, USA
22	Aug	2020	Waterford and Lismore (Diocese), Ireland
27	Mar	2021	Wau (Diocese), South Sudan
21	Mar	2021	Weetebula (Diocese), Indonesia
20	Sep	2020	Weihai [Weihaiwei] (Prefecture Apostolic), China
22	Mar	2021	Wellington (Archdiocese), New Zealand
13	Apr	2021	Western Sahara {Sahara Occidental} (Prefecture Apostolic)
10	Feb	2021	West Indies (Patriarchate), Spain
24	Sep	2020	Westminster (Archdiocese), England, Great Britain
15	Dec	2020	Wettingen-Mehrerau (Territorial Abbey), Austria
17	Nov	2020	Wewak (Diocese), Papua New Guinea
11	Dec	2020	Wheeling-Charleston (Diocese), West Virginia, USA
12	Feb	2021	Whitehorse (Diocese), Yukon, Canada
25	Jul	2020	Wiawso (Diocese), Ghana
27	Jun	2020	Wichita (Diocese), Kansas, USA
27	Jul	2020	Wien {Vienna} (Archdiocese), Austria
21	Aug	2020	Wilcannia-Forbes (Diocese), Australia
13	Jul	2020	Willemstad (Diocese), Netherlands Antilles, Antilles
05	Sep	2020	Wilmington (Diocese), Delaware, USA
02	Mar	2021	Windhoek (Archdiocese), Namibia
04	Dec	2020	Winnipeg (Archdiocese), Manitoba, Canada
07	Jul	2020	Winnipeg (Ukrainian) (Archeparchy), Manitoba, Canada
02	Mar	2021	Winona-Rochester (Diocese), Minnesota, USA
19	Aug	2020	Witbank (Diocese), South Africa
23	Jan	2021	Włocławek (Kujawy, Kalisze) (Diocese), Poland
06	Sep	2020	Wollongong (Diocese), Australia
04	Sep	2020	Wonju (Diocese), Korea (South)
28	Mar	2021	Worcester (Diocese), Massachusetts, USA
22	Jun	2020	Wrexham (Diocese), Wales, Great Britain
17	Jul	2020	Wrocław {Breslavia} (Archdiocese), Poland
19	Jan	2021	Wrocław-Gdańsk (Ukrainian) (Diocese), Poland

28	Jan	2021	Wuchang [Wuchang] (Diocese), China
17	Nov	2020	Wuhu [Wuhu] (Diocese), China
05	Mar	2021	Würzburg (Diocese), Germany
23	Oct	2020	Wuzhou [Wuchow] (Diocese), China
26	Jul	2020	Xai-Xai (Diocese), Mozambique
12	Jul	2020	Xiamen [Hsiamen, Amoy] (Diocese), China
31	Jul	2020	Xi'an [Sian, Chang-An] (Archdiocese), China
11	Feb	2021	Xiangtan [Siangtan] (Prefecture Apostolic), China
05	May	2021	Xiangyang [Siangyang] (Diocese), China
09	Jun	2020	Xianxian [Sienhsien] (Diocese), China
05	Mar	2021	Xiapu [Funing] (Diocese), China
01	Dec	2020	Xichang [Ningyüan] (Diocese), China
10	Jul	2020	Xingtai [Shunteh] (Diocese), China
10	Apr	2021	Xingu-Altamira (Diocese), Para, Brazil
26	Jan	2021	Xining [Sining] (Prefecture Apostolic), China
20	Feb	2021	Xinjiang [Kiangchow] (Prefecture Apostolic), China
06	Nov	2020	Xinjiang-Urumqi [Sinkiang] (Prefecture Apostolic), China
30	Oct	2020	Xinxiang [Sinsiang] (Prefecture Apostolic), China
24	Nov	2020	Xinyang [Sinyang] (Diocese), China
29	Sep	2020	Xiwanzi-Chongli [Siwantze] (Diocese), China
30	Aug	2020	Xochimilco (Diocese), México, México
07	Apr	2021	Xuanhua [Süanhwa] (Diocese), China
12	May	2021	Xuân Lộc (Diocese), Viet Nam
20	Mar	2021	Xuzhou [Süchow] (Diocese), China
19	Nov	2020	Yagoua (Diocese), Cameroon
05	Apr	2021	Yakima (Diocese), Washington, USA
04	Apr	2021	Yamoussoukro (Diocese), Côte d'Ivoire
27	Jul	2020	Yan'an [Yenan] (Diocese), China
26	Feb	2021	Yanggu [Yangku] (Diocese), China
11	Oct	2020	Yangon (Archdiocese), Myanmar
18	Nov	2020	Yangzhou [Yangchow] (Prefecture Apostolic), China
15	Aug	2020	Yanji [Yenki] (Diocese), China
02	Sep	2020	Yantai [Yentai] (Diocese), China
05	Aug	2020	Yanzhou [Yenchow] (Diocese), China
03	May	2021	Yaoundé (Archdiocese), Cameroon
18	May	2021	Yauyos (Territorial Prelature), Peru
05	Nov	2020	Yei (Diocese), South Sudan
11	Apr	2021	Yendi (Diocese), Ghana
31	Aug	2020	Yibin [Suifu] (Diocese), China
21	Feb	2021	Yichang [Ichang] (Diocese), China
11	May	2021	Yiduxian [Iduhsien] (Prefecture Apostolic), China
17	Oct	2020	Yinchuan [Ningsia] (Diocese), China
15	Oct	2020	Yingkou [Yingkow] (Diocese), China
24	Aug	2020	Yixian [Yihsien] (Prefecture Apostolic), China

16	Jul	2020	Yokadouma (Diocese), Cameroon
28	Feb	2021	Yokohama (Diocese), Japan
22	Feb	2021	Yola (Diocese), Nigeria
01	Jul	2020	Yongjia/Wenzhou [Yungkia] (Diocese), China
26	Nov	2020	Yongnian [Yüngnien] (Diocese), China
04	Jun	2020	Yongping [Yüngping] (Diocese), China
01	Feb	2021	Yopal (Diocese), Colombia
17	Nov	2020	Yopougon (Diocese), Côte d'Ivoire
04	Jul	2020	Yoro (Diocese), Honduras
07	Jan	2021	Youngstown (Diocese), Ohio, USA
24	Nov	2020	Yuanling [Yüanling] (Diocese), China
04	Aug	2020	Yucatán (Archdiocese), México
12	Sep	2020	Yuci [Yütze] (Diocese), China
03	Jul	2020	Yueyang [Yochow] (Prefecture Apostolic), China
28	Dec	2020	Yujiang [Yükiang] (Diocese), China
22	Nov	2020	Yurimaguas (Vicariate Apostolic), Peru
03	Nov	2020	Yuzhno Sakhalinsk (Prefecture Apostolic), Russian Federation
26	Oct	2020	Zacapa y Santo Cristo de Esquipulas (Diocese), Guatemala
02	Mar	2021	Zacatecas (Diocese), México
21	Aug	2020	Zacatecoluca (Diocese), El Salvador
16	Oct	2020	Zadar (Zara) (Archdiocese), Croatia
29	Nov	2020	Zagreb (Archdiocese), Croatia
31	Aug	2020	Zahleh (Maronite) (Eparchy), Lebanon
17	Jun	2020	Zahleh e Furzol (Melkite Greek) (Archeparchy), Lebanon
12	Feb	2021	Zamboanga (Archdiocese), Philippines
24	Oct	2020	Zamora (Diocese), Michoacán, México
03	Apr	2021	Zamora (Diocese), Spain
26	Jan	2021	Zamora en Ecuador (Vicariate Apostolic)
20	Jun	2020	Zamość-Lubaczów (Diocese), Poland
28	Nov	2020	Zanzibar (Diocese), Tanzania
22	Aug	2020	Zaragoza (Archdiocese), Spain
24	Sep	2020	Zárate-Campana (Diocese), Argentina
29	Jun	2020	Zaria (Diocese), Nigeria
31	Oct	2020	Zé-Doca (Diocese), Maranhão, Brazil
30	Jul	2020	Zhaotong [Chaotung] (Prefecture Apostolic), China
04	Nov	2020	Zhaoxian [Chaohsien] (Diocese), China
10	Jul	2020	Zhengding [Chengting] (Diocese), China
20	Feb	2021	Zhengzhou [Chengchow] (Diocese), China
13	Feb	2021	Zhoucun [Chowtsun] (Diocese), China
27	Sep	2020	Zhouzhi [Chowchich] (Diocese), China
21	Jun	2020	Zhumadian [Chumatien] (Diocese), China
04	Sep	2020	Zielona Góra-Gorzów (Diocese), Poland
14	Dec	2020	Ziguinchor (Diocese), Senegal
18	Sep	2020	Žilina (Diocese), Slovakia

20 Dec 2020   Zipaquirá (Diocese), Colombia
03 Feb 2021   Zomba (Diocese), Malawi
06 Apr 2021   Zrenjanin (Diocese), Serbia

Count of structures by type

- 9 Apostolic Administration
- 13 Apostolic Exarchate
- 39 Apostolic Prefecture
- 82 Apostolic Vicariate
- 597 Archdiocese
- 44 Archeparchy
- 5 Archiepiscopal Exarchate
- 2130 Diocese
- 110 Eparchy
- 36 Military Ordinariate
- 8 Mission Sui Iuris
- 9 Ordinariate for Eastern Faithful
- 5 Patriarchal Dependent Territory
- 9 Patriarchal Exarchate
- 11 Patriarchate
- 3 Personal Ordinariate
- 1 Personal Prelature
- 7 Suburbicarian See
- 11 Territorial Abbey
- 40 Territorial Prelature
- 3169 Total

Printed in Great Britain
by Amazon